A History of Holywell and Greenfield

Rowland Tennant

bridge books

A History of Holywell and Greenfield
First published in Wales by
BRIDGE BOOKS
61, Park Avenue, Wrexham
LL12 7AW

©2007 Text Rowland Tennant
© 2005 Typesetting and layout, Bridge Books

All rights reserved.
No part of this publication may be reproduced,
stored in a retrieval system or transmitted in any form or
by any means, electronic, mechanical, photocopying, recording
or otherwise without the prior permission of the
copyright owner.

The right of Rowland Tennant to be identified as the author of this work has been
asserted by him in accordance with the Copyright, Designs and Patents Act 1988.

ISBN 978-1-84494-039-4

A CIP catalogue entry for this book is available from the British Library

A full on-line catalogue of Bridge Books publications is available at
www.bridgebooks.co.uk

Printed and bound by
Cromwell Press Ltd
Trowbridge

Contents

	Notes	4
	Foreword	5
	Preface	9
1	Shaping the Community	13
2	The Town and Its Services	33
3	Religion	60
4	Roads, Railways and Sea Transport	108
5	Industry	124
6	Education	155
7	Businesses and Residences	168
8	Notable Families and People	192
	Bibliography and Notes	196
	Index	200

Notes

Ordnance Survey grid references are quoted throughout this publication to assist the finding of a location, place, building, etc. Such references are given with the district's prefix 'SJ'.

Within the text, references numbered 1–155 relate to published works detailed in the Bibliography. References relating to Flintshire Record Office documents have are prefixed by the letter 'R'.

Equivalent contemporary values of the pound sterling are shown alongside some of the original income, expenditure, costs, etc. The chart used for these calculations was published and supplied by the Bank of England an relates to values as of February 2007.

Foreword

> Holywell, or Treffynnon, takes its name from its famous well, the largest spring in Great Britain. It is pleasantly situated on a hill overlooking the estuary of the Dee. When the lead mines were at their best and the numerous industries along St Winifred's stream were flourishing, Holywell was one of the busiest towns in North Wales.
>
> *Flintshire [Cambridge County Geographies]* by J. M. Edwards (Cambridge, 1914).

This was the observation of J. M. Edwards, the Headmaster of Holywell County School whose book *Flintshire* was published in July 1914, on the eve of the outbreak of the Great War (1914–18). At this time, Holywell was a large industrialised and commercial centre which had contributed much to the social, cultural, economic, industrial and religious history of north-east Wales. Crucial to this importance was its geographical location, close to the navigable river Dee, sheltered on the edge of a large limestone plateau blessed with mineral ores such as lead and calamine, abutting the coal reserves along the Dee shoreline, and a plentiful water supply issuing from the well of St Winefride. Its location had attracted settlers since before written records began and it was an area over which men had fought, marking the border zone between the English settlements based at Chester and the Welsh tribes of the Flintshire hills.

During the Dark Ages, the kings of Mercia had attempted to define their border and protect themselves against Welsh incursions on their land by building large earthen dykes, most notably Wat's Dyke which skirted the town on its eastern side and which can still be identified running through the Strand woods. Several centuries later Offa, King of Mercia built his dyke which skirted the town on its western edge. Between these two building phases, the land upon which the town of Holywell later developed changed hands from being in the possession of the Welsh tribes to the control of the powerful English tribe of Mercia. This battle between two opposing groups was to mirror the history of the town over the next few centuries, as this land was constantly fought over and the boundary between the two forever shifted. Holywell was very much a border province and within close proximity of the town, there is archaeological evidence of Roman, Saxon, Viking and Norman settlement, intermixing with the native Celtic tribes. This period was also to witness the religious importance of the area with the discovery of the healing qualities of the well of St Winefride and the later establishment of a monastery at Basingwerk.

During the medieval period, the town began to develop as a commercial centre although exactly when and why the town migrated from its original valley location clustered around the well up the hill to its present location along High Street is uncertain. Certainly the town was not of significant geographical importance to Edward I who bypassed the area in favour of settlements at Flint and Rhuddlan. What brought about the development of the town was its industrial ventures. By the eighteenth century, it was the home to numerous and varied industries, while within the town, commercial undertakings took place such as printing, banking and trading. Holywell began to emerge as a prosperous and important town, its population being swelled by immigrants from all over the British isles. By the early nineteenth century, it had the largest population of any town in north Wales; Samuel Lewis noting in his *Topographical Dictionary* of 1843 that its inhabitants numbered 10,834. Of the town itself he commented:

> The streets are spacious and well paved; the houses are handsome and well built; and the whole town is well lighted with gas, and abundantly supplied with water by wells.

Holywell was approaching the height of its prosperity but it was a prosperity based upon less than firm foundations. With the development of steam power, the importance of the water-wheel declined and factories could now be located in areas which did not possess a powerful stream to act as a constant source of power. This diminished the importance of the Greenfield valley. Holywell undoubtedly possesses a rich past and it occupies an important place in the annals of the history of north-east Wales, and indeed within that of Wales itself. Yet, despite this historical significance, no detailed history of the town has ever been written. Thomas Pennant provided a brief outline history of the town in his *Tour in Wales* which appeared in 1778, which he later expanded into his more informed study of the *History of the Parishes of Whiteford and Holywell* in 1796. His writings commenced a process of academic research, yet while Pennant recorded a wealth of local data about these two large parishes, he did not write a detailed history of the town itself. Others have attempted similar ventures such as J. Poole who compiled his *Gleanings of the Histories of Holywell, Flint, Saint Asaph and Rhuddlan* in 1831, which provided a cursory overview of the history of the town. In the various published tours of gentleman travellers the town has received a mention and aspects of its history have been noted, but much of this material had been copied from previous authors and especially from the works of Pennant. Indeed, all these publications just touched upon aspects of the history of the town.

The renaissance in the study of local history in the last quarter of the twentieth century has witnessed the appearance of a number of important works dealing with aspects of the town's history. Extensive archaeological excavations of the industrial ruins in the valley during the 1970s resulted in the publication by Ken Davies and Christopher J. Williams of *The Greenfield Valley*, which appeared in 1977. During the 1980s several pictorial publications whetted the appetite of those interested in local history through such works as *Holywell in Times Past* (1983) by Marjorie R. Isgar, which was closely followed by a series of books by David R. Wilkes *Holywell & Greenfield in Old Photographs* (1983), *Holywell & Greenfield: A Pictorial Past* (1984) and

Holywell and District: a portrait in old picture postcards (1992). Such publications have done much to foster an interest in the history of Holywell and Greenfield, but they have only examined Holywell's past in fairly recent times, not least since the invention of the camera. Numerous academic articles have appeared in the *Flintshire Historical Society Journal*, *Clwyd Historian* and *The Welsh History Review*, to name but a few. But what the town lacks is a detailed *history* in the full academic sense. Of all the works mentioned above this new publication by Rowland Tennant comes closest to meeting this criteria. While not a chronological history in the strict sense, Rowland's *A History of Holywell and Greenfield* provides a detailed survey of the town and the valley, areas which are so closely intertwined that they cannot really be dealt with as separate studies. As Samuel Lewis wisely noted: 'the commercial importance of Holywell is commensurate with its manufacturing pre-eminence', and the map of the town and valley produced by John Wood in 1833 certainly demonstrates the importance of industry and commerce.

After analysing the geology of the area in order to ascertain the reasons for the siting of the town, Rowland proceeds to provide an outline history in which he chronicles the most significant events in the history of Holywell and Greenfield. He then adopts a thematic approach and, through the discussion of selective themes, illustrates the rich history of the town and its valley. The industrial activity obviously takes prominence, with a look at the copper, brass, zinc and lead works, the cotton and woollen mills, the breweries and mineral water factories, which provided the vast array of jobs and which accounted for the dramatic rise in population from the 1770s onwards. As the town grew larger, it attracted associated building works such as civic and public buildings, parks and recreation areas, cultural domains such as libraries, music halls and later, cinemas. The Cottage Hospital took care of the sick, while those who fell on hard times could seek relief in the Lluesty workhouse. The migration of workers brought a variety of different religions, hence the Roman Catholic and Protestant churches and the array of Nonconformist chapels. Through this detailed study, Rowland has lavished his readers with an encyclopaedic survey of the important buildings and sites in both Holywell and the Greenfield valley. He has chosen to conclude his survey with a look at some of the noted families and persons who have coloured and shaped the history of the area. It is an engrossing read and one that it highly recommended. You will not be disappointed!

Dr R. Paul Evans
Wrexham (but a native of Carmel!)
April 2007

A present-day view of Holywell from Pen-y-Ball Hill.

Preface

It is my hope that the contents of this book will enrich the reader's knowledge of at least some of the unique history that Holywell and Greenfield have witnessed over many centuries. May the years to come prove to be enriched by further prosperous times for the district.

I am very pleased to have written this, my second book, on the subject of local history in the district in which I have had the pleasure of living for over seventy years. My first publication in 2003 was *A History of Six Villages* — those being Brynford, Carmel, Gorsedd, Lloc, Pantasaph and Whitford. The villages are virtually adjacent to Holywell and, indeed, all have, over the centuries, added to the history of the town itself. Holywell and Greenfield have a history which is very varied and rich — indeed, it is quite unique in Britain. I hope that the content of this book helps to convey that to you. The research needed to gather facts for the numerous aspects of this publication has been quite immense — but most certainly greatly rewarding. I have been amazed by the quantity of historical facts uncovered relating to so many topics and I hope that the book will act as a written record of the district for those who follow us in the years to come.

The town of Holywell was at first gradually created by the religious events. Through the lives of St Beuno and St Winefride in the seventh century, the shrine of the Holy Well became internationally known. By the seventeenth century, some travel maps were produced with the specific purpose of outlining routes for pilgrims wishing to come to St Winefride's Holy Well from religious places such as St David's and Shrewsbury. The Cistercian monks established Basingwerk Abbey in the mid twelfth century and quickly became owners of a great deal of land and property. The chapter dealing with religion will illustrate what a tremendous impact the Cistercians had on the lives of the population over the four hundred years they were active here; a long period of time for the growing population of the district to be dependant upon a body of men for so many aspects of their needs — including religion, health and employment.

The thirteenth century was the time when the town itself really started to become established following the early establishment of weekly trading markets by the Cistercians, to which people from a wide area were attracted. Industry began to play an ever-increasing part of the town's life from the fourteenth century and the remarkable story of the district's industry is related here.

By the eighteenth century, an industrial revolution had started in the Greenfield

Valley, drawn there by the fast flowing reliable waters from the Holy Well. Added to this was the availability of coal from the nearby coastal mines and the Halkyn Mountain range which was producing lead, with an abundance of calamine, which was utilized in some industries. From that time until the beginning of the twentieth century, the combination of religion and industry caused a huge growth in the population of the district. However, the early twentieth century heralded the beginning of many changes. Some blamed the dramatic stoppage of the water to St Winefride's Well in 1917 as the reason for a decline in the number of pilgrims coming to the town. This reduced volume of water running down into the Greenfield Valley was also the end to its industrial revolution. There were unquestionably many other factors which had influenced these topics for many years previously — the stories of which are contained within this book.

As stage-coaching increased, Holywell became an important staging point on one of the north Wales routes. The introduction of the railway between Chester and Holyhead in 1848, resulted in the building of the station at Greenfield, thus making the district far more easily accessible to a much larger part of Britain. The twentieth century saw a huge alteration in the way the population lived. Rail and road transport changed, and travel increased; the town had its own railway station opened in 1912.

Large industries were established outside Holywell — Mostyn Ironworks, Shotton Steelworks and, at Flint, Courtaulds Artificial Silk factories. In 1936, Courtaulds opened the world's largest Rayon Staple factory at Greenfield. During those years the town and district prospered and there was major housing development. Alas, these modern industries, and others, either closed or severely cut back on their workforce during the later years of the century. On the commercial and retail front, supermarkets had come into being in the middle of the century, resulting in the loss of trade and closure of small shops and businesses.

Thus has Holywell suffered, but with such a tremendous history, we should look positively at present-day events and trust that prosperity will return again. Most certainly, Flintshire County Council's current Townscape Heritage Initiative is something to be praised, and already new life and business is emerging from it.

It is of paramount importance that I acknowledge the many individuals who have most readily helped me with their own knowledge and given suggestions as to where details on particular subjects might be found and confirmed. As with my first book, I do not think it would be correct to name any of those people with thanks — it really would be an impossible task to name them all and, without doubt, leaving out one person would be unjust. Thus, to all of those people, I offer my deepest thanks; without them the publication would most certainly have had far less history recorded in it. I am deeply indebted to the staff of the libraries at both County Hall in Mold and in Holywell, for not only being so helpful in providing books and documents from their own holdings, but also for their assistance in obtaining for me many books from national sources. I am also happy to offer thanks to the staff of the Flintshire Record Office for their valuable assistance.

It has been absolutely necessary for me to have invaluable help in the finalisation of the publication in two areas. One was the arduous and time-consuming task of proof reading over 93,000 words. That has been carried out by a person who does not wish to be named, but to whom I must extend the greatest of thanks. I have also been greatly honoured by the fact that Dr R. Paul Evans offered to provide the Foreword for this book. We know only too well that through his early life in the area, coupled with his intimate knowledge and writings of Thomas Pennant and Moses Griffith, he has proved to be an historian of whom the district can be justly proud. Paul is now editor of the *Flintshire Historical Society Journal*. My sincere thanks are offered to him for devoting very precious time towards this publication.

My dear wife Irene has been a tower of strength to me during difficult times and I therefore dedicate this book to her, with my deepest thanks.

Finally, whilst every effort has been made to double-check my research where possible, inaccuracies will no doubt be found. For any such errors, do please accept my sincere apologies.

Rowland Tennant
2007

Chapter 1
Shaping the Community

The spelling of the name 'Holywell' is seemingly a natural one, having come about as the town gradually formed after *c*.620 AD, when the events surrounding St Winefride and the Holy Well occurred. The Welsh name, *Treffynnon*, translates into 'Town of the Well'. But why is the English pronunciation of it Holly Well? An extremely eminent friend of mine has the thought that it may have come about from the fact that Bryn Celyn holds the answer. The hill on which the western side of Bryn Celyn stands runs southerly to the area almost opposite the well and for centuries after 620 AD, before any buildings were erected there, the hill could have been covered in holly. The English translation of *Bryn Celyn* is Holly Hill. If that was so, we could get 'Hollywell'.

At a height of 350 ft above sea level, the old Town Hall [SJ 1858 7591] in High Street really signifies the centre of Holywell. The River Dee is about $1^{1}/_{2}$ miles north-east, at the end of the Greenfield valley. It is in this latter area that the township of Greenfield was first established in 1535, out of the previously named district of Fulbrook. Although Holywell was not mentioned in the Domesday Book, Fulbrook was. Its entry was: 'land for 1 plough, which 3 villagers and 2 smallholders have. Woodland for $^{1}/_{2}$ a league long and 40 perches wide'.

St Winefride's Well.

Whilst the place-name Greenfield could signify an area of fields, Canon David Thomas says: 'Greenfield is an inept rendering of the name *Maesglas*, based on a misconception of the meaning of the second element in the compound. The first element *maes* — field, in its wider sense, e.g. battlefield. The second element is not the adjective *glas* variously translated as 'green' or 'blue', but the noun *clas*, meaning an abbey, a convent, a monastic community, a cloister. In this compound the 'c' is mutated to 'g', making *Maesglas*, which would translate as 'abbey field', or better, 'abbey land'.[7]

Canon Ellis Davies, in his *Flintshire Place Names*, gives us an explanation of how the name Basingwerk was possibly created. Split the word up into parts. 'Bas' was most possibly derived from the name 'Bassa'. Bassa being the grandfather of Cenulf, Offa's successor, the Mercian king who succeeded Æthelbald. 'Ing' is from the old English word *ingas*, meaning 'sons', 'descendants' or 'dependants'. 'Werk' is from the old English word *weorc*, meaning a 'work', an 'earthwork' or a 'fortification'.[30] Thus, because of the foregoing and the fact that the northernmost point of Wat's Dyke terminated at today's Greenfield, it is my belief that the place was named by the Mercians as Basingwerk [SJ 1952 7760]. The word Mercian is derived from the old English word *merce*, meaning 'boundary folk'. However, it has to be said that there are conflicting thoughts by historians about the original site of Basingwerk (not Wat's Dyke). Whilst some contend that it was at Greenfield, others place strong argument that it was, in fact, at Hên Blas (Coleshill, Flint) [SJ 223 736].

Geology

The area's geology can be traced back to the last Ice Age when ice gouged out the valley into its present shape. Holywell and its surrounding district are on the gentle slopes of the Halkyn mountain range, which extends from near Mold in the east, to Dyserth in the west. Holywell's centre, and its valley, nestle in a shallow area. In the Middle Ages, the hills were mostly covered in thick forest.

In the Carboniferous period, some 330 million years ago, because of a warm and shallow marine environment, rather like that of the Bahamas today, great thicknesses of limestone accumulated, forming the greater part of the Halkyn Mountain range; the limestone thickness is estimated to be some 770 metres (2,500 ft). It lies on Silurian age beds, which are some 400 million years old. Within the limestones, of which there are several varieties (as a result of variation in composition) are shale beds which are the products of mud brought into the lime-rich seas by rivers. Sometime after the limestones and shales were deposited, the area was subjected to earth movements. These flexed the area and produced the charactistic jointing in the limestones. This, together with the layer or bedding, breaks the rocks naturally into blocks. Around fifty million years ago, the joints, and also some faults (high angle breaks through the rocks along which movement has shifted the layers out of line), were invaded by hot fluids carrying mineral elements in solution. The result was the crystallisation of these elements along the joints and faults in the limestone, forming mineral veins. Since the minerals, lead and zinc in particular, are bound up in other minerals such as white calcite, and with the limestone, these rocks are described as ores. The lead is argentiferous (silver-rich) in parts, and it was this mineral which drew the Romans to the area to set up mines.

The mountain range falls in height on its more north/north-east section and, around Holywell, the carboniferous limestone gives way to millstone grit sandstones of the middle carboniferous age, named the Holywell Shales. Their average thickness is some 125–190m (400–600ft). At their northern end, the Holywell Shales are overlaid by extemely fine-grained sandstone called Gwespyr Sandstone, which, in places, attains a depth of some 100m (300ft). The coastal plain along the Dee has coal measures beneath it which extend partially up the valley towards the town under relatively impermeable rock, thus the stream running down the valley does not sink through. However, because the limestone on the hills is porous, the rainwater seeps through the land surface and there are therefore virtually no rivers or streams on the surface until the lower parts of the hills where the limestone ceases. The water filters through the limestone into subterranean water tunnels and lakes, some of which are very large. As the limestone gives way to the grits and sandstones, water outlets are often found in the form of springs and wells. By far the largest example of a spring emerging from the Halkyn Mountain range was that at St Winefride's Well; the rate of water issuing from it was 25,000 gallons per minute. With a fairly constant temperature of 40°F the stream very rarely froze or flooded. Thus it was in the eighteenth century that industrialists flocked to the valley and created an industrial revolution. Another important water outlet has been The Level, below the Holway, whilst Roft's Tob Spring, located behind present-day St Peter's Estate, [SJ 190 757] was another major source of water supply for the town's households.

The limestone, the shale and the sandstone have all been used extensively in and around the town for buildings and walls; evidence of all that will come to light in later chapters of this book.

Early Times

Small pre-Christian settlements of people in the district would naturally have lived near springs for easy access for their water needs. Wood, cut from the hillside woodlands, would have given them fuel for fires as well as creating clearings for them to live in. Their basic occupations were hunting and agriculture. These type of people must have been living around the area where [St] Beuno was given land in the

A roadside wall made of Holywell Shale.

early seventh century by his brother-in-law, Tyfid, on which to build his first church. Geographically, it was a sheltered spot, at the head of the 1½ mile valley leading to the River Dee.

The following five topics highlight how exceptionally important the area known as Basingwerk (Greenfield) was in the earliest recorded history of the district — rather amazingly, the area does not seem to have been collectively highlighted in bygone years in the writings of travellers or, indeed, historians. This text tries to convey the thoughts of historians as to whether Basingwerk was at first at Hên Blas (Coleshill), or at Fulbrook (Greenfield) .

[1] The Roman Period — around 50–55AD, is the era where we can find the earliest known history of Holywell and Greenfield. In those days, the River Dee inlet at Greenfield Dock came further inland, up to the bluff that can be seen to the north of (the later) Basingwerk Abbey. At that point, the land falls steeply to what is now a car park. Sir John Edward Lloyd, in his 1911 book *A History of Wales*, wrote that the sea here barred a furtherance of a coastal road westwards.[27] The Romans created a route westwards from their strategic stronghold at Deva (Chester) to their military base at Segontium (Caernarfon). Using today's place names, it is quite probable that this north Wales road went south from Chester to Balderton, then via Bretton before it dropped down to the coast below Hawarden (in those days there was marshland between the modern-day Sandycroft and Saltney — as is suggested by their names). The road then followed the marshland coast to Greenfield. The important aspect of the route as far as Holywell's history is concerned, is the fact that, the Basingwerk Bluff [SJ 1965 7753] caused a natural barrier, forcing the road to go inland. I would suggest that the point where the Roman road turned in as being at SJ 1972 7745 — at about the point where the footpath from east of the car park joins with the higher land. That land has of course been utilised and altered for the old railway line to Holywell (eliminate from your vision the A548 coast road and the rail bridge with connecting land build up, the sea would have reached just beyond those). From that point the Roman road went up the Greenfield Valley to just below what became the site of the Meadow Mill.[15] It then bore west, passed what was, in the nineteenth century, Meadow Cottage [SJ 1905 7705], over the moor (near Moor Farm) before reaching the Golch (Carmel), then continuing towards Gorsedd for St Asaph and beyond.[15]

Thomas Pennant wrote that in the digging of the foundations for the Meadow Mill Works, there was the discovery of 'A Roman hypocaust, furnished with various flues, with the superincumbent tiles of a fine red colour … this proves that they had a stationary settlement in this place, probably of merchants concerned in the mineral [lead] works, which they had on the adjacent mountain …'[22] M. V. Taylor, in the 1922 *Flintshire Historical Society Journal*, gave another interpretation to this discovery: 'If the road … is Roman, the hypocaust is probably Roman … . And if it is Roman, it may be a house, tile-kiln, a building connected with lead-smelting, or it may even be the bath-house of a fort now disappeared.' In my own publication *A History of Six Villages*, I gave evidence that the Romans had mined in the Carmel district. Included in this was the detail of a Roman pig [ingot] of lead, of *c.*60 AD, which was discovered in 1951 when the new Carmel school was being built. Twentieth century archaeologists have confirmed that there had been a large Roman smeltery at Pentre Ffwrndan, Oakenholt, Flint, sited alongside the Leadbrook stream. Lead was shipped from there to Chester up the River Dee, where the Romans were building their legionary fortress.[124] Now, here is a point to debate: with proof that the Romans built a road (which included a length between Carmel and Basingwerk); that they leadmined in Carmel; that there has been evidence of some type of Roman settlement and/or activity by [the later] Meadow Mills; that, in those days, the inlet from the Dee came up to the Basingwerk Bluff, might there not also have been a possibility that there was at least a small smelter at the Meadow Mill site, and that they shipped lead from the Basingwerk Bluff to Chester? Bear in mind that when factories such as Meadow Mills were built during the eighteenth and nineteenth centuries any evidence of Roman remains would have been eradicated.

Following the departure of the Romans from Britain, the Saxons began to invade the country from the fifth century. In time, they came into north Wales. Local to this area, they formed two small settlements — one at Bagillt and one at Mertyn [near Whitford].[30]

[2] Borderland fighting between the Welsh and English over the centuries greatly affected the district around Holywell. One of the earliest major events was the construction of Wat's Dyke, which historians generally believe was built in the eighth century by the Mercians, during King Æthelbald's reign. The dyke was built as an embankment with a ditch to its east. Whilst there is now no original evidence left of where the dyke's northernmost point was, I contend that it would have been located just to the east of the important Basingwerk Bluff — which would have been the point where the Roman road turned inland. Of the bluff, Sir Cyril Fox wrote: 'the dyke terminated close to the little plateau on which Basingwerk Abbey was [later] built. The site was an important one — a flattened spur flanking the Holywell ravine and close to a cliff overlooking the estuary of the Dee.'[28] Today, a section of the dyke is clearly visible (and is way-marked) on the hillside east of the Flour Mill Pool [SJ 1915 7698]. After this stretch it is lost, but it would originally have continued to, and crossed, the site of today's Basingwerk High School, then along Strand Walk. Crossing Pen-y-Maes Road by the house named Bryn Offa, it followed a course, via Rose Hill, to Garth-y-Foel where it crossed the dingle and at the top turned south-east towards Northop. Termination was at the River Morda, a Severn tributary, near Welshpool.

A great deal of mystery surrounds the early unwritten history of Wat's Dyke:

- who, or what, was Wat?
- around which period in time was the dyke built?
- why was it built so close to Offa's Dyke?

I have researched the subject in great depth and have come to the following possible conclusions:

A section of Wat's Dyke in Strand Woods, [SJ 192 771] to the east of Meadow Mill.

- Bearing in mind that the Saxons came over from the area of modern northern Germany, I found that the German word *watt* translates as 'mud flats'. The tidal inlet at the Basingwerk bluff would have certainly had mud flats on it when the tide went out. Secondly, in the mid seventh century, there was a Mercian King Wat in the southern English kingdom.[34] Even with no written evidence for or against it, was he responsible for the dyke? It could have been that, because of Æthelbald's high authority, he used King Wat as a subject king, and moved him to the north Wales borderlands to supervise the building of the dyke. Alternatively, was there another Wat of significance?

- With no documents available from those days, we can only speculate on dates. However, Hill and Worthington in their book *Offa's Dyke, History and Guide* believe that Offa's Dyke never went the full distance from Prestatyn to Chepstow, and that other smaller dykes ran some of the distance. For instance, in the north, Whitford Dyke covered the length from Newmarket (Trelawnyd) to the Ysceifiog parish boundary near Pantasaph. It is maintained that this dyke was of different construction from Offa's Dyke. They further believe that Offa's Dyke covered the length from Treuddyn to just north of Hereford.[34] Wat's Dyke was again of different construction. The Clwyd County Council publication of 1991 *The Archaelogy of Clwyd*, also refers to the Whitford Dyke.[6]

- Importantly, all the dykes were along the disputed borderlands between England and Wales. There were differences in the methods of their individual construction, all of which surely confirms that they were constructed by the Mercians who were the boundary folk.

After the crown of England fell to the Norman, William the Conqueror, in 1066, one of his first moves in attempting to conquer Wales, was to place three borderland centres (Chester, Shrewsbury and Hereford) into the hands of Norman barons —

Hugh d'Avranches (also known as Hugh Lupus and Hugh the Fat) being made Earl of Chester in 1070. This gave him access into north Wales, which naturally proved to be important in the history of Holywell and Greenfield. The years under the succeeding kings, William II to Edward I, witnessed fighting along the borderlands between the English kings and the Welsh princes.

[3] Basingwerk Castle. In 1157, the Welsh prince, Owain Gwynedd, moved his forces across Tegeingl and encamped at Coleshill. At the same time King Henry II arrived at Chester with an army. The two sides fought the battle of Ewloe, and Owain defeated the king's men. However, the Normans re-grouped and Owain retreated to St Asaph. Henry then built a castle at Basingwerk in the same year. Although Thomas Pennant wrote that vestiges of a stone castle could be found in the foundation of a wall near the turnpike road,[22] I agree with the Friends of the Greenfield Valley (who are presently endeavouring to pinpoint the site) that it was usual for motte and bailey castles to be built in that era; such a castle was built at Prestatyn in the very same year (part of the mound is still there, [SJ 0724 830]). At Greenfield, on the eastern side of the lane leading up from the A548 main road (the old turnpike road) to Basingwerk House, there is a significant mound with at present a car park to the east of it. That mound could well be the site of the elusive motte and bailey castle. We must bear in mind that both lane and car park came into being during modern times and have been cut into the base of the hillock on which the castle may have stood. History relates that after 1157, there was further fighting and, in 1166, Owain seized Basingwerk Castle and destroyed it. The castle was never rebuilt and the site was left to the Basingwerk Cistercians[26 & 30] who were resident in the abbey, on the flat plateau, just yards away from the possible position of the castle.

[4] The Cistercian Monks (a more detailed history is to be found in Chapter 3). The Savigniac monks had built a chapel at Hên Blas (Coleshill) in 1131, but when the

The possible mound of the site of Basingwerk Castle

Cistercian Order superceded the Savignac's, they moved from Hên Blas and built the first parts of a new abbey above the Basingwerk Bluff, at Fulbrook [Greenfield] in, or just after, 1147. The site was immediately to the east of what had been the Roman road, as well as Wat's Dyke.

[5] The case for the site at Greenfield as having always been named Basingwerk, as opposed to the site at Hên Blas, Coleshill. (a) If (as outline in the introduction to this chapter) the name Basingwerk was derived from the Mercian name 'Bassa', with its northernmost part sited at [later] Greenfield then, to me, the Hên Blas site is ruled out. (b) Basingwerk Castle, built in 1157, was adjacent to the abbey built in, or after, 1147 at Greenfield. That is supported by the fact that Henry II gave the castle site to the Cistercians after the castle was destroyed in 1166 by Owain Gwynedd. There is no record of the Cistercians having had lands at Hên Blas as late as 1157.

The Lordship (Manor) of Holywell, Fulbrook and Greenfield

The Cistercian Order at Basingwerk Abbey was in a rather unique position because of their position on disputed borderland. As a result of this, during the twelfth and thirteenth centuries, both English kings and gentry, as well as Welsh princes, granted them lands which resulted in the creation of a lordship. The first example was when Ranulf II, Earl of Chester, gave them the lands of Fulbrook on which they built the abbey — the grant also included many acres in the vicinity of the Greenfield Valley. Other examples of land gifts were: Prince Llywelyn ab Iorwerth (who died in 1240), gave the monks property at Gelli (above Whitford); Dafydd, the son of Prince Llywelyn, granted them not only Holywell church but also the shrine and pilgrimage chapel of St Winefride, in 1240.[20] Through being lords of the manor for some 400 years they were able to build up other assets and trade from rental income. Nicholas Pennant, the last abbot, had foreseen the coming of the dissolution of the monasteries, and, just before 1536, gave away a great deal of lordship land to other members of the Pennant family; the Crown duly took over the residue. Although Nicholas Pennant's gifts were contested by the Crown, they did not succeed in reversing his actions.

King James I granted the lordship to John Eldred and George Whitmore after which the manor passed through three more sets of gentry before 1809, when Robert, the Earl Grosvenor, obtained the title.[29] From then, and until the Law of Property Act, 1922, which abolished copyhold tenure, the rents from the manor were duly received by the Grosvenors. In 1926, the Vesting Deed in Tenure caused, as elsewhere in Britain, the end of lordships.

To return to the fighting between the English and Welsh in this district; the Basingwerk abbots and monks had complained to Archbishop Hubert Walter between 1193 and 1209 that in the wars with the princes of Wales they have lost their church in 'Hallewell' which was valued at £100.[19] As a consequence of this, in 1209, the Earl of Chester, Ranulf III, built a castle on the hill just to the south-east of the Parish Church [SJ 186 7625].[1] The site of the castle could well have been chosen to help protect pilgrims to the Holy Well during those troubled times. However, its life was short-lived because in 1210, when King John was in Ireland, Prince Llywelyn ab Iorwerth entered the Earl's dominion and destroyed the castle.[1] It was never rebuilt, but the site became known as Bryn-y-Castell (Hill of the Castle). Some people believe that hill was where St Winefride's family lived, just above the site where St Beuno had built his church. Dwellings built in 1861 to the west of New Road, looking east, are called Castle View and are still inhabited.

As already stated, Holywell was not mentioned in the Domesday Book, but, when Robert of Shrewsbury compiled *The Life of St Winefride* in about 1143, he implied that Holywell was a daughter church of Whitford, and the annual payment of two shillings made to St Beuno's (Holywell) *ex'a donna de Holywell*, up to, at least the dissolution, may have been made in acknowledgement of such a connection. Reference to Holywell can be found in a deed of 1093 in which Adeliza, wife of Hugh Lupus, Earl of Chester, adds 'the Church of Haliwell' to previous bequests to the monks of St Werburg's, Chester. Thus, it is obvious that the shrine and church were known between 620 AD and 1093. St Winefride's Well and Church had become fact around 620 AD, although there are no surviving documents until the twelfth century.

Community Shaping

The Statute of Rhuddlan (otherwise known as The Statute of Wales), was signed in 1284 by King Edward I, resulting in the creation of *cantrefi* (the Welsh administrative districts). The statute included the condition that: 'There shall be a Sheriff of Flint under whom shall be the Cantref of Tegeingl, the land of Maelor Saesneg, the land of Hope, and all the land attached to our castle and Village of Rhuddlan.' The Lordship of Holywell and Fulbrook was sited within Tegeingl. The Anglo-Saxons had established shires, and the official appointed to control them was a 'reeve' — hence the title sheriff (shire-reeve).[4] The old Marcher lordships of Mold and Hawarden were not included in the statute, but Henry VIII added them when he introduced his Act of 1542 which distributed the Marcher lordships among the counties.[4] Holywell was put under the lordship of Holywell, Fulbrook and Greenfield.[4] Central government was watched over by the monarch, and justice was controlled by his appointed judges who visited local parishes (see Chapter 2).[3] The Act also created the 'Parish Vestry' which carried out the town's administrative work up to the middle of the nineteenth century when [see Chapter 2] many Acts relating to various aspects of local administration were passed and control passed to such committees as the local Board. The Reform Act of 1832, placed Holywell in the Flint Parliamentary District which had one member of Parliament. The county of Flintshire was created in 1889 and Holywell was included in this.

On 5 March 1894, the Local Government Act was passed and Urban District Councils were created in towns such as Holywell, replacing the old Parish Vestries. For rural areas, Rural District Councils (RDCs), as well as (Community) Parish Councils, were established — local examples being Holywell RDC, plus the Brynford, Whitford and Ysceifiog Parish Councils. Ecclesiastical duties for the Anglican Church remained with the Church authorities but most of the other work done by the Parish

Vestries became the responsibility of the new civil Parish Councils. With County Councils having been established in 1888, there were therefore two levels of civil council for Holywell from 1895.

The Holywell community boundaries of today encompass lands in, and adjoining, all the following areas: Holywell town, including the district to the east at Milwr; west along the Holway; Bryn Celyn, between the works of W. Hall & Co. Ltd and the Old Plough Inn, alongside the Holywell to Greenfield road; and, below Bryn Celyn, Greenfield, with its coastal boundaries covering the area east from the bottom of Pen-y-Maes Road [SJ 2038 8680], and west, to the bottom of Isglan Road [SJ 1835 7858].

The communities of Holywell and Greenfield developed from religious and industrial foundations. The fact that St Winefride's Well attracted so many people and pilgrimages to the area would unwittingly have acted as an advertisement to the district's advantages for any potential industrialist. It is well worth mentioning that all the industrialists who built the larger factories came to the valley from places outside the district while the local gentry were involved in lead and coal mining, mostly on their own lands.

Holywell became a market town from 1292 when Edward I granted a charter to the monks of Basingwerk Abbey for the right to hold weekly markets and an annual three-day fair in the town. The latter had to be held on the religious festival of Trinity-tide.[21] In the weekly sales, they sold their produce, which included good ale. The markets increased in size with merchants and farmers coming into the town with their own merchandise to sell, exchange and barter. In return for organizing and controlling those events, the Cistercians had the right to collect taxes and charges from stall-holders (which became a valuable source of income for them). Naturally, St Winefride's Well, with its famed healing powers, would have been of great benefit to Holywell. In those days it was common practice for pilgrims to visit markets and fairs where there were holy wells.

The wider, lower end of High Street, extending from Bank Place entrance down to Cross Street, was the area where markets and fairs were held. The extra width would not only have been needed for the stalls, but also for traders with carts carrying goods to turn around. In the early days, a concentration of dwellings and inns, all of wooden construction, with thatched roofs, would have lined either side of this street.

It is often asked 'why is the parish church so low down from the town?', and it must be remembered that it was the town which was established, after the church, on the relatively level area of land at the top of the steep ascent from the site of the original church which St Beuno had built. From the religious establishments of St Winefride's Well and the Parish Church, Well Street was formed and High Street was created.

After the dissolution of Basingwerk Abbey in 1536, the markets ceased and others were established. Letters Patent granted to Sir John Egerton (lord of the lordship of Holywell and Fulbrook) on 20 June 1703, allowed a good corn market to be established. It is important to highlight the historic significance of Exchange House (4 High Street). Evidence which has come to light during the last fifty years makes it

A History of Holywell and Greenfield 23

Looking down High Street in 1887, the clock in the foreground was to commemorate the coming-of-age of Sir Pyers Mostyn, Bart, of Talacre. In front of the Cross Street shops, at the bottom of the street, is a column which could possibly have been the site of the market cross.

abundantly clear that this large building was the nerve centre for the operation of the markets and fairs from medieval times until at least the nineteenth century. It may have been that the ground floor had an open front for a while, thus the inside housed facilities for exchange trading. The corn market declined, but a general weekly market continued to be held, mainly dealing in meat and provisions.[13 & 23] From the mid nineteenth century, weekly markets were held on Fridays and fairs were held on the first Friday of the month.[11] J. Lloyd Price, a local businessman and a civic leader said that 'In 1830 Holywell was *the* market town of Flintshire. It was the central mart for merchandise of every description, and commanded the attendance of vendors and purchasers from far and near — from Cwm, Newmarket, Gwaenysgor, Llanasa, Dyserth, Prestatyn … to the very confines of Abergele on the one side, and on the other from Tremeirchion, Caerwys, Ysceifiog, Rhosesmor, Halkyn, Northop and to the very suburbs of Mold.'[11] Nationally, many market towns used to have a market cross installed in them — they very often had a religious significance. It appears that Holywell had one which was stragically sited at the western end of the market area, at the junction of Cross Street, and the top of Well Street. A close look at the 1887 print (facing) reveals a pillar in front of the lower Cross Street shops. I believe the pillar would have held Holywell's Market Cross. If so, that would have been the reason for the naming of that street — not just because of the junctions connected with it. This supposition is verified by Alfred Rimmer in his book *Ancient Stone Crosses of England* where he says that monastic Orders, particularly the Cisterians, sent a monk of friar into towns on market day to preach to the assembled traders at a cross. This symbolic central point also served as the point where the monks collected any tolls due for the privilege of selling goods in the market. It would appear, therefore, that, just after 1292, the Basingwerk Cistercians built a cross at the spot detailed above which ceased to be of religious significance after the closure of the abbey in 1536. It however remained *in situ* until at least 1887.

An indoor market was built in 1879 (behind the present Old Town Hall), with space for sixty-three stalls. During the twentieth century, a market business was run there for many years by a man named Joe Baker. Open air market stalls are now held in High Street on Thursdays and Saturdays. A livestock market operated between Coleshill Street and Bagillt Street from the late nineteenth century to around 1970.

Coal mining started in the thirteenth century around Mostyn and soon expanded along the coastal area to Bagillt. Although lead mining was

An enlarged detail from the 1887 view of High Street showing the market cross column.

carried out over centuries along the Halkyn Mountain range, this book only includes that carried out in the immediate Holywell area. The Holloway Level Mines were certainly within the confines of Holywell and are written about in Chapter 5. The abundance of water from the Holywell stream was the main reason why industry started to be created in the Greenfield Valley from the times of the Basingwerk monks. In the eighteenth century, the valley developed as an industrial centre and the population increased enormously. The industries created five reservoirs in the valley by building dams to hold back the Holywell Stream. The dam sluices provided water to turn large water wheels, thus creating power for machinery. The reservoirs were: Battery Pool (otherwise known as the Greenfield Mills Pool), Meadow Mills Pool, Lower Cotton Works Pool (later known as the Flour Mill Pool), Parys Mine Pool and Paper Mill Pool.

In 1810 it was recorded that 'The town till the beginning of the last century was very inconsiderable, the houses few, and mean, the greater part being roofed with thatch.'[13] Historic statistics prove how the population increased dramatically in just two centuries. Caution should be taken when making comparisons over the years, primarily because the original population statistics were based on the religious parish of Holywell which included the parishes of Bagillt (until 1839) and Brynford (until 1853). These two parishes were carved out of it, thus reducing the statistical returns for Holywell. Edward Llwyd wrote in his survey of Holywell c.1669: 'There are in Holywell betwixt houses & cottages 120.' In 1686, the Diocese of St Asaph recorded 274 families.[13] By 1795, the Parliamentary returns stated that 5,567 persons lived in Holywell.[13] The population had risen to 8,969 by 1831.[18] The 1847 Report on the State of Education in Wales said that the Parish of Holywell contained 10,834 inhabitants. This was a 95% increase in the fifty-two years from 1795 — proof of how industry developing so rapidly had brought new inhabitants to the district during those years. Because of the population explosion, there was also a tremendous increase in dwellings. There were numerous courtyards and alleyways in the town and the number of High Street shops and hotels/boarding houses increased. By the end of the eighteenth century there were eleven alleyways, which all ran at right-angles from the main street. Today, only Panton Place, the Mews and Bank Place still exist. Most of the side streets had at least ten to thirteen properties. As time went on, these alleyways had further side-alleyways and dwellings built. A very interesting fact about the town's High Street is that, despite the fact that the town has had (and still does have) many religious buildings, there has never been one erected along it; they were all positioned on the periphery of the town.

By 1901, the parliamentary figures disclosed that population numbers had dropped to 6,873[18] — presumably due to the closure of many factories in the Greenfield Valley. The 2001 Census recorded a population of 10,761 for the Holywell Town Council district.

It is interesting to read the comments of writers and travellers whose views were often so diverse and even controversial:

'The Water Poet', John Taylor, wrote in 1652, of the hill down to the Holy Well:

The hill descending is plentifully furnished with beggars of all ages, sexes, conditions, sorts and sizes, many of them are impotent but all are impudent and richly embroidered all over with such Hexameter poudred Ermins as are called lice in England.[71]

There is an interesting commentary regarding St Winefride's Holy Well from the journal of a person who travelled greatly during the latter part of the seventeenth century and hailed from aristocracy. She was a nonconformist and named Celia Fiennes. Visiting 'Holly Well' in 1698, she wrote:

St Winefred's Well, is built over with stone on pillars like a tryumphall arch or towere on the gates of a Church; there is a pavement of stone within ground 3 sides of the Well which is joyn'd on the fourth side by a great arch of stone which lies over the water that runs off the Well, its many springs which bubbles up very fast and lookes cleane in a compass which is 8 square walled in with stone; in the bottom you see as Crystall are 9 stones layd in an oval on which are dropps of red coullour some almost quite covering the top of the stone, which is pretended to be the blood of this holy saint whose head was struck off here, and so where her body laid this spring burst forth and remaines till now, a very rapid current, which runs off from this Well under a barre by which there are stone stepps for the persons to descend which will bathe themselves in the Well; and so they walke along the streame to the other end and then come out, but there is nothing to shelter them but are exposed to all the Company that are walking about the Well and to the little houses and part of the streete which runs along by it; but the Religeuse are not to mind that; it seemes the Saint they do honour to in this place must beare them out in all things, they tell of many lameness's and aches and distempers which are cured by it; it's a cold water and cleare and runs off very quick so that it would be a pleasant refreshment in summer to washhe ones self in it, but its shallow not up to the waste so its not easye to dive and washe in; but I thinke I could not have been persuaded to have gone in unless might have had curtains to have drawn about some part of it to have shelter'd from the streete, for the wett garments are no covering to the body; but there I saw abundance of ye devout papists on their Knees all round the Well; poor people are deluded into an ignorant blind zeale and to be pity'd by us that have the advantage of knowing better and ought to be better; there is some small stones of a reddish coullour in the Well said to be some of St Winefrede's blood also, which the poore people take out and bring to the strangers for curiosity and relicts, and also moss about the bancks full of great virtue for every thing - but it's a certaine gaine to the pooore people, every one gives them something for bringing them moss and the stones, but least they should in length of tyme be quite gather'd up they take care to replenish it dayly from some mossy hill and so stick it along the sides of the Well — there is a good streames runs from it and by means of steepe descent runs down and turns mills; they come also to drinke of the water which they take up in the first square which is walled round and where the springs rise, and they say its wonder full operation; the taste to me was but like good spring water which with wine and sugar and leamons might make a pleasant draught after walking amongst those shady trees of which there is a great many and some straight and tall like a grove but not very uniforme, but a sort of irregular rows …. From thence I went back to Harding [Hawarden] which is 8 very long miles; at Holly Well [Holywell] they speake Welsh, the inhabitants go barefoote and bare leg'd a nasty sort of people, their meate is very small here, mutton is noe bigger than little lamb, what of it there is was sweete; their wine good being neare the sea side and are well provided with fish, very good salmon and eeles and other fish I had at Harding.'[71]

Traveller and writer Daniel Defoe, in his 1724–5 *A Tour Thro' the Whole Island of Great Britain*, described Holywell as a small village by the well.[8] However, to indicate the immense growth of industry during the remainder of that century, the Revd Bingley, in his 1798 writings *Tour in North Wales* said:

> … this town is of great commercial importance. The numerous manufactures in its vicinity, and its easy access to the sea, have rendered it the great mart of this part of the kingdom. The town is spacious, but irregular; and pleasantly situated on the slope of a mountain which extends nearly to the water. Many of the houses are good, and give it an air of considerable opulence.[2]

Dr Samuel Johnson, touring north Wales in 1774, wrote:

> Holywell is a market town, neither very small nor mean. The spring called St Winefred's Well is very clear, and so copious, that it yields one hundred tuns of water in a minute … perhaps thirty yards of its eruption, turns a mill, and in a course of two miles, eighteen mills more. The well is covered by a lofty circular arch, supported by pillars; over this arch is an old chapel, now a school … the [outside] bath is completely and indecently open. A woman bathed while we all looked on.[26]

In 1796 a mineralogist named Arthur Aikin visited Holywell and observed it to be:

> a town of considerable importance on account of the extensive lead mines in the neighbourhood, and the various manufacturers that are here carried on. Upon entering the town from Downing Hall his party noticed a troop of cavalry who were quartered there.[152]

An interesting statement! I can only presume the troops were passing through the town — not previously reading of such in Holywell at that time.

The Revd Richard Warner, on a second walk through Wales in 1798, found that: '… the town has many good houses and respectable families in it … the social principle flourishes here in great vigour, and good neighbourhood is the motto of the place.'[154]

John Marius Wilson, writing in the *Imperial Gazetteer of England and Wales* (1870–2) repeated the words of Warner about the industrial valley:

> … not withstanding all the unpleasantness, noise, and bustle in the town, produced by numerous manufactories, the scene may be called picturesque. This is the only instance of that sort of beauty we have ever seen blended with so much mechanism, and so many specimens of human art. It is a deep glen, with well wooded banks on each side, having the Chester channel in the distance. The works are kept in such excellent order, that one of the first emotions occurring to the mind is that of wonder, at so much work carried on with so much cleanliness.[149]

J. Poole in *Histories of Flintshire*, 1831, wrote of Holywell:

> The streets though much improved of late years are still irregular, High Street is very spacious and contains many excellent houses and elegant shops …. Holywell ranks the first in the principality of Wales, both in a commercial and manufacturing point of view. Its inhabitants are intelligent and enterprising, and few places can boast of society being better cemented, or good cheer and hospitality more uniformly practised.[23]

The White Horse Hotel (now the HSBC Bank) was for many years a main posting house on the Holyhead to London route. In October 1832, thirteen-year old Princess Victoria [later Queen Victoria] was a passenger in a stagecoach which stopped at the hotel to change horses — she was travelling from Anglesey to Chester. A record of the event stated:

> Both sides of the road for miles were lined with anxious spectators to see their future Queen, who was welcomed with loud and reiterated huzzas. During the time of changing horses at the White Horse Hotel the party was again received with the loudest acclamations and loyal attachment by the inhabitants of the town and those of the surrounding country …. Triumphal arches were erected in the streets, and the waving of flags, handkerchiefs etc were seen from every window and avenue.[33]

Robson's Commercial Directory of 1840 highlights just how busy and important Holywell was then.

> Friday is market day, it is one of the largest markets in North Wales, upwards of 60 butchers regularly attend from various parts of the country. Hucksters from Chester and Liverpool meet the country people, and other hucksters from Denbighshire and Carmarthenshire [Author's note: I suspect this should have read 'Caernarfonshire'] at this market, by means great quantities of poultry, eggs, etc. , are regularly forwarded to those large towns.

High Street became cobbled, possibly in the early part of the nineteenth century. In *Black's Guide to North Wales*, 1855, it was said:

> The streets are irregular but spacious and well paved and lighted with gas; and the number of thriving shops and substantial houses, some of which are elegant, give indications of prosperity and opulence.[9]

Worrall's Directory, 1874, said: '[Holywell] consists of several good streets lighted with gas, and containing many first-class retail establishments'. J. Sproule, writing in his *Official Handbook to North Wales* in 1859. stated:

> The closing of some cotton factories threw a shade over the town, leaving houses empty and hands unemployed, but they have gradually been absorbed by the growing demands of other departments. (The chief of these 'other departments' was woollen manufacturing).[139]

But the 1860 *Imperial Gazetteer* recorded: 'In winter weather, the streets are excessively dirty. The houses are of brick, and of very indifferent construction.'

Despite those comments, there were atrocious living and sanitary conditions in the dwellings, particularly those off High Street.

The actor and playwright, Emlyn Williams, described High Street at 8.45 a.m. in 1917, '… as a wide, cobbled street, alive with people' in the day 'it was bustling High Street'.[16]

Well Street extends from the original Greenfield Street (adjacent to where the present-day Plas Dewi flats are located) to the top corner of the eighteenth-century wrought-iron gates of St James' Parish Church. From Greenfield Street, New Road (to

A History of Holywell and Greenfield   29

Well Street, c.1906. Note the branch leading to Chapel Street on the left, with the round memorial (now in the War Memorial Gardens, off Panton Place).

its junction with Whitford Street) must have been constructed during the eighteenth century. Well Street continues past the old vicarage, the Catholic Presbytery and the Roman Catholic Church. At the top end, there used to be the Convent and the Convent School. Well Street was, therefore, over many years the centre of ecclesiastical life; it was also, during the nineteenth century, the hub of civic and commercial life.

A major disaster occurred in Holywell on 5 January 1917, when the water feed to St Winefride's Well stopped. Since 1897, an underground tunnel was being gradually cut from Bagillt up into the hills in the Halkyn area in order to release flood waters from the lead mines, to enable the further expansion of the mining. As they cut into the Pant Lode below Pentre Halkyn, they unexpectedly hit a subterranean lake, with the result that its waters diverted down the new tunnel to Bagillt. Besides the well drying up, the industries in the Greenfield valley lost most of their power supply. In addition, the population of the town lost a large part of its supply of domestic water. Frantic efforts were made by the Town Council, the well authorities and the various industries to resolve the problem. The Town Council, the Holywell Textile Mills and Grosvenor Chater all joined together to get alternative supplies. Problems with the water supply had been voiced much earlier. In the introduction to the 1903, *The Life of St Winefride*, by Father Philip Metcalf, concern was expressed about lead mining adits draining away water from the sacred spring. Lady Anna Marie Mostyn (of Talacre) succeeded in obtaining a Parliamentary restriction on some areas of tunnelling and, in recognition of her work, she was made a member of the Bardic Circle at the 1904 National Eisteddfod in Rhyl (taking the title *Rhiain y Ffynnon* — the Lady of the Well).

On 22 September 1917, with government aid, a new, but much-reduced supply was routed to the Holy Well. The scheme involved the installation of a pipeline from the nearby water outlet from the Holway Level Mines. A special pump had to be installed at the Roskell Shaft higher up the level. However, the volume of water was far less than before and the well did not have anything like the surge it previously had. As time went by, when there was a drought, supplies could virtually cease, aggravated by the fact that eventually the pumping system at Roskell's shaft had to be abandoned. The mining tunnel company was sued.

The district known as Bryn Celyn (Holly Hill) became established in the latter part of the eighteenth century as a result of the industrial expansion in the area. Battery Row cottages were built, as were numerous other dwellings, on the hillside to the west of the main road. A National School was built there in 1819; Mount Gilead New Connection Methodist Chapel was erected in 1830. Close to these establishments a bowling green was opened, and the Alexandra Inn and Sycamore Stores were built alongside the main road (all pre-dated by the Royal Oak Inn). Bryn Celyn Stores and Post Office served the area until its closure in 1977.

On the southern hillside above the town of Holywell, Fron Park Road, the first by-pass road for the town was opened in 1932. It not only relieved the town of through traffic, but also opened up land for private housing development. Individual, larger houses were built alongside the by-pass and avenues of dwellings were laid out

Bryn Celyn, c.1908, showing Crescent Mill, Battery Pool and cottages, and Mount Gilead Chapel.

leading down from it. By around 1937, Dewi Avenue and Gwenffrwd Avenue had joined a new road named North Road. Over to the east, Park Lane was created.

Prior to that, the building of a large council houses estate had been started in the Strand area and this was added to after the Second World War. At about the same time, School Lane council house estate was built. The Holway council estate was developed in the late 1950s.

Many other private estates and individual dwellings were built in the district as the years passed. The larger private estates, including Pistyll, Wedgewood Heights, Coed-y-Fron and the Maxwell estate, developed in the second half of the twentieth century

The Holywell Townscape Heritage Initiative.
At the start of the twenty-first century, Flintshire County Council decided to create the Holywell Townscape Heritage Initiative (THI) and a Regeneration Officer was appointed. The scheme's main aim was to restore some of the authentic historic character of Holywell and encourage economic regeneration and growth. Holywell was chosen because of the substantial number of fine historic buildings that existed in the town and because it had suffered both social and economic set-backs during recent years.

Work was started in 2001 and many key sites were targeted with the aim of restoring their original character and features, and re-opening closed properties. The upper storeys of some buildings are now being used again, either as office accommodation or quality apartments. Shop fronts and interiors are being sympathetically renovated and restored to give back their original image, bearing in mind that such features must also be of service and appeal to today's needs.

Substantial funding is necessary for such a large scheme, arranged through the partnership of the County Council and other bodies, including CADW, the National Lottery, the Heritage Lottery Fund, the Welsh Development Agency, the Welsh Assembly and individual property owners. Flintshire County Council was one of the first bodies in Britain to have an application for a substantial amount of money approved for this type of scheme by the Heritage Lottery Fund, setting the standard for other similar schemes in Wales.[110]

Evidence unearthed by the scheme has shown that the buildings between the lower eastern end of Pen-y-Ball Street, linking with Cross Street, and the southern side of High Street, have elements of buildings dating from at least the sixteenth century and the stuctures of other town buildings are originally of wood.

Chapter 2

The Town and its Services

To try to understand how the civil life of Holywell developed from the earliest times, it is essential to have an outline of how and when, the more notable national laws were established. For four centuries from the mid twelfth century the people of Holywell were very fortunate in having the Cistercian monks of Basingwerk Abbey in their midst. Most importantly, the Order aided the poor and the sick, and provided some work for the population.

The Courts of Quarter Sessions were instituted in 1363.[36] The Justices of the Peace, appointed by the Crown, met four times a year and had great powers, visiting local parishes to ensure justice, order and peace.

After Basingwerk Abbey closed in 1536, a series of laws were passed, aimed at assisting the poor.[36] This was all in the days when the Parish Vestry carried out the administration of the town. In 1597, an Act was passed which called upon every parish to appoint overseers of the poor, as well as to provide 'Parish Houses' (an early form of workhouse). The most important Act passed was the Elizabethan Poor Law of 1601 which was intended to make it a duty for every parish to raise funds from the population by means of levies.[37] It is unknown when the system commenced in Holywell. The Act consolidated most of the previous Acts, and remained virtually unchanged until 1834 when The Poor Law Amendment Act was passed.[36] That year, the Holywell Local Poor Law Board was set up, before Holywell was the chief town in Flintshire for such purposes. Covering the same area as this board was the Registration District of Holywell (which had four sub-districts, namely, Whitford, Holywell, Flint and Mold). In 1871, the Local Government Board was created in the town, which absorbed the Poor Law Board, and was also responsible for the local public health service.[10] The Public Health Act of 1875 created Sanitary Districts, which were, in reality, the existing Poor Law Unions.[4]

Changes in the way of life nationally during the late eighteenth and early nineteenth centuries meant that it was necessary for Parliament to devote attention to various aspects of people's everyday lives. There were serious hazards to public health, a lack of sanitation, and growing problems with crime and education was in serious need of assistance and regulation.[38]

The important Holywell Local Board was established in 1862, consisting of a chairman, twelve members, a clerk and a surveyor.[38 & 39] Between them, they managed the affairs of the town from their offices in Well Street. The Board that year designed the official Holywell seal, which incorporated an engraving of the Holy Well, and the motto *Llwyddiant i Dreffynnon* (Success to Holywell). However, it was the passing of the Local Government Act of 1888 that was the real start of our modern local government system. That Act created County Councils[3] — Flintshire County Council being one. The first meeting of the 'Provisional Council' in Flintshire was held in Mold on 3 January 1889. At a subsequent meeting on 20 February 1889, the Clerk was instructed to obtain a seal for the county. Following elections for County Councillors, the first full Flintshire County Council meeting was held on 1 April 1889.[4] In 1894, the Local Government Act was passed which created Urban and Rural District Councils and Parish Councils [Brynford and Whitford being local examples].[3] The last meeting of the Holywell Local Board was held on 31 December 1894 and the following day Holywell Urban District Council held their first meeting in the Well Street offices of the old Holywell Board. Its chairman was local-born surgeon, Dr James Williams, of Castle Hill; the Clerk to the Council was a solicitor, Mr William Davies.[41]

The intention is not to record the responsibilities of the respective Councils as, since 1888, there have been innumerable changes in the structure, responsibility and authority of the councils. In 1929, the Ministry of Health abolished the Boards of Guardians (including that for Lluesty) and their functions were transferred to the County Councils, although the Poor Law remained in force.[37] Through the revolutionary National Health Service Act of 1948, the Poor Law was eventually superseded by National Assistance.[37] Hospitals became the responsibility of Regional Health Authorities. Since that time there have been numerous changes to the way in

Holywell High Street, just after 1900.

Station Road, Greenfield, just after 1900 (note the Royal Hotel on the right hand corner)

which hospitals and health services have been developed and, again, it is beyond the scope of this book to go into the complex detail of this subject. Thankfully, the deplorable conditions experienced in Holywell in the eighteenth and nineteenth centuries are now long gone and the district enjoys excellent facilities, some governed by the County Council, whilst others are controlled by Welsh Water.

On 1 April 1974, a national reorganisation of local government took place. The boundaries for both Flintshire and Denbighshire, which had remained unchanged since they had been set up in 1536, were altered and a new county named Clwyd was created – merging the two old counties. There were some variations to the overall boundaries, and the old split of Flintshire into two separate geographical parts was lost. Within the new county, both Holywell UDC and Holywell RDC ceased to exist, to be replaced by a governing body created to cover the districts of Holywell, Flint and Mold, known as Delyn Borough Council (the name Delyn being derived from the two main rivers within its boundaries, namely the Dee and the Alyn). The other new body set up to manage Holywell and Greenfield's more domestic affairs was Holywell Town Council. A new light, structured building was erected in Coleshill Street which accommodated some of Delyn Borough Council's services. The Town Council was at first given some temporary office accommodation within that building, but eventually had to provide their own separate premises. To meet that problem, cottages at lower Bank Place were converted to provide suitable permanent accommodation for a meeting room and office, where the clerk and the council continued to be housed. Delyn Borough Council gradually transferred services from the Coleshill Street building to their other offices in Mold and Flint.

36 *A History of Holywell and Greenfield*

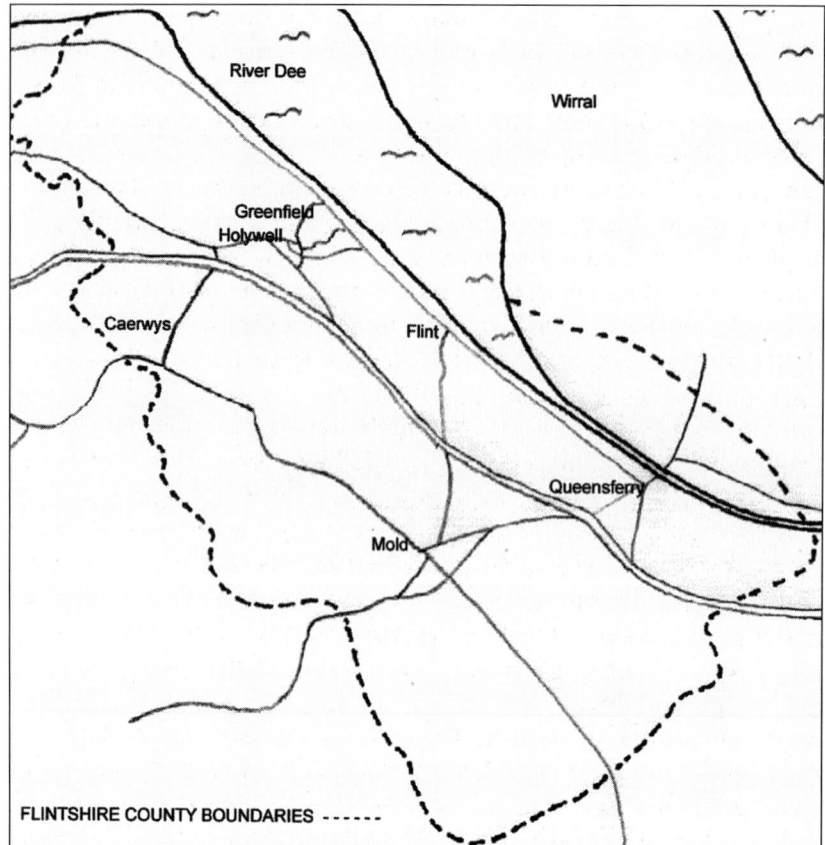

Holywell and Greenfield within the boundaries of the new Flintshire County from 1st April 1996.

On 1 April 1996, further local government changes were made by central government. Clwyd County Council ceased to exist and was replaced by three new areas of county control — Flintshire County Council, Denbighshire County Council and Wrexham County Borough Council. The boundaries of the new counties were different from those of the old authorities which bore the same names. Delyn Borough Council also ceased to exist and its duties were merged into Flintshire County Council. In 2000, the County Council closed what had been the Delyn Borough Council building in Holywell and it was demolished in August 2002.

Municipal, Public and General Services Buildings
The Town Hall, Market Hall and Assembly Hall [SJ 1852 7590]
The Town Hall was erected between 1893 and 1896, on land given by Earl Grosvenor. The architect for all three buildings was R. Lloyd Williams, then county architect to Denbighshire County Council; the builder was Abel Jones of Rhyl.[41] The front of the high-Victorian, Gothic-style building,[42] of stone construction with a freestone clock

tower with octagonal belfry, gave the town a magnificent building which enhanced the town centre. Offices on the ground floor and an assembly room above gave the Council excellent facilities. Before the whole complex was constructed there had been a Market Hall to the rear of the site which had taken six years to build, opening on 24 June 1879. It had twenty-eight greengrocery stalls, five fish stalls and, to their rear, twenty-nine butchers stalls. When there was a catastrophic fire at the woollen mill in 1883, the Market Hall was used to accommodate the mill hand-looms. In 1885, the Market was replaced by a new Public Assembly Hall which was opened by Dame Edith Wynne. Over the succeeding years, great public use was made of the hall with its dressing rooms, cloakrooms and grand wooden block floor for a wide variety of social events and meetings. Later, good toilet facilities were introduced and an additional room was added for refreshments. In its latter years, the hall could comfortably seat around 450 people. The town's first cinema, 'The Empire Electric Picture Palace' was opened in the hall. However, in 1922 the new 'Prince of Wales Theatre' was built in Station Road. As a consequence, the Empire had to close.

Built into the front wall of the Town Hall in 1922 were two memorial tablets to remember servicemen from Holywell who had lost their lives in the First World War. The cost of £130 had been raised by public subscription. Engraved above the tablets, in granite, are the Arms of Holywell District Council. The unveiling ceremony, on Easter Sunday 1922, was carried out by John Williams, a local man who had been badly wounded and crippled in the war.

Before the Second World War, all trading from the Market Hall was run by one businessman, named Joe Baker, who hailed from Merseyside. For many years, his distinctive character, with a keen eye to trade at low prices, was something which attracted shoppers to his market. Whilst there was no set pattern to his displays, it always seemed that whatever you asked for he immediately found. When the hall closed in 1986, he transferred his business to premises in Halkyn Street. After the 1992 pedestrianisation scheme, other people were allowed to operate outdoor market stalls in the High Street and Tower Gardens.

In 1986, Clwyd County Council and Delyn Borough Council decided to demolish the Public Assembly Hall, as well as a major part of the Town Hall and Market. The only part of the Town Hall left was the front façade on the High Street. Behind this, a retail shop was built. The Assembly Hall land, together with other adjoining land, was developed into a car park with a supermarket to the western side. An electrically driven water wheel, with a stone wall surround, was erected here in April 1987. The Town Hall façade was given a Grade II Listed status by Cadw in 1991.[44]

The Town Clocks
The first major clock that we know about was 4 ft in diameter and was erected in 1814, outside his High Street watchmaker's shop, by Edward Jones. It remained in constant use until 1867[11] when Sir Pyers Mostyn (8th Baronet), of Talacre, presented the townspeople with a clock on a free standing wooden tower sited outside the Cross Keys Hotel to mark the coming of age of his son, William. It was unveiled on 14

August 1867. The clock remained there until October 1893, when the mechanism was removed from the tower and, with some alterations, was mounted onto the tower above the central entrance of the front wall of the Town Hall which was then being built. Its situation meant that it could be seen from both ends of the High Street. Sir Pyers died on 14 May 1882, and William succeeded to the title. He subsequently died on 10 May 1912 and was buried alongside his father in St David's Churchyard, Pantasaph.

In 1900, a new clock was provided on the Town Hall which had two black-faced, round dials, with white hands and numerals. After the end of the First World War, the dials were changed – this time they were white and the hands and numerals black. This change meant that the clock could be read more easily from a distance. With just routine maintenance, the clock remained in continuous use until 1990 when a major renovation programme had to be carried out, which included replacing the original manual winding mechanism with an electrical system. The clock has now given service to the public for well over a century.

The War Memorial Gates and Gardens, Panton Place [SJ 1858 7575]
At the Panton Place entrance to the Memorial Gardens, a magnificent pair of wrought-iron gates, manufactured by the Caernarfon Iron Works, were installed after the Second World War. In stone pillars to each side of the gateway are two memorial tablets to the 110 Holywell men who died in the two World Wars. The gates and associated stonework were given a Grade II Listing by Cadw in 1991.[44]

Within the memorial garden is a 5 ft 6 ins high, 3 ft diameter, rounded stone pillar with spiral steps to its rear which bears the date 1855. This was removed from its original site, alongside the wall at the junction of Well Street and Chapel Street, when the town's inner ring road was constructed in 1985. Although no documentary evidence has been traced, it is widely believed that it was erected in 1855 to commemorate those Holywell men who had lost their lives in the Crimean War (1854–56). Other local reminders of this conflict can be found where the route of Crockford's mineral tramway left the Level and crossed the Holywell/Greenfield road, north of the Textile Mill, by means of a stone-pillared wooden trestle bridge named Inkerman Bridge. Close to the bridge was a residence named Alma Cottage. The battle of the River Alma took place on 20 September 1854 and the Battle of Inkerman on 5 November 1854.

The Greenfield War Memorial is sited in specially laid out gardens at the road junction between the A548 Coast Road and Dock Road. The Gwespyr stone memorial was provided by the Greenfield Victory Club to commemorate the lives of the twenty-five Greenfield men who died fighting in the First World War. For the sixteen men who lost their lives in the Second World War, a Welsh slate plaque was added near the base of the original memorial.

A war memorial to the employees of Courtaulds, Greenfield, who died in the

Facing: Holywell Town Hall in the first few years of the twentieth century. The entrance to the Cross Keys Hotel can be seen on the left.

The War Memorial Gardens and Gates leading from Panton Place.

battles of the Second World War was placed on the outer front wall of the main office block. This was thankfully saved when the factory closed and re-erected within Holy Trinity Church, Greenfield.

Fron Park [SJ 1855 7565]
When Fron Park Road was constructed, land adjoining it became available for housing development and the Urban District Council resolved to create a leisure park for the town, between what were to become the housing avenues of Gwenffrwd Road and Park Lane, with the by-pass acting as the southern perimeter [note the rather elaborate iron boundary fencing to the three sides]. At this point it is interesting to record how extensive the lands of 'The Fron' had been from at least the middle of the nineteenth century. On their southernmost boundary, Fron Hall was built by Richard Sankey, adjacent to Coed-y-Fron [SJ 184 754], and the estate ran basically north to a line where North Road was built by 1935, west to Dewi Avenue and east to Park Lane. The plans for the Fron Park project were drawn up by the UDC's surveyor and architect for twenty-two years, Philip Llewelyn Dykins, of Gerddi Beuno [there is a memorial window to him and his wife in the Parish Church].[45] At first, a small stream ran through the park but, unfortunately, this has since almost dried up. The first facilities provided were a children's playing area, two bowling greens and two tennis courts, together with two buildings — one providing changing/locker rooms and the other being a bandstand. In 1968, Holywell UDC voted to construct a heated

swimming pool in the north-eastern section of the park, alongside which a leisure centre was later built resulting in the loss of much of the open area of parkland.

The Swimming Pool and Leisure Centre [SJ 1855 7565]

The town's first baths, named 'The Westminster Plunge Baths', were provided in 1865 next to St Winefride's Well. The spacious modern swimming baths were built by Marples Ridgeway (Contractors) Ltd on the north side of Fron Park in 1969 (just south of the Community Centre/Youth Club [SJ 1869 7571]). The building and baths themselves cost £160,000; internal furniture and fittings cost a further £40,000. Shingler Risdon Associates were the architects, and the premises were officially opened on 23 September 1969 by Martyn Woodroffe, Swimming Silver Medalist in the Mexico Olympic Games, 1968. A gym/exercise room named 'Silhouette' was added to the building and officially opened on 4 March 1991, by Nevil J. Brackenbury, the Mayor of Delyn Borough Council.

An excellent leisure centre was added to the complex in 1985. Attached to the swimming pool building, its amenities provided a snooker room (with six tables), a squash room and a public room for general use. There is also as a cafeteria and a licensed bar. On 16 March 1987, Diana, Princess of Wales, visited the Leisure Centre in her capacity as Patron of Birthright. She witnessed special displays by local fitness groups and gymnastic displays that had been organised by the charity.

Libraries

We have to look back as far as 1838 for what appears to have been the first form of public library in Holywell. *Robson's 1840 Commercial Directory* records:

> A Society has been formed, called the Royal Geological and Natural History Society, for the purpose of diffusing useful knowledge and science, and to promote the intellectual improvement of all branches of society; it has only been in existence two years, and the library and museum are well stored with books and curiosities.[43]

Flintshire Record Office, Hawarden, hold 'A Subscription Book for Holywell Circulating Library covering the years 1838 to 1868' (although it is not known how long this circulating library lasted). It was sited in Panton Place, and, in 1874, the Holywell Literary Institute and Reading Room was listed as being there.[43 & 47] The Urban District Council opened a room on the upper floor of the Town Hall as a library in 1905, but in 1910, their library was in a former working men's club, off the High Street. This is believed to have been what was later Post Office Lane, and from which premises, the council provided a library service until 1965.

Although the Flintshire County Council Library Service had been established in 1925, Holywell UDC decided to continue independently with their own library service.[4] However, following the Public Libraries Act of 1964, the UDC library became an integral part of the County service the following year. The County Council continued to use the Post Office Lane premises until 1975 when they built a new modern library off North Road [SJ 1852 758].

Holywell Library, 2006, housing its ultra-modern facilities.

The new premises covered an area of 4,879 sq ft, about six times the size of the old library, at an overall cost of £55,000. The builders were Messrs Spooner, of Hull.[48] The opening ceremony was carried out on 11 September 1975 by Councillor Mrs M. E. Risley, the Mayor of Holywell, who unveiled the commemorative plaque. Between January and August 2005, the building was extended and completely refurbished and modernised. During that period a temporary library was conducted from the nearby Youth Centre. When the project was completed and opened, as the Holywell Library and Learners' Centre, on 1 September 2005, it provided two new training suites equipped with the latest ICT facilities, which enabled local learning providers to offer various courses and training opportunities for the public. Additional computers were added to those that had been introduced to the library, around 2000 under the government's New Opportunities Funding Project. A gallery was also incorporated into the building for displays of such subjects as local art, crafts and local history. The whole project cost £576,000 and was financed by Local Regeneration Funding from the Welsh Assembly.[46] The official opening ceremony was carried out on 14 October 2005 when HRH The Duchess of Gloucester unveiled a commemorative plaque.[46]

Law and order
Police
Prior to the establishment of the modern police forces, parishes appointed a constable to help with local law and order. In Holywell, transgressors were incarcerated in a square building curiously named the 'Round Building',[11] sited at the junction of Well Street and Chapel Street.

County constabularies were established in 1856 and the Flintshire Constabulary was formed by the Flintshire Quarter Sessions on 5 March.[4] The County Council Act of 1888 meant that the police came under the control of the Standing Joint Police Committee.[4]

From 1855, the Holywell police station was at the rear of the County Court Building. In the late 1920s a new police station was built to the east of the Court building [SJ 1877 7571]. At first, it also housed the superintendent, but later the building was converted for use as a police station only and a private house in the town was purchased for the superintendent. Extensions added to the building in later years included a cell-block. During the winter of 2006–07 the cell-block was demolished, and the interior of the station underwent major alterations and refurbishment.

Greenfield has its own police station, built on the corner of School Lane and the main Holywell road, shortly after Holywell's police station was erected. It served the local area until the early 1970s when a decision was made to close it and the building was subsequently sold.

In December 2003, the County Council (on behalf of Flintshire Rural Partnership) installed a closed-circuit TV security system in the town to assist in reducing crime. Eight strategically placed cameras were linked to a central monitoring county unit in County Hall, Mold. Out of an overall cost of £314,000, the Welsh Assembly Government granted £179,000, the remainder of the cost being borne by Flintshire County Council and Holywell UDC.[46]

County Court, Halkyn Street [SJ 1877 7571]
Courts known as 'Quarter Sessions' came into being after 1363 and in Holywell, after the building of St Winefride's Chapel, sessions were held there. The 1846 County Court Act showed Holywell in the 29th Circuit of Towns.[43]

The robust, Italianate-style County Court building was erected in 1855. Single-storeyed, its front is divided into three short rusticated portions, with arched doorways. There is a venetian window in the centre, with a pediment containing the Arms of the Crown. The original accommodation was described in *Worrall's Directory* of 1874 as having 'a fine court room, with rooms for the judge, attorneys, high bailiff, and registrar; and an office for the latter. The Court had a dais over the judge's panelled bench. In September 1998, the building ceased to be used as a court and cases were then dealt with at Mold Magistrates Court. A development company purchased the premises and converted it into office units. The building was Grade II listed by Cadw in 1991.[44]

The police station, complete with cells and a lockup, was situated immediately behind the Court.[43] The building was subsequently converted into use as a solicitor's office, and has remained so to this day.

Registrar of Births, Marriages and Deaths
A law passed in 1538 made it the responsibility of the parishes to maintain parish records of the baptism, marriage and death of all local people. The earliest records available for Holywell Parish date from 1677. Nationally, by the end of the eighteenth century, it had become apparent that records were by no means being maintained for a large proportion of the population (due to the growth of Nonconformity) and

stricter measures were introduced to provide accurate data of the country's population. The first Act passed to provide better statistics was the Census Act of 1800; data was then available giving more accurate statistics. Since 1801, a census has been taken every ten years (with the exception of 1941). The Act for the Compulsory Civil Registration of Births, Marriages and Deaths followed in 1836. This encompassed the system of parish registration; however it also meant that individuals no longer had to register through the Established Church if they did not wish to do so. To cope with this new system Register Offices were opened in each registration district. In Holywell, the first office was in Well Street. By 1870 it was in Panton Place.

In 1966, a purpose-built, brick building was erected in Park Lane [SJ 1868 7570] alongside the Health Clinic, which, as well as being used for the registration of births, marriages and deaths was also used for civil marriage ceremonies. Provision was also made in the building for accommodating the Clerk of the Courts for the Holywell and Caerwys districts.

Other public services
Ambulance Service
The volunteer St John's Ambulance, which had its premises off Station Road, provided Holywell with its first ambulance service in the 1940s. The ambulance was garaged at Robert's Garage in Bagillt Street. In 1948, with the creation of the National Health Service, the Ambulance Service H.Q. was transferred to Lluesty Hospital. In 1955, the Flintshire Ambulance Service took over the unit, still at Lluesty, but the following year saw the building of a new, purpose-built Ambulance Centre alongside the present Fire Station. Tremendous advances in the service and technology of the county's ambulance service have been witnessed since then.

Fire Service
The only means of dealing with fires before the twentieth century was by handchains feeding buckets of water to the fire. Consequently, there must have been many disastrous results in the district because of a lack of organization, as well as a shortage of readily available water. Before the 1937 Fire Brigades Bill, which was responsible for the implementation of the Auxiliary Fire Service, Holywell UDC had only provided the voluntary firemen with a handcart to transport the equipment which consisted of a standpipe, hose and small sundries. After the Act, an outbuilding to the rear of the Assembly Hall was opened as a fire station and trailer pumps were purchased (which were towed by private cars!).[32] The outbreak of the Second World War resulted in the government passing a Bill on 22 May 1941 which created the National Fire Service and the County Council became the controlling body. In a short while, the Council provided a wartime brick building with concrete roof, at the junction of Whitford Street and the A55 trunk road [SJ 1815 7617], which served as a fire station.[32] Nissen huts were added to both sides of the station building. In 1965, the Council replaced the wartime structure with a purpose-built brick building.[48]
Cemeteries

For centuries, burials in Holywell took place in the parish churchyard. In 1847, a new cemetery, named 'St Peter's Cemetery', was opened adjacent to the junction of Coleshill Street and Crossroads. By this time, the subject of burials had become a serious matter due to the growth of Nonconformity and the wish of the Roman Catholic communities to be independent of the Anglican Church. Consequently, the Burial Act was passed in 1855 which made local municipal councils provide cemeteries for the use of anyone. Earlier, Pantasaph Roman Catholic Cemetery had been opened in 1852, and a cemetery for the Welsh Nonconformists was opened at Seion Chapel, Carmel, in 1855.

In 1909, Holywell UDC bought land and passed plans for a public town cemetery on the hillside above the junction between Whitford Street and the Holway [SJ 1805 7595]. A new entrance to it was made when the Fron Park by-pass road was opened in 1932. A cemetery chapel, built of limestone with slate roof and belfry was built early in 1910. The chapel was heated by means of a coke-fired stove. Both cemetery and chapel were opened later that year. The graveyard was designed to provide separate areas for the different denominations, i.e. Anglican, Catholic and Nonconformist. As the years passed, use of the chapel ceased, but the building still stands, although it is now used for the storage of equipment used in the upkeep of the cemetery.

In 1914, Holywell UDC decided that it was necessary for Greenfield to have its own public cemetery, which was opened at the top of School Lane, Greenfield [SJ 1908 7595]. As with the Holywell Public Cemetery, sections were provided for those of different religious denominations. An extension was added to the cemetery in 1969. Because space for further burials was limited, another cemetery [SJ 1907 7595], to the west of the original one, was opened by Flintshire County Council in September 1998. This became known as Greenfield N[o.] 2 Cemetery.

Water drainage and sewerage
On account of its geology Holywell was very fortunate in the past by having a number of wells and springs providing sources of water and an early example of such was described by Thomas Pennant in 1796:

> In an adjacent field of mine, called Roft Tob, was a valuable spring which was running to waste ... I (by the assistance of Mr Donbavand) caused, in the year 1794, a pillar to be erected, into which the water was collected, and raised to a height convenient to be received into vessels placed there, to supply, with ease and expedition, the wants of the inhabitants.[22]

The Roft [otherwise known as 'Roff'] Tob (nobody knows the origin of this name) pump was behind the houses of today's St Peter's Estate [SJ 1908 7567]. The other major supply of water for the town was adjacent to St Winefride's Well. Whilst some residents carried their water in buckets, some men placed a specially shaped yoke across their shoulders and carried two large buckets of water suspended on chains. A blind man named Joe Barker, for some twenty years from around 1900, would fill a

36-gallon wooden water barrel at Roft Tob. The barrel was on a wheeled chassis, which, in turn, was pulled by a donkey. Joe went about the town, selling water for a penny or two.

Lluesty workhouse had its own Bamford Water Lift Pump, the supply for that came from yet another strong underground spring. At the north-eastern end of The Mews, off High Street, the outer side of a high cast-iron water tank can be seen — the inner half is within the end property. This was installed to collect rain water from the roof gutters of The Mews buildings and locals could obtain water from a tap near the base. Presumably the end property was built around the pre-existing tank. There is a similar, but smaller, tank behind the dwelling on the eastern end of Strand Park.

Although several directory writers described High Street in good terms throughout the nineteenth century, they did not highlight the exceptionally poor homes and health conditions prevailing in the town. As far back as records can be traced, this was always a major problem for the district, as indeed it was for most other towns. Unfortunately, there were terrible outbreaks of diphtheria, fevers, and especially cholera in Holywell, from which over 200 people died in at least four major outbreaks between 1832 and 1866. So bad was the situation that in 1849 the Bishop of St Asaph declared that Thursday, 18 October, be observed throughout the Holywell parish as a Day of Humiliation and Prayer. All classes were invited to join in the supplication, and shops, public-houses and so on were asked to have a total cessation of business for the day. Services were held in the Holywell, Greenfield and Bagillt churches.[R103]

The squalid and appalling sanitary conditions in which the local population lived continued until at least the middle of the nineteenth century. Despite government legislation to deal with sewerage, drainage and to provide clean water supplies,

Joe Barker, the blind man, supplying water in Brynford Street for the townspeople.

Holywell parish and the subsequent Local Sanitary Committee did not comply in any significant manner. It was only after the Government Medical Officer, R. Thorne, issued a report on 14 May 1897, stating:

> There are probably few districts in England and Wales of which the sanitary condition has occupied the attention of the Local Government Board more frequently, or with less satisfactory result than the tract of the flat marshy land extending along the south bank of the Dee estuary.

After the Holywell UDC was formed in 1894, far more attention was paid to the matters referred to above. For any reader wishing to have a much deeper knowledge of conditions in the town during the 1800s, the publication *Living Conditions in nineteenth century Holywell*, by Tim Jones, is very strongly recommended. During September 1912, a scarlet fever epidemic hit the town as a result of which schools were closed until the following January.[12]

For many years the district has obtained its water supply from the Alwyn Reservoir on the Denbigh Moors. From there, the water travels via a large main to a branch near Cilcain which feeds a water pumping station at Rhosesmor, and from there, a large underground reservoir at the summit of Moel-y-Gaer. A water main from that reservoir goes to the Pen-y-Ball area, and a further branch feeds the concrete reservoir on the hilltop above Holywell.

As the twentieth century unfolded, mains drains were installed in the district, however, as before, their outlets were into the River Dee. In 1963, Holywell UDC decided that, because of the problem of untreated sewerage being pumped into the Dee, a new sewerage plant was needed at Greenfield. In 1972, a £200,000 scheme for a full-treatment works was put forward to the Welsh Office. There then followed a long drawn-out period of disagreement between the parties involved and it was not until the late 1970s that the new treatment plant to the west of Dock Road, some 200 yards from the river, was built and brought into service.

Refuse and recycling
As with most other small UK towns, until the twentieth century there had been no major system or collection of household waste in Holywell, but, as the century unfolded, refuse started to be disposed of into old quarries. By the 1930s, a household collection service had been started by Holywell UDC and they opened up a waste tipping area in the valley to the east of the road from Holywell to Riverbank, Bagillt. This area had the advantages of a large acreage, as well as depth from the road into which the waste was dumped. This waste, as it built up, acted as a re-inforcement for the road above. By the mid 1970s, the area was full and was levelled and landscaped. With the changes in local government in 1974, Holywell UDC became absorbed into the new Delyn Borough Council and waste was taken to a landfill site at Y Ddol, near Afonwen. When that closed in 1987, a site at the old Courtaulds Castle Works, Flint, was used until 1993, when waste was transported and tipped at two sites in Buckley.[50] Following further local government reorganisation in 1996, Flintshire County Council

became the controlling body for the household waste from the whole county.

By the 1970s, the use of individual containers for recyclable waste had started and, by the end of the century, items such as paper, glass, textiles and metals were part of the collections. Containers were placed in car parks as well as supermarket parking areas. The County Council opened a site on the Castle Industrial Park, Flint, which included skips for garden waste as well as general waste such as wood and household electrical items.

A major step for recycling green garden waste came about in January 2003 after a dedicated composting waste facility was opened by Flintshire County Council within the site of the old Courtaulds N°. 4 Unit factory in Greenfield. A two-acre raft of concrete with full water interception facilities, a weighbridge, an industrial chopper and trammel screeners had cost £270,000 — all funded by the Welsh Assembly Government. The facility was officially opened by Sue Essex, National Assembly Minister for Environment, Planning and Transport, on 30 January 2003. Households within trial districts of the county had been provided with brown 'wheely bins' for their green waste, and the council started a collection service, from which the wagon emptied its contents at the new site. After a special process, taking twelve to sixteen weeks, the green waste becomes a usable soil conditioner. At first the Council used the product in the county's parks, but from November 2003, arrangements commenced to sell it commercially. This facility was immediately widely acclaimed as an excellent environmental commitment by the Council.[46 & 50]

On 17 October 2005, a £750,000 recycling park was opened alongside the composting site at Greenfield. This park, the largest in Flintshire, has ten split-level bays for a variety of household waste items. The Welsh Assembly gave £250,000 towards the cost; the balance coming from Flintshire County Council. The project was further proof of the county's commitment to provide user-friendly facilities to meet national recycling targets.[46]

Gas
Although it was a young Scotsman, named William Murdock, who, in 1801, first introduced gas lighting in Britain by illuminating Soho Street in Birmingham, it was a Moravian named Wintzer (later named Winsor), who came to London in 1807 and lit part of Pall Mall by gaslight. He named his company the Chartered Gas Company, which, by 1812, had expanded and was re-named the London Gas Light & Coke Company.

In 1824, a plot of land was purchased at Greenfield from the Commissioners of Woods and Forests for the purpose of erecting a gas works [SJ 1965 7767]. One year later, the British Gas Light Company installed a gasometer there with the specific undertaking to supply gas lighting to the townships of Holywell, Greenfield and Bagillt.[51] The works were reputedly to be the third in the UK.[18] Unfortunately, the aspirations of the gas company were not fulfilled and, three years later, they offered the whole plant for sale for £5,000. A sale, however, was not achieved, but a lease on the works was arranged with a Mr Webber. He died in 1834 and, after nine years, his administrators passed the complex back to the British Gas Light Company. It was in that year that the Holywell vestry voted for the provision of gas lighting in the area from Bagillt Street to Marldir, from Chester Street to Perth-y-Terfyn, from Pen-y-Ball Street to Malt Kiln, from Whitford Street to Pen-y-dre and as far as the town boundary in Greenfield Street. The total installation cost was £90, chargeable to the rates. Greenfield township did not have gas lighting until after a meeting of ratepayers on 20 February 1860, when they sanctioned an expenditure of £132 for the work to be carried out.[51] When the railway station at Greenfield was opened in 1848, it was lit by gas from the nearby gasworks. Gas engines superceded some water wheels and steam engines in the industrial Greenfield Valley, and, needless to say, gas quickly replaced candle and paraffin lamps in the district.[51]

In 1928, the first gas showroom was opened in shop premises on the central northern side of High Street. This was re-sited to 2 Cross Street in the mid 1950s.

Electricity
The Electric Lighting Act of 1882 signified the commencement of electric power and light across the nation. By an Act of 1904, the North Wales Power Company was given the right to supply electricity to Flintshire. However, it was the Electricity Distribution of North Wales & District Ltd, who purchased electricity from North Wales Power Company and then sold it to Holywell UDC for the purposes of lighting and power.[48] A major example of a commercial enterprise which switched over to electricity in 1913 was the Holywell Textile Mills. A sub-station erected in 1926, and bearing the name North Wales Power Company, is still to be seen to the east of Greenfield Road, just before School Lane.

Nationally, on 1 April 1948 regional electricity boards were created under the Government's nationalisation programme — Holywell's supply coming from The Merseyside and North Wales Electricity Board (MANWEB).

Postal Services
Holywell's first post office was sited in Panton Place where *Pigot's Directory* for 1822 stated that the London and Chester mails arrived every afternoon at three, and departed every afternoon at five. The Bangor, Conwy and St Asaph mails arrived every morning at two, and departed each evening at half-past eight. At the back of the post office was a courtyard which had an arched entrance (which still survives) alongside the Red Lion public house.[43]

By the early 1860s, Holywell Post Office was following the General Post Office pattern and provided money orders, as well as a National Savings Bank. In 1868, it also became a telegraph office.[43] In the late nineteenth century, the telephone service was added to the facilities provided by the town's post office. When the main Chester to Holyhead railway opened in 1848 (which included the station at Greenfield), mail ceased to be carried to and from the town by stagecoaches and the railway took over, as was the case all along the north Wales coast. Sometime around 1880, the town's post office ceased to operate from Panton Place and operated from newly constructed premises at 48 High Street (the building now occupied by Barclays Bank [SJ 1866 7581]).

In 1925, the General Post Office acquired the premises next to the post office in High Street, which had previously been a Jesuit College. The present-day post office building was constructed on this site. A public-counter service was provided on the ground floor and the first floor was equipped to serve as the telephone exchange for the surrounding district. The postal sorting office, with a rear yard and vehicle garage, was built at the back of the building. The complex was opened in 1926.

During the 1950s, with the use of telephones rapidly extending, the High Street exchange could not cope with the volume of calls and a new telephone exchange was built on Fron Park Road.

Unfortunately for both Holywell and the postal delivery staff, the Royal Mail closed the town's sorting office in the mid 1990s. An industrial unit at Flint was converted into a large sorting office to cover the needs of both Holywell and Flint districts. Yet again, this was a set back for Holywell.

Greenfield's first post office was sited alongside the coast road to Mostyn, next door to the Crown & Anchor Inn, at the junction of the Holywell and Mostyn roads (by the tollgate). This opened in about 1855; *Slater's Trade Directory* for 1856 stated: 'Letters arrive by foot-post from Holywell every morning at half-past six, and are despatched thereto every evening at six.' After the turn of the twentieth century, the post office business was transferred to new premises located up the hill from the main road, before a further move to the New Shops Precinct.

Bryn Celyn Post Office opened for business in 1930, the premises having been a general store for many years previously. Mrs Foulkes held the position of the first post-mistress (latterly with one of her daughters), until her retirement in 1977. The shop and post office then closed and the building was later demolished as part of a road widening scheme.

Holway Post Office, also a general stores, opened in the early 1930s, and was sited just past the site of the old turnpike gate. After the general business closed in 1958, the post office business was transferred to premises further up the Holway.

Citizens Advice Bureau
The offices of Holywell district's first Citizens' Advice Bureau (CAB) were opened in Well Street in 1967 by the chairman of Holywell RDC, Councillor Bob Fazackerley. Following the closure of the town's library in Post Office Lane during 1975, the CAB offices were transferred there. Over the years, many people have given freely of their own time to provide such a vital service and sincere thanks are most certainly due to them.

Welfare and Health
Poor Houses
For many years, until the dissolution of the monasteries in the 1530s, the monks of Basingwerk Abbey had assisted the poor people of the Holywell district. Help for such citizens also came from local charitable gentry and the 'better-off' population. Monasteries had provided hospital facilities and supplied charitable food and alms for the poor and destitute in hard times. The removal of this resource was one of the factors in the creation of the army of 'sturdy beggars' that plagued late Tudor times, causing instability. This problem was of national concern, and led to the passing of the Elizabethan Poor Laws of 1597/98.[122] In places such as Holywell, the administrators of the Poor Law were the parish overseers, who included the vicar, the church-wardens and some of the gentry. Their main objects were to provide relief for the aged, the sick and the infant poor. In addition, through poor houses, work was to be provided for the able-bodied poor. However, problems continued to arise and, in Holywell, the only real aid came from a special poor box placed in the church. The building of poor houses nationally came about very slowly but an Act of 1722 helped parishes to refuse aid to able-bodied people. On 8 September 1739, the Holywell committee formed plans to have a poor house built on Castle Hill (above the Parish Church). Because they did not wish to substantially increase the rates, some gentry donated money for this purpose but, as a result, only a small poor house, capable of housing six inmates, could be built. It was named 'Mr Phillip's Poor House' after the first master. One aim of the poor house was to teach the inmates the virtues of discipline, thrift and sobriety and it is believed some form of medical service was also provided. The residents made clothes from local fabrics. Although there were financial problems, it seems the house continued to be used because, in June 1779, the vestry opened a second house in an old cottage and a house superintendent was elected to control it. The paupers who were allowed to live there had to attend prayers twice a day and take part in church worship on Sundays. Other strict rules were in place to keep the house and the occupants in good living standards. It is not known when these Poor Houses ceased to exist but, in later years, conditions seemed to deteriorate everywhere and food riots occurred in both Flintshire (including Holywell) and Denbighshire between 1800 and 1830.

An excellent and detailed history of the poor houses and of Lluesty Workhouse is to be found in *The Holywell Workhouses*, by Tim Jones (published in 1996).

Lluesty Workhouse and Hospital [SJ 1895 7500]
Following the Poor Law Amendment Act of 1834, Poor Law Unions were created throughout England and Wales. On 25 February 1837, the Holywell Union was established with a board of twenty-seven guardians. It embraced Holywell and thirteen other parishes and took over the responsiblity for the relief of the poor. The Board of Guardians held their first meeting two days later and immediately set in motion plans to build a workhouse, to accommodate up to 400 inmates, off the Ysceifiog turnpike road on the outskirts of Holywell [Brynford Road, from Brynford

Street to the tollgate did not exist then]. The Poor Law Commissioners authorised £6,200 for its construction and the design was of a cruciform layout. There was separate accommodation for males and females, and inmates were also categorised as either infirm or able-bodied.[53] The building, in places up to three storeys high, was of limestone construction and building work was carried out between 1838 and 1842. The builder was Daniel Parry, a local firm, but the Guardians also employed poor people to do manual work. The design was by John Welch.[42] Of a final cost of £9,000, the Poor Law Commissioners contributed £6,200.[R101] The premises were named Lluesty, meaning 'shelter'. The workhouse opened on 9 November 1840.

Meetings of the Guardians were usually held on alternate Fridays. Among the original staff appointed were a medical officer, a schoolmistress and a chaplain. Religious services were held daily, morning and evening. For the able-bodied, efforts were made to find local work for them. The mental health of many inmates caused problems, but in 1865 the more serious cases were transferred to the Denbigh Asylum, which had opened in October 1848.

On planning workhouses, the authorities tried to provide them at a space of a day's walking distance from each other (e.g. St Asaph and Holywell) in order that tramps and so on could find a meal and shelter for at least a night. However, they had to work for that accommodation by carrying out tasks such as breaking up stones into pieces which were small enough to be passed through a barred window in a special building.

Over the years, alterations and improvements were carried out to the establishment and, soon after 1880, the Visiting Committee approved a scheme to have additional buildings constructed which would increase the accommodation for inmates by 162. At the same time, it was proposed that a purpose-built chapel be erected.[R102] This chapel, designed by John Douglas of Chester, was built onto the west end of the workhouse in 1883/84.[42 & 43] Of Early English Gothic style, the chapel was built of rubble masonry with red sandstone dressings and a slate roof.[42]

The welfare and education of children always seems to have been a subject of major importance to the Lluesty Board of Guardians and, in 1895 they had a children's home built over the road from the chapel. They also had workshops erected in the workhouse for the purpose of training young people in such trades as woodcraft, tailoring and shoe-making. Arrangements were also made to send some children to Holywell's elementary schools around the turn of the nineteenth century. In 1912, the Guardians were granted permission to install lifts, and oil lamps were replaced by electric fittings.[R102]

In 1913, a red-brick infirmary was built to the east of the workhouse which was run in conjunction with the workhouse itself. The builders were Sibeons of Holywell, and the architect was J. H. Davies, Chester. The foundation stone was laid on 15 August 1913 by Mrs John Jones, Pistyll, Holywell. In 1917, the government informed the Guardians that they had to take soldiers wounded in the war into the infirmary and they were allocated £2,500 for this purpose. The wounded started to arrive in January 1918 and, in all, 477 military patients were treated there. The premises

The frontage and main entrance at the former Lluesty Workhouse.

gradually returned to being an infirmary for the poor but, as time passed and living conditions improved, provisions were made for the public in general to benefit from it.

With the introduction of the National Health Service in 1948, the workhouse ceased to be used as such, and it was converted into more hospital accommodation and an X-ray department was added. The workhouse inmates were discharged to such places as nursing homes and psychiatric units. In 1956, extensions costing £78,000 were carried out at the hospital which included a bed lift, a new kitchen, further storage areas, as well as staff dining accommodation.[54]

By 1960, Lluesty had become a geriatric hospital for Flintshire, with sixteen wards capable of accommodating 170 patients. The chapel was converted into a rehabilitation unit in 1977. Changes in the structure of the hospital system in the region led to the Health Authority starting to close down wards in 1980, and the original Infirmary unit finally closed in 1993. The hospital buildings, including the chapel, were Grade II listed in 1991.[44]

The Flintshire Dispensary [SJ 1876 7582].
With no hospital in Holywell, September 1825 saw the Flintshire Dispensary opened in rented premises in Bagillt Street, situated across the road from the present Robert's Garage, some twenty yards towards Pen-y-Maes. This charity was managed by a committee and had a doctor and a voluntary nurse in daily attendance, carrying out surgery if necessary. It was for outpatients only, there being no bed facilities. Even in

its earliest days it was a busy place — it is noted in their fourth annual report (1829) that 3,816 patients had received attention in those first four years. An early list of subscribers and donors makes interesting reading as, apart from the general public, many of the wealthier inhabitants of the district were listed as well as people from far away. The local mining companies were also well represented, a reminder to us of the terrible conditions endured by lead and coal miners who suffered from breathing and chest problems, stomach and bowel difficulties, as well as body injuries incurred in the course of their work. The dispensary must have witnessed some awful scenes. The largest fund raising effort was an annual ball which was held in The Royal & White Horse Hotel (today's HSBC bank building).

The demands on the dispensary continually increased and, at the turn of the century, the committee had to start looking to either enlarging the premises, or finding a new and larger building. This dilemma came to the notice of Edwin Jones J.P., a tailoring businessman in London, who had been born in Holywell on 11 August 1837. He wrote to the committee on 6 July 1907 offering to buy both land in the town and pay for the cost of building a hospital. His offer was gratefully accepted. Out of four possible sites available, it was decided that Maes Offa, a field bordering Pen-y-Maes Road at the corner of the Strand, would be best suited, and it was duly purchased from Mr G. Freeman. The opening of the Cottage Hospital meant that the dispensary was not required and the building was eventually demolished.

Holywell Cottage Hospital [SJ 1880 7585]
Building work on the Cottage Hospital commenced in early 1908 by Sibeons (Builders) of Holywell. The architect was Samuel Evans of Mold. On 28 May 1908, the benefactor, Mr Edwin Jones and his wife, travelled from London to lay the foundation stone with due ceremony, the inscription reading: 'Flintshire Dispensary and Cottage Hospital, a gift to his native town by Edwin Jones, Clapham Park, London, 28th May 1908'. The stone is sited below the front window of the male ward.

The opening day of the hospital on 6 October 1909 had fine weather and it can be justifiably argued that the day was witness to the greatest benefit with which the people of Holywell and district have ever been gifted. From the Town Hall, Mr & Mrs Jones were preceded in procession by the Flannel Mills Band and the Town Council members. Hundreds of joyous people, including children, stood along the route, which was decorated with bunting. The Council had already widened the road up the hill. Mrs Jones declared the building open and unlocked the main door. A hymn and short service followed, after which Mr Jones gave the deeds to hospital trustee, Mr H. A. Cope. Celebrations continued later in the town.

It is interesting to record that Fron Deg (to the rear of the dwellings on the western side of Brynford Road) later became the house where some of Mr Jones's family lived in the earlier part of the twentieth century. Although not confirmed, I have been told that Mr Jones lived there for part of his retirement.

By 1926, it was necessary to lengthen both the male and the female wards, in order to increase the total number of beds to sixteen. The building contractors were Messrs.

Albert Bibby Lloyd of Flint, and the cost was £1,900. The re-opening day was 25 May 1927. To appreciate the standard of workmanship, it is worthwhile comparing the original photographs of the hospital with those taken after the enlargement. The original front bay windows, the plaster designs above them and the original foundation stone were all re-used and sited, as previously, at the front.

As the years progressed, further improvements and additional facilities were added, including an X-ray unit in 1932 and, in 1934, four side-wards at a cost of £2,300 (making it a twenty-bed hospital). The opening ceremony was carried out on Friday, 11 May 1934, by Her Grace the Duchess of Westminster. 1942 witnessed a new X-ray clinic being built as a separate building to the hospital. In 1945 an emergency annexe was added to the main building.

When the National Health Service came into being in 1948, the hospital committee decided not to join and tried to keep the Cottage Hospital going by local public subscription funds. This, however, proved unsuccessful and, in 1949 they joined the NHS. A dayroom was added in 1972, and further extensions were added to the X-ray clinic for other outpatient clinical work in the years 1974, 1985 and 1989.

In 1980, the Clwyd Health Authority re-named the hospital the Holywell Community Hospital, but the public still affectionately called it the Cottage Hospital. In 1998, the house named Gwenllys and land, together with a cottage to the rear of the hospital were purchased by the Health Authority to enable them to build a new hospital. It should be recorded that Holywell had been promised a new community hospital for many many years.

On Saturday, 25 November 2006, the Cottage Hospital main building was closed after all patients were transferred from it to Lluesty Hospital. The minor injuries unit was also transferred to Lluesty that day. However, the building housing the

Holywell Cottage Hospital as it was upon completion in 1909.

outpatients unit, complete with X-ray department, will continue to serve the area until the new Community Hospital is opened in 2008.

Community Hospital
In the early 2000s a decision was taken that, from three possible sites, the site of the promised new community hospital would be just off Halkyn Road on a green field area to the east of the new Bodowen Surgery. However, time went by without any firm and final decision being made to actually start. Eventually, on 22 August 2006 the Welsh Assembly Government gave the go-ahead for a forty-four bed hospital to be constructed at an approved cost of £11.4 million, part of which would be funded by the sale of Lluesty Hospital, the Cottage Hospital and the property named Gwenllys. The new complex was planned to include all the facilities carried out at the clinic alongside the Cottage Hospital, as well as a rehabilitation centre, a minor injuries unit, social services and a dental unit. Added to the overall structure would be a surgery to replace the aged Panton Place Surgery. Site preparation work started on 9 October 2006 and four days later, Dr Brian Gibbons, the Welsh Assembly Government Health Minister, officially cut the first turf, witnessed by a large number of people. Dr Gibbons said 'For all those people who have worked so hard, they will now see the fulfilment of their ambition. Holywell is part of the largest ever capital investment since the creation of the NHS in 1948'. John Saunders, chairman of the Good Companions of Holywell Hospitals, said 'We started campaigning forty-three years ago. It's absolutely marvellous we're here to witness this'. Tribute was paid by Mrs Sandy Mewies, the Delyn AM, to the Good Companions and the Councillors who had worked endlessly to achieve a new hospital at Holywell. The contract for the main construction of the hospital was awarded to Nor-West Holst.

Ante-natal and Post-natal Clincs
These clinics were adjacent to the north-east of the Grammar School. This pre-fabricated concrete building was erected as an air-raid shelter during the Second World War. When the war ended, the structure was converted for use as a clinic and continued to serve as such until 1955 when a modern clinic was provided in Park Lane by the County Council.

Health Vistiors' Clinic, Park Lane. [SJ 1868 7570]
This purpose-built brick building with a slate roof, was constructed and opened in 1955. Its services included a dental department and a Schools Nursing Officer who worked in conjunction with the clinics regarding vision, hearing and head lice problems.

Llys Gwenffrwd Elderly Persons' Home, Brynford Street [SJ 187 755]
As part of Flintshire County Council's policy to provide elderly persons' care-homes in the county, Llys Gwenffrwd was built in 1971. Councillor Mrs Mair Risley performed the official opening.

During 2003, the residents' thirty rooms were re-furbished and upgraded, some having en-suite facilities added. A new wing was also added to act as an intermediate place for people between hospitals and their own home — the aim being to help the sick so that they could return to their own environment and cope for themselves more easily. On 20 November 2003, HRH the Duke of Kent visited to officially reopen the home.[46]

Warden Assisted Accommodation
This modern type of assistance was first provided in the town in 1970 when the Panton Place houses were converted into flats for elderly and disabled people. More of these flats were later built in Holywell and in Greenfield.

Surgeons, Chemists, Dentists and Doctors' Surgeries
Whilst we know that the health of the district certainly benefited during the Middle Ages from the presence of the monks at Basingwerk Abbey, the first record of a surgeon and apothecary in Holywell has been traced as that of a William Coyney, who served the town between 1746 and 1773. Whilst there must have been others, the details of only one other are known as he was described on a marble tablet in St James's Parish Church: 'In memory of Thomas Simon, Surgeon, who departed this life 22nd August 1803, aged 39'. Although *Pigot's Directory* of 1835 lists six surgeons in the town, no other records of their places of practice are shown, nor do any records of such appear to have survived until the 1881 census. That census also tells us that there were other health workers about the town. *Sutton's Directory* of 1889 named Brynford House, and a house at Castle Hill, as housing surgeons. It also informs us that there was a dentist in Panton Place (the first mention of that profession in the town). However, since that date there have always been dentists recorded and, at the present time, there are two dental practices – one in Brynford Street, the other in Panton Place. Of the two chemists and druggists in High Street during the nineteenth century, one was the very notable and benevolent Humphrey Roberts, who had practised for many years from his High Street shop until shortly before his death in early 1848. In his will he bequeathed (through Viscount Fielding and the Hon. E. M. Lloyd Mostyn) the sum of £500 to be invested, with interest payable, via the Parish Church Wardens and overseers, to the poor of the parish. The Apothecary's Hall at 35, High Street was most probably the first chemist in the town. The more recent residents of the area will remember the building as 'Seftons the Chemist'.

Bodowen Surgery: This is the earliest doctor's practice for which a good history can be traced. It opened in 1890 at 7 Brynford Street, founded by Dr John Owen Jones. Born about 1860 in Cyffylliog, he qualified in Edinburgh in 1886. He became a house surgeon at Holywell's Flintshire Dispensary in 1889 and then founded Bodowen Surgery where he at first lived (BOD meaning 'dwelling place', OWEN was, of course, from his name). Dr Jones also owned the house to the left, the Volunteers Arms public house on the corner, and a cottage in Halkyn Street (behind the Volunteers Arms) in which his coachman, William Roberts lived. On 15 August 1900

Dr Charles Edward Morris became his partner, and Dr Jones moved to Llwyn Onn in Halkyn Road. In later years, Bodowen became a very busy practice and naturally has had many changes in doctors.

One of Dr Owen Jones's five children, Arthur, qualified as a doctor and, after experience in other establishments, joined Bodowen in 1930. Unfortunately his father died the following year. In 1951, Dr Morris left Bodowen and opened another practice at 21, Brynford Street.

As the years unfolded, the Bodowen premises became far too small and a new purpose designed surgery was built alongside Halkyn Road [SJ 189 755] in 1992 (opposite Llwyn Onn). It was officially opened by Dr David Williams on 27 February 1993.

Pendre Surgery: Dr Charles Morris established a new practice at 21 Brynford Street in 1952. His son, Dr Jim Morris, joined him and the practice prospered. By 1970, the premises had become too small, and the three partners at that time, Drs Martin Parry, Curley and Gruffydd O. Jones, purchased Pen-y-Dre House in Coleshill Street [SJ 1885 7575] and converted it into a surgery, moving there from Brynford Street on its completion. In 1982 and in 1998 the partnership made alterations and extensions to the premises.

Panton Place Surgery [SJ 1865 7580]: In 1939 Dr B. D. Chowdhury first rented these premises, but was able to purchase them in 1947. Dr O'Connor become a partner, but they split in 1951 and Dr O'Connor left. The practice grew and the partnership built a second surgery at School Lane, Greenfield. Unfortunately, due to the amount of vandalism, this surgery (which then included Dr Sahar as one of the partners) was forced to close.

Plas-yn-Dre Surgery, Bagillt Street [SJ 1880 7585]: Opened in the late 1940s by a Dr Gamble, who served the community for about ten years before emigrating to Australia.

Pennant Surgery: In 1998, Dr Kapur, formerly a senior partner in the Panton Place surgery, set up his own practice and had a brand new surgery built on land to the rear of Robert's Garage.

Whilst the above text gives a general history of the district's surgeries, it is important to highlight how dramatically their service to the public has changed over the last two decades. Computer systems were slowly introduced and now, not only is almost everything recorded and controlled by sophisticated computer links within the local surgeries, but there are also direct links with Glan Clwyd Hospital. Additionally a triage sister has been introduced into the surgeries. Such sisters not only carry out specialized nursing duties but also, when a sick patient telephones in with an urgent need, they determine whether the patient can be given immediate advice over the phone or needs either her help or that of a doctor. There are presently a total of fifteen doctors in the town; in addition there are sisters, nurses, pharmacists and administration staff.

The Good Companions
Although a completely voluntary body of local people and not an organisation run by local government, the Good Companions must be included here. The organisation was started in 1964 by Sister Jean Saunders of Lluesty, who was concerned at the lack of amenities for the hospital's patients. She immediately had the support of her husband, friends and colleagues. They extended their help to Holywell and Flint Cottage Hospitals (although Flint formed its own committee in 1980). The untiring efforts of the Good Companions for well over forty years have raised funds running into hundreds of thousands of pounds — all used for purchasing hospital equipment, patient amenities and so on. There can hardly be a family from the Holywell district which has not gained some aid or advantage from this committee's efforts. To all the committee members concerned over the years a very big 'Thank You' is undeniably due. In 2004, Sister Saunders was awarded the MBE in recognition of her services to the community.

CHAPTER 3

Religion

Religion has played an important role in the life of Holywell for over fourteen centuries. Indeed, few towns can have such a remarkable religious history. The main people and events can be summarised thus:

- Early seventh century: Beuno (later a saint) built his first north Wales church in Holywell.
- Legend says Winefride, Beuno's niece, was beheaded, but was miraculously restored to life.
- Mid twelfth century: Basingwerk Abbey was built by the Cistercian monks. They were given lands and were a dominant body in the area for four centuries.
- Mid sixteenth century: St Winefride's Well, the only shrine remaining intact after the Reformation.
- Late sixteenth century: The Jesuits came and kept Roman Catholicism alive in Holywell.
- Sixteenth–eighteenth centuries: Catholicism and Anglicanism were the religious bodies.
- Mid eighteenth century: Nonconformism spreads to Holywell and its various bodies built chapels in the town.
- Mid twentieth century: Evangelism emerged in the town.

The Age of Saints
The Age of Celtic Saints in Britain is generally accepted as having been between the mid fifth and the eighth centuries. After the Romans left at the end of the fourth century, there was a Romano-British community in the south-east of Wales, especially around Caerwent, from which we can trace the beginning of the Welsh Celtic Christian missionaries. These religious leaders established churches and monasteries — known as a *clas* — some of which were named after them. However, in many places, even though these 'saints' were not directly involved with them, churches, wells, caves, etc were named after them through the centuries.

The Age of Saints started in the south of Wales and St David was probably the most famous. He died on 1 March c.589. North-east Wales witnessed St Kentigern coming from Strathclyde in 560 to form a monastery at Llanelwy. When he returned to Scotland in 573, he was succeeded by one of his disciples, Asaph, and several churches and religious places were named after him — Llanasa, Pantasaph and Ffynnon Asa being the best known examples. At the start of the seventh century, a man named Beuno went from his home in south-east Wales to Caerwent, where he studied the scriptures. He was ordained and the King of Powys granted him the right to establish a church in the district of Berriw. However, he soon moved north and founded a church at what was to become Holywell just before 620. Beuno later moved on across north Wales and founded a monastery at Clynnog Fawr, south of Caernarfon. He died there on 21 April *c*.642. In Holywell, besides the famed St Winefride's Well, a nearby well was named St Beuno's Well, the adjoining hillside was called Gerddi, a well at Tremeirchion was named Ffynnon Beuno and some nearby prehistoric caves also carry his name. The church at Whitford, now known as St Mary's, was originally dedicated to St Beuno. Indeed, based on the evidence we have, Beuno was really the north Wales counterpart of St David. In 1848, the large St Beuno's College at Tremeirchion was built for training Jesuit priests.

Roman Catholics, Basingwerk Cistercians and Anglicans
As with so many other Celtic saints, there is no original documentary evidence of the lives and activities of Beuno and Winefride. The first known writings which relate to the legend of St Winefride were compiled *c*.1130 under the title *Vita prima*, by an anonymous author, possibly for the monks of St Werburgh's Abbey, Chester. Then, in 1138, Robert, the prior of Shrewsbury Abbey, wrote *Vita secunda* Winefride.[57] With regard to St Beuno, the oldest surviving record is a fourteenth century Welsh document, prepared by an anchorite in Cardiganshire, that is believed to be an abbreviated version of an earlier, but lost, Latin *Vita*.[57]

Because the origins and connections between Beuno and Winefride are difficult to follow, it is perhaps necessary to include here their geneology, along with that of St Eleri and St Tenoi:

> Bugi ap Gwynllyw (a nobleman of Powys) married Peren (the daughter of Lleuddun Luyddog of Dinas Eiden [Edinburgh]. The landholdings of Lleuddun's family included areas between the lordship of Tegeingl (which included Holywell) and Gwytherin. Bugi and Peren had a daughter, Gwenlo, and a son, Beuno.
>
> Gwenlo married Tyfid ab Eiludd and they had two children, Gwenfrewy (Winifride) and Owain.
>
> Beuno was thus the brother-in-law of Tyfid, by whom he was given land on which to build a church (Holywell).
>
> Gwenlo's mother, Peren, had a sister, Tenoi, who married Dingad ap Nudd Hael. They had a son, Eleri and other children who came to be regarded as saints. The district of Gwytherin contained two religious communities, one male, the other female. Eleri became the abbot of the male community and Tenoi became the abbess of the female community. When Tenoi died, Winefride succeeded her as abbess at Gwytherin.

62   *A History of Holywell and Greenfield*

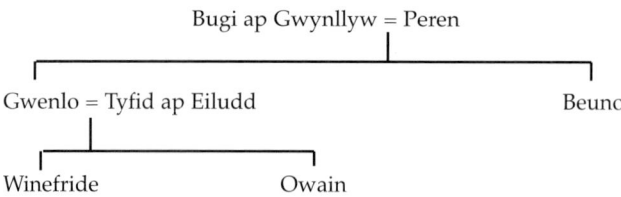

The first church [SJ 185 762]
The site which Beuno chose for the building of his church nestled at the bottom of a steep hill. It is thought that Tyfid, Gwenlo and Winefride may have lived on the hill above the church, perhaps where Holywell castle was built in 1209.[19] If we eliminate Well Street, New Road, and all the adjacent buildings from our minds, we can then imagine the thatched dwellings of a small community that would have been settled on the slopes of that hillside. The church would most probably have been constructed of either wattle and daub, or of oaken boards thatched with reeds. From that time there has always been a church on the site — today it is the Anglican Parish Church of St James the Apostle.

Exactly when the first stone church was constructed cannot be established, but it is known that during the second part of the fourteenth century a spacious stone church was erected. The pillars which support the present-day galleries are, at least, of that era.[52] They had originally supported arches for the roof. However, because three of the pillars on the north side have capitals which differ from the others and are not so well finished, they suggest that they belonged to an older, stone-built church. Thomas Pennant, said:

> The pillars, plain themselves, and with plain capitals, which support the nave, are original; and by the specimens given by Dr Ducaral, in his *Norman Antiquities* … appear to have been in use among the Saxons and the Normans. The arches, which might have confirmed my suspicion that the church was built in the Norman reign, are taken away, but the style continued till about the year 1200.[22]

Thus, wattle and daub type structures may have been replaced by stone as far back as the twelfth century. Until 1770, the church at Holywell was always dedicated to St Winefride. The fact that some historic documents prior to 1500 refer to the 'chapel of St Winefride' as well as a church can be misleading, however, this issue is clearly described in the action of when, in 1240, Prince Dafydd ap Llywelyn, granted the Holywell church and the shrine and pilgrimage chapel of St Winefride to the monks of Basingwerk. At the beginning of the thirteenth century, the Abbot of St Werburgh's, Chester, told Archbishop Walter that: 'In the wars with the princes of Wales they [the monks of Basingwerk] have lost their Church at Hallewell which was £100 value'.[19] A charter of 1240 by Prince Dafydd ap Llywelyn, granted the Cistercian monks of Basingwerk 'their grange at Fulbrook [by Holywell stream] … and the church of Holywell with the chapel of Coleshill'. Another example is an entry in the *Calendar of*

Papel Registers for 1427 asking for 'alms for the repair of the chapel of St Winefride the Virgin, called Holliwell … whose buildings are collapsed'. This was referring to the towered church of St Winefride.[57] In 1484, Richard III gave 10 marks* annually for the 'yearly sustentation and salarie of a prieste at the Chappelle of Saint Wynefride'.

The sixty-foot high, three-stage, square, west tower was built of Gwespyr stone (believed to have come from the Moor Quarry [SJ 181 773][58]), in part of the late fourteenth century church. At an unknown date, it had a crenelled parapet added.[44] The tower is supported by stepped buttresses on the outside[44] and the main entrance was originally built into the west side of the tower base. The doorway has a single stone lintel and a spiral stone stairway leads up to the belfry. There is just one bell in the tower, manufactured by A. & A. Randall of Gloucester. It rests on a wooden frame bearing the date 1682 and the names of the two churchwardens — Thomas Mostyn and Edward Butler. Slots in the frame indicate that there may at sometime have been two more bells in use.

The Legend of St Winefride
It is generally believed that Winefride lived in Holywell *c*.620. Thomas Meyrick, in his 1878 book, *The Life of St Wenefred*[60] thoroughly researched her history and concluded that she would have been aged 14 or 15 at the time of her near martyrdom which he also said took place in 620. As already mentioned, there is no surviving record of her until the twelfth century, at a time when England was witnessing a great number of monasteries being built by various monastic orders. Ranulf de Gernon, who was Earl of Chester between 1129 and 1153, had contacted the French Savigniac monks to open up the chapel in what was then the *cantref* (district) of Tegeingl in 1131. The creation of Basingwerk Abbey in 1157 by Cistercian monks was the result. These early records state that Winefride was visited by a prince, named Caradoc, who came from Penarlag (Hawarden) and tried to seduce her. She fled towards St Beuno's church where a service was being held. Caradoc is said to have then drawn his sword and cut off her head. Beuno came to her and, whilst praying, replaced her head. She was restored to life and a great spring erupted at the spot. Some versions of this legend say that the ground swallowed up Caradoc after he had taken his sword against Winefride. Ieuan Brechfa, a fifteenth century genealogist, found that Winefride had a brother, Owain. Rather than the mythical story, it is possible a more probable fact was that Owain could have slayed Caradoc in revenge.[57]

The controversial element of the legend, the beheading of St Winefride and her restoration to life by Beuno, is naturally disputed. The Revd Christopher David (Roman Catholic curate at Holywell, 1955–64) wrote in 1971:

> The story of her head being cut off and her resuscitation to life is commonplace in Celtic hagiography and inherently unlikely. The legend of the Saint was not written down for 500

---

* A mark, then an English monetary unit, was equivalent to thirteen shillings and four pence which, in 2006, would be around £310.

years after her death. It is not surprising that for this and other reasons it became embroidered.[19]

During the Age of the Saints, many religious buildings were established close to a spring or stream — water was obviously essential for them. The shrine of St Winefride's Holy Well is the only one in Britain to have survived the Reformation, and is still internationally known and visited by people from around the globe. As the road signs for Holywell proudly say, it is 'The Lourdes of Wales'. In addition, it is one of the so-called 'Seven Wonders of Wales'.

Winefride wished to become a nun and Beuno gave her religious education. It is said that he sat on a stone, now named St Beuno's Stone, located in the outer plunge bath, and told Winefride her future.[57] After Beuno left Holywell and went to Clynnog Fawr, Winefride went into a convent in Gwytherin where she became an abbess and remained until her death c.660. She was buried in the convent churchyard but, in 1138, her remains were moved by the Black Monks of Shrewsbury, first to St Giles's Church outside that city's walls (whilst a shrine was prepared for the remains at the Abbey). They were eventually transferred to the Abbey itself.[60] She was later to become the patron saint of that town.[61] During the era of Henry VIII and his chief minister, Thomas Cromwell, her relics were destroyed. However, one finger bone was saved; half of which is now in Holywell and half in the Abbey of St Peter and St Paul in Shrewsbury.[61]

The feast of her martyrdom is kept on 22 June; that of her death is on 3 November. In 1398, Robert Walden, Archbishop of Canterbury, ordered St Winefride's feast to be kept with Nine Lessons in Canterbury Province which was the start of national acknowledgement of her as a saint.[61] In the fourteenth century, long-distance pilgrimages to the well increased — the main one being from St David's. The fourteenth century maps in Professor William Rees's *Historic Atlas of Wales* and *South Wales and the Border in the Fourteenth Century*, provide such evidence. Later, the maps of John Speed indicated the routes from St David's as well as from Shrewsbury.[61] The monks of St Werburgh's, Chester, as well as the Cistercian monks of Basingwerk Abbey, gave lodgings to pilgrims bound for the shrine in Holywell.

Monarchs, Gentry and Notable people who have visited the Holy Well

1119: Earl Richard, the Countess of Adeliza's son.[57]

1189: Richard I (the Lionheart).[57]

1415: According to the chronicler Adam of Usk, King Henry V, with great reverence, went on foot in pilgrimage from Shrewsbury to St Winefride's Well in thanksgiving for his victory over the French at Agincourt.[57]

1439: Isabel, the Countess of Warwick gave her gown of russet velvet to deck the image of St Winfride in the chapel.[61]

1461:The Welsh poet, Tudur Aled, told of the visit by Edward IV. The monarch placed some moss from the well upon his crown in token of his devotion to the saint.[57]

23 July 1684: The Duke of Beaufort, in his appointed position as Lord President of the Council of Wales and the Marches, visited the well before staying with Sir Roger Mostyn at Mostyn Hall.[33]

29 August 1686: Accompanied by Queen Mary (of Modena), King James II, who was a Roman Catholic, came to crave the prayers of St Winefride that they might be blessed with a son. The King presented the chapel with part of a dress worn by Mary, Queen of Scots, at her execution, and the Queen gave £30 towards the fabric of the building.[19]

1819: Prince Leopold of Belgium (later King Leopold), staying at Eaton Hall with Earl Grosvenor, visited the well before going to Holywell Races.[33] The Prince's mother was Queen Victoria's sister.

1932: The Archbishop of Westminster made a private visit to the well.

19 June 2005: Cardinal Cormac Murphy O'Connor, Archbishop of Westminster and leader of the Roman Catholic Church in England and Wales, visited the Well to officially open and bless the new facilities which had been created there over the previous five years.

Owners of the Holy Well, the Church and Lady Margaret's Chapel.
The countess Adeliza, wife of one of William the Conqueror's henchmen, gifted the church of 'Haliwel' to the monks of St Werburgh's Abbey, Chester[57] (the place-name Haliwel is Anglo–Saxon and means Holy Well).

In 1240, the Welsh prince, Dafydd ap Llywelyn, following his gain of the disputed lands in the district from the English, gave the church and the well to the Cistercian monks of Basingwerk Abbey. The Cistercians remained in control of the Shrine and the Church, plus, later, the well-chamber and Chapel above, until the dissolution of the abbey in 1536.

Upon the Basingwerk Abbey's dissolution, Henry VIII had the well and chapel handed over to a servant, William Holcroft, who was instructed to collect alms at the chapel and send them to him. This proved impossible because of troubles caused by former abbot Nicholas Pennant and others.

In 1873, the Jesuit Father J. B. Di Pietro was granted a lease on the Well crypt and its associated buildings from Holywell Local Board in the sum of £162 p.a.[19 & 151] Due to subsequent local government changes, the legal owners of the Well, the Holywell Board has been succeeded by the Holywell UDC, Delyn Borough Council and now Flintshire County Council. The leasing of the Well to the Catholic Diocese for Holywell has continued throughout.

St Winefride's Chapel and Well Chamber Building [SJ 185 762]
The Well Chapel forms an upper storey to the Well Chamber beneath. Its Gwespyr sandstone is believed to have come from the Moor Quarry and was built during Abbot Thomas Pennant's time (1481–1522). The abbey received an annual grant of ten marks to maintain a chaplin at the pilgrimage chapel.[68] Whilst some believe this unique structure was built just prior to 1500, the actual period was *c.*1500–10, by the munificence of Lady Margaret Beaufort, the daughter and heiress to the first Duke of Somerset, and grand-daughter of John of Gaunt, Duke of Lancaster.[65] Born on 31 May

1443, Margaret was only twelve years of age when King Henry V married her to Edmund Tudor, the Earl of Richmond.[65] Edmund's father was Owen a member of the Tudor family of Penmynydd, Anglesey. Edmund's mother was Catherine, the daughter of King Charles VI of France. Edmund died in October 1456, after one year of marriage leaving Margaret with an unborn baby. She was taken by Jasper Tudor, Edmund's brother and Earl of Pembroke, to the safety of Pembroke Castle. There, on 28 January 1457, she was delivered of a son, Henry. In 1471, King Henry VI and his brother, Edward, were murdered in the Tower of London. Margaret's son, Henry Tudor, therefore became the sole male heir of the House of Lancaster. However, the Yorkists staked their claim on the throne and Richard III became king. To protect Henry, Jasper took him to Britanny. In the meantime Margaret married again, this time, to Sir Henry Stafford. He died in 1471. In 1473, Margaret married for the third time, her new husband being Thomas Lord Stanley (later the 1st Earl of Derby).

Henry Tudor came to Milford Haven in 1485, determined to gain the throne of England. Being of Welsh descent, he marched through Wales to muster support to fight Richard III. Lord Mostyn gathered his forces and, with Lord Stanley, joined Henry at Bosworth Field in Leicestershire.[22] In the ensuing battle, Richard was killed and Henry was declared King Henry VII of England. His stepfather placed the crown on his head. Thus, Lady Margaret Beaufort was the mother of the King.

After Thomas Stanley died, Lady Margaret lived the life of a nun having appointed John Fisher (later Bishop of Rochester) to guide her spiritually.[19] She made many charitable donations, including the magnificent building erected in Holywell.

The Well Chamber (with the Chapel above) and the Parish Church of St James, 1742.

She was buried in the Henry VII Lady Chapel in Westminster Abbey and the epitaph on her tomb reads:

> Margaret of Richmond, mother of Henry VII, grandmother of Henry VIII, who gave a salary to three monks of this convent and founded a Grammar School at Wimborne, and to a preacher throughout England, and to two interpreters of scripture, one at Oxford, the other at Cambridge, where she likewise founded two colleges, one to Christ, and the other to St John, His disciple.
> Died 29th June 1509.[65]

Henry VII also had a statue of St Winefride erected in the Lady Chapel.[65] Lady Margaret is also depicted in a beautiful stained glass window in St Winefride's Church.

The Well Chamber, open to the north, has heavily moulded piers which carry the complex tierceron vault beneath the Chapel. The well itself is polygonal in shape and has a maximum depth of six feet. The centre of the vault has a pendant boss, portraying six scenes from the life of St Winefride. There are also many other bosses and sculptures, an important one in the ceiling of the crypt depicts three pomegranates in a shield, surmounted by the crown of Catherine of Aragon, the first wife of Henry VIII.[44] This architectural feature gives weight to the belief that the whole structure was erected between 1500 and 1510 as Henry and Catherine did not ascend to the throne until 1509. An effigy of St Beuno can be seen in the ceiling of the crypt, which also carries a stone carving of Lady Margaret and Lord Thomas Stanley. This profile can raise the question: was it created whilst Thomas was still alive, or, if after, was it to act as a memorial to him? The present fine statue of St Winefride, in an original niche, replaced the original. Outside the well basin itself, are three outer bays. The building, complete with the chapel above, is considered to be unique in Europe and it is also thought that the architect was Robert Vertue, the architect of the Royal Chapel: the ground plan of the star-shaped well chamber matches exactly that of the east end of the Lady Chapel in Westminster Abbey.[151]

During the seventeenth century, a plunge pool was constructed into which flowed the water from the well. The Well House residence for the custodian, together with a gatehouse to the Well and the Westminster Plunge Bath were built of Gwespyr sandstone in 1865 — the whole project costing the town over £3,000. In 1875, wooden changing cubicles were provided (which were removed in 1963) and in 2001, four new changing cubicles, with facilities for the disabled, were bought.[151]

In January 1930, the Holywell Roman Catholic authorities completed the purchase of the site and premises of the former St Winefred's Brewery, which had been put up for auction on 7 October 1929, following the death of the owner, J. Lloyd Price. The premises had a 185 foot frontage to the main road between the Well House and the Holywell Textile Mills. After demolishing the old works, the land was cleared and levelled to provide much needed open space to the north end of the well. In 1962, a new house was built for the well custodian on land adjacent to the Holywell Textile Mill. It was named Plessington House, after Father John Plessington, a Holywell

Jesuit priest. Around 1978, the disused Westminster Bath had hardcore placed on the area behind Plessington House and an elegant shop and entrance were built on the site. The other half of the bath had a suspended wooden floor placed over it on which a store-room was built. Delyn Borough Council carried out an extensive remodelling of the land and buildings around the Well frontage: the gatehouse entrance onto the old courtyard was altered to create a chapel for use as a small place for quiet reflection and prayer.[151] Two magnificent stained-glass windows, depicting St Winefride and St Beuno, were installed in the chapel. The storeroom at the shop was converted into an Exhibition Room in 2003 and now houses a magnificent display which includes life-size figures of Saint Beuno and Saint Winefride, as well as ten illuminated boards giving the history of the site. Among the other features one can see numerous carefully restored crutches that had been discarded by pilgrims who believed themselves to have been healed by the water. Cures are still reported today by infirm pilgrims and visitors. The shrine currently welcomes over 25,000 pilgrims and visitors a year.

Between the 2002 and 2005, the 1865 Well House was restored and converted into the Museum of the Pilgrimage and a library. The latter provides archive and research facilities for students of all ages. On Sunday, 19 June 2005, the Archbishop of Westminster, Cardinal Cormac Murphy-O'Connor, visited Holywell and led an historic procession of some 2,500 pilgrims from St Winefride's Church to the shrine and celebrated an open-air Mass before officially opening the new complex. The Cardinal was accompanied by the Archbishop of Cardiff and by the Bishops of Wrexham and Menevia.

Some of the exhibits which can be seen in the museum are:

- A small portion of a finger bone relic of St Winefride which was identified in Rome in 1852 and which was brought to Holywell in 1854.
- A silver reliquary monstrance which was made to display the above relic and was presented to the Shrine in 1913 by the Bishop of Menevia, Francis Mostyn. The Bishop was a member of The Mostyns of Talacre who were supporters of the Shrine for over 300 years.
- A circular silver case, obtained by the Shrine in 1930, specially designed for The Relic of the True Cross in order that it could be displayed in the Mostyn Reliquary.
- The lidded silver ciborium named The Petre Ciborium was given to the Shrine as a votive offering in 1720 by Baroness Petre. A ciborium is a vessel made to contain consecrated Hosts (the bread for Holy Communium) outside Mass times.
- The Clifford Chalice and Paten were presented to the Shrine in 1856 by the Catholic Clifford family as a thanksgiving for the safe return of their son Henry Hugh Clifford from the Crimean War.
- A tiny Portable Altar which may have been used during Penal Times when Mass had to be said in secret.
- A small piece of the Arch Gwenfrewi which was a late-eighth century tent-shaped chest at Gwytherin. Between 1698 and the middle of the nineteenth century the Arch was sawn up into small pieces and sold to pilgrims to Gwytherin. The piece in this museum was acquired by John Griffith Wynne in 1849 and presented to the Shrine in 1859.

- St Winefride's Coffin, a dug-out chest which was associated with the Arch Gwenfrewi and visitors to Gwytherin were told that it was where St Winefride's relics were housed. It remained in Gwytherin over the centuries but when that church closed the Church in Wales let the Holywell Shrine hold it on long-term loan.
- The Unknown Martyrs. A chestful of human bones was found in Holywell presbytery in 1878 and is firmly believed that they are the remains of two seventeenth century martyrs. As has already been written, Holywell priest, John Plessington, was hanged, drawn and quartered at Chester in 1679. It is widely believed that one set of these bones was his.
- The five remaining 'Corvo Banners' are displayed in the museum. They depict: the martyrdom of St Winefride; St Augustine of Canterbury; St Gregory the Great; St George; and St Ignatius of Loyola.

The Chapel, otherwise known as the Beaufort Chapel, is 52′ x 20′ and has a four-bay nave, with aisles to three eastern bays and a one-bay chancel with a three-sided apse.[44] The windows are curved-headed with ogee lights, and the roof is camber-beamed with arched braces: the beams, purlins and rafters are moulded.[44] Bosses, quatrefoils and corbels all add to the attractiveness of the interior. Outside, there is a frieze depicting animals and various badges of the Houses of Stanley and Tudor. Architecturally, the structure is late-perpendicular and may have been the work of a Royal Master Mason.

The stained-glass east window depicts scenes commemorating the life of St Winefride. To the left of the central panel is the name 'Stanley Shield', and, to the right, Henry VII. In the upper part of the same window there are various heraldic motifs.[67] The building work would have been supervised by Thomas Pennant, the abbot of Basingwerk Abbey and guardian of the Church and Well between 1481 and 1522.

Little has been discovered about the use of the building during the turbulent years after the Reformation. However, after 1685, the Protestants took over control of it and Thomas Pennant (the writer) records that the Chapel had been used as the hall for holding both the great and the quarter sessions.

> I remember Matthew Skinner, esq., chief justice of Chester, holding the assizes there; and I also recollect a quarter sessions; the hall having been properly fitted up for the purpose. But the distance from the centre of the county was found to be inconvenient, that after these instances they were removed to Flint, and finally to Mold, where they still continue.[22]

In 1723, a wall was built between the sanctuary and the nave and a false roof added which covered both the flat roof of the nave and the aisle roof, obscuring the clerestory windows.[19] The chapel was then used as a school and vestry meetings were also held there.[45] In 1841, due to the numbers using the Parish Church, and an increased demand for Welsh services, the Bishop of St Asaph granted a licence for Welsh services to be held there. It is not known when the chapel ceased to be so used. During the 1960s the Holywell Musical Society held concerts in the building. The chapel was given a Grade I Listing on 26 July 1951.[44]

In 1952 the Representative Body of the Church in Wales conveyed the Chapel (only) into the guardianship of the Ministry of Works.[20] Major restoration work was carried in the years from 1952, utilising some of the stone from the ruins of Downing Hall. Further remedial work was carried out prior to 1991. The perimeter wall and parapet top, adjacent to the main road, was rebuilt in dressed Gwespyr sandstone in 2000.

Associations with other religious houses
The Abbey of Saints Peter and Paul, Shrewsbury
Around 1138, St Winefride's relics were taken to Shrewsbury from Gwytherin by Prior Robert and the abbey's monks. The relics were first placed in the church of St Giles, before being moved to the abbey. The cult of St Winefride's then increased to the extent that a shrine was built in the abbey during the late fourteenth century by Abbot Nicholas Stevens.[69]

On a panel below one of the abbey's windows are the images of St Winefride and St Beuno. Although the main cloister was demolished in 1836 to make way for a road, the handsome early fourteenth century Grinshill stone refectory pulpit survived and is now on the opposite side of the road from the abbey. On one of the three panels are the figures of St Winefride and St Beuno.[34] The largest abbey bell weighed 34 cwt and was known as St Winefride's Bell. Unfortunately, it cracked in 1730 and was melted down.[63]

The Lady Chapel, Westminster Abbey
Within this chapel, which was erected in 1519, there is a statue of St Winefride who is depicted as a young woman with long loose hair and turban; she is reading from a book and has a palm branch in her right hand. At her feet is a block with a female head on it, alluding to her head having been cut off.[65] The black marble tomb of Lady Margaret Beaufort is also within this chapel. Also, within Westminster Abbey library, are Lady Margaret's prayer book and one of her travelling trunks.[65]

St Werburgh's Abbey, Chester
St Werburgh had been born *c.*650 and was the daughter of Mercian King Wulfere. She became first a nun, and later a renowned abbess because of her reforms and holy life. Following her death, she was buried in Hanbury, Staffordshire, and many miracles were reported from there. Subsequently, her relics were moved to the abbey in Chester, where a shrine was made (it survives in the present-day cathedral) which duly became a place of pilgrimage and was thus on a pilgrimage route for those going to the St Winefride's.

Throughout Britain, from the time of the dissolution in 1536 (under Henry VIII) to the reign of William III in 1685, there was a long drawn-out period of changing attitudes and beliefs swinging between Protestantism and Roman Catholicism. As an example, Thomas Goldwell, Bishop of St Asaph, (died 1585) refused to accept

Protestantism and restored pilgrimages to St Winefride's Holy Well. Since 1685, all British monarchs have been of the Protestant faith. Thus, those in Holywell who wished to teach and worship in the Catholic faith faced an exceptionally difficult task until 14 July 1808 when the Flintshire Clerk of the Peace finally granted permission for public use of 'Ye Olde Star' as a place of Catholic worship. The Catholic Emancipation Act of 1829 eventually gave Roman Catholics equal religious and political rights.

The Society of Jesus (the Jesuits)
The Jesuit Order was founded by St Ignatius of Loyola and, although he met with six young men in Paris on 15 August 1534, it was not until 27 September 1540 that Pope Paul III approved their draft outline of the Order.[64] It then grew rapidly, assuming a prominent role in the Counter-Reformation.[64] From around 1574, the Jesuits began to play an important role in Roman Catholicism in Holywell. Not only did they keep the Roman Catholic faith alive, but they also ensured that pilgrims still came to the shrine of St Winefride, despite the efforts of successive governments to stop them. St Winefride's Holy Well was the only shrine in England and Wales to survive the Dissolution and the substantial numbers of pilgrims who came to the Well during the years of persecution were one of the most important factors in keeping Catholicism alive in Britain. The Revd Christopher David, Catholic curate of Holywell, 1955–64, tells us:

> The first and most remarkable of the priests who worked in Holywell in the reign of Queen Elizabeth I was John Bennet … who arrived in 1574. He was caught and condemned to death in 1582 at a trial that apparently took place in the Chapel over the well since an epidemic was raging in Flint. But his life was spared and, after an imprisonment of three years he was banished. He re-entered the country and returned to Holywell in 1587 where he worked under various aliases until his death in 1625.[19]

Protestant Elizabeth I tried to stop pilgrimages to the well, as her instruction to the Council of the Marches of 13 June 1579 stated:

> To discover all Papist activities and recommend measures for suppressing them … to pay particular attention to the pilgrimages to St Winefride's Well and in view of the claim that the water is medicinal to appoint two men to test its properties; if not medicinal the Well should be destroyed ….[70]

The Queen's wishes were to be of no avail and the numbers of pilgrims coming to the well actually increased. As was said about the Welsh in 1590, 'They doe still goe in heapes to the wonted wells and places of superstition'. In 1625, the Bishop of Bangor told the House of Lords: 'There is a great concourse of people to St Winefride's Well. In an old chapel near, a public Mass is said continually'.[70] On the celebration of St Winefride's Day in 1629 it was reported that there were around 1,500 people present at the well, including prominent gentry from afar, as well as about 150 priests.[70]

In 1636, a serious attempt was made by the government to prevent the access of pilgrims to the well. The Chief Justice of Chester, Sir John Bridgeman, ordered that the iron posts around the well (which supported pilgrims in the well) should be taken away, that the image of the saint be disfigured, that all hostelries except two be closed, and that all pilgrims who went to the well should have their names taken and be reported to the next assizes.[70] It was subsequently announced that the posts had been removed and the shrine whitewashed. The innkeepers had refused to accede to the order and were subsequently fined. The statue was taken from the site but the richly carved canopy and niche remained untouched.[19]

In 1639, Jesuit George Petre, the youngest son of Lord Petre, bought the Star Inn (which was sited where the Presbytery is now) and the adjoining land for the purpose of creating a pilgrim's hospice.[70] There was, however, stiff opposition to the plan from other Catholics and the idea was abandoned. George Petre then moved to Ireland.

After the Civil War, there was a period when the premises fell into disrepair. In 1670, the mission of the Fathers of the Society of Jesus in North Wales was constituted and made Holywell its centre. On 19 July 1679, Father John Plessington, the priest-in-charge at Holywell, was executed in Chester — for no other reason than that of preaching religion and, for a time, pilgrims were discouraged from travelling to the well. In 1686, King James II and Queen Mary paid a special visit to the Holy Well and things seemed to be improving. The Queen's gift of £30 towards the upkeep of the building was handed to a Jesuit, Father Thomas Roberts, prompting a legal case which found in favour of the King, who then gave the chapel to the Queen and she, in turn, wrote to Sir Roger Mostyn:

> It having pleased the King, by his royall grant, to bestow upon me ye ancient chapel adjoining to St Winefride's Well; these are to desire you to give present possession, in my name, of the said chappell, to Mr. Thomas Roberts, who will deliver this letter into your hands. It being also my intention to have the place decently repaired, and put in good use, I further desire that you will afford your favour and protection, that he may not be disturbed in the performance thereof. You may rest assured, that what you do herein, according to my desire, shall be very kindly remembered by Your good friend, Mary Regina. May 8th 1687, Whitehall.

A Christopher Tootal then recorded:

> Mr Brian, chaplin at the Cross Keys in Holywell town, gave me an account on June 22 1687, that after he had procured a lease of Holywell Chapel and the possession given him by the landlord, the Jesuits' agent demanded the key of Mr Brian; but he refused to deliver it. Whereupon they broke open the door and delivered possession thereof to the Jesuits. For redress of this wrong done to Mr Brian he had recourse to the landlord, who fairly owned that his lease was good and duly executed, but withall declared that in regard it was the Queen's pleasure that the Jesuits should have the chapel for their use, he was not willing to incur her displeasure by opposing the proceedures.[19]

The Cross Keys was later sold and converted into a house.

There is a stone laid in the side of the Well-basin commemorating restoration work. Dated 10 June 1687, it bears the Jesuit monogram IHS (Jesus, Saviour of Mankind). Unfortunately for them, the Jesuit's possession of the shrine was short lived, because, on 10 June 1688, the Queen gave birth to a son, believing that St Winefride had answered their prayers. The Protestants, however, believing there was the threat of another Catholic king encouraged William, Prince of Orange, to land at Torbay on 5 November and King James fled the country on Christmas Day. In Holywell, the Protestants broke into the Star Inn and removed books and a cross, which they burned in the town's Market Place and for some three years, Father Roberts had to sleep outdoors.[19]

The names of Ye Olde Star Inn and the Cross Keys both have Biblical origins. As one may imagine, Ye Olde Star Inn refers to the Star of Bethlehem. The Cross Keys can be traced back to Matthew 16 in the Bible where Jesus is quoted as saying to Peter:

> And I tell you, you are Peter, and on this rock I will build my church, and the powers of death shall not prevail against it. I will give you the keys of the kingdom of heaven and whatever you bind on earth shall be bound in heaven, and whatever you loose on earth shall be bound in heaven, and whatever you loose on earth shall be loosed in heaven.

Thus, the crossed keys in the arms of St Peter represent the keys of earth and heaven. The golden key symbolises losing and the silver key symbolises binding.[71] There is an excellent plaster cast of the Crossed Keys within St Winefride's Church.

Although there were times when the building was not occupied because of opposition to the Jesuits, the superiors of the Society continued to work from Holywell until about 1773.

After 1685, all British monarchs were Protestant and St Winefride's chapel came under Protestant control. The difficulties of trying to teach and worship in the Roman Catholic faith in Holywell continued until 14 July 1808, when the Clerk of the Peace for Flintshire granted permission for public use of 'Ye Olde Star' as a place of Catholic worship.[19] Thus, arguments and differences between all those wishing to worship in a rightful place and officially recognized place of worship came to an end. Nationally, the Catholic Emancipation Act was passed by Parliament in 1829.

In March 1869, Father Joseph Mann, S.J., accepted an offer to purchase the house which occupied the site of the Cross Keys. Included in the purchase were several small cottages and a malt kiln and a convent and new hospice were built on these site. The total cost was £550.[72]

In 1875, the area around the outer bath was fitted with wooden cubicles for bathers to change in. Large screens were also erected to give privacy to bathers from passers by.[19]

In 1886, a magnificent replacement statue of St Winefride was installed into the empty niche of the earlier statue, due to the generosity of R. Sankey, JP, of The Vron, Holywell.[70] The statue shows the saint as an Abbess, carrying a crook and the palm of martyrdom. Around her neck is a thin line depicting where her head was said to have been severed. The Sankey family were prosperous business people in the Holywell area, and Richard Sankey was, at the time of his gift, serving as the Chairman of the Holywell Magistrates and as a land tax commissioner. When he died, aged 76, on 22 September 1899, he was buried in the family vault in St David's Churchyard, Pantasaph.

74   *A History of Holywell and Greenfield*

The Jesuits continued to serve Holywell's Catholic community until 30 September 1930, when they handed their ministry over to the secular priesthood which came under the control of the Diocese of Menevia.[72] On 18 March 1987, the Diocese of Wrexham was created and Holywell was embraced into it.

The Roman Catholic Church, Well Street [SJ 1855 7509]
The first part of this church was built in 1832, to the design of renowned Catholic Church architect, J. J. Scholes; the entrance was then from New Road (Well Hill). Gwespyr sandstone was used for most of the exterior walls; the roof was slated and slanted.[44] According to the 1851 religious census, the building could accommodate some 300 people.[10] In 1909, because of a large increase in the number of worshippers, the building was greatly altered and extended. The contract for the work was awarded to T. W. Sibeon of Holywell. Externally, the principle alteration was the moving of the front entrance from New Road (Well Hill) to Well Street. This neo-classical entrance was reached by stone steps which had a parapet wall to their front. A crucifix finial is pedimented to the centre.[44] Some of the new exterior walls were of cement rendered brickwork; the bell-tower is at the northwest. Internally, the magnificent veined white marble altar was moved from the east to the west. At the eastern end, above the lobby, a gallery was built to house the organ and accommodate the choir. A chapel, dedicated to St Winefride, was added to the south-western side of

Employees of T. W. Sibeon, builders and contractors, carrying out work in 1909 around the original New Road entrance to St Winefride's Church.

the church and decorated in the Byzantine style. To the west of the chapel altar is a statue of St Winefride on a granite pedestal. It was sculptured by Joseph Swynnerton and blessed by Pope Leo XIII in the grounds of the Vatican.[66] A beautiful large stained-glass window was later added to the west in memory of Gertrude Manners Harden.

During 1911 to 1912, a Lady Chapel was built of Gwespyr sandstone on the north-western side of the premises. Internally, above the beautiful white marble altar, is a statue of Mary holding the baby Jesus. This was all donated by Mrs G. M. Harden in memory of her husband.

The church has some fine stained-glass windows, one of which commemorates Lady Margaret Beaufort. A further window is a memorial to the Jesuit priest John Plessington who was executed at Chester.

A striking memorial is that of three members of the Sankey family who were so very dedicated and generous to the Catholic Church and who devoted so much of their lives to the business world of the town: Mary Sankey (the wife of Richard Sankey, senior); their son Charles Sankey; and Richard Sankey, junior. There is an additional memorial to Mary Anne, the widow of Charles Sankey. The church was listed a Grade II building in 1991.[44]

The Catholic Presbytery, Well Street [SJ 1855 7509]
Part of this building was built before the seventeenth century as 'Ye Olde Star Inn'. As already related, the premises were purchased in 1639 with the intention of them being converted into a hospice, but after thirty years, it became the official residence of the Jesuits.[19] The main entrance was from a steep slope on New Road (Well Hill). After permission was given on 14 July 1808 for the premises to be a Catholic chapel, they were suitably altered and used as such until the Catholic Church was built alongside in 1832.[44] Since then, there have been alterations but the original cellars used by the public house are still in being.[44] The premises were made a Grade II listed building in 1991.[44]

The original St Winefride's Roman Catholic Hall and School, New Road (Well Hill) [SJ 1848 7607]
These buildings were erected, as the plaque still on the roadside wall records: 'by Rev. Father Charles Beauclerk, S.J., in 1895'. Built when Catholicism in Holywell was experiencing great advancement, including a growth in the numbers of visiting pilgrims, the premises were intended to provide the dual purpose of parish use as well as children's school. The slate roof bears an interesting feature in different coloured tiles; the letters 'WVM' and 'AMDG' stand for 'Winefride Virgin Martyr' and '*Ad Majorem Dei Gloriam*' (To the Greater Glory of God) – the latter being a Jesuit motto. The building remained in constant use until 1975 when the need for refurbishment and the demands of a modern, dual-purpose building, resulted in two new schools being built in Whitford Street; one serving the Roman Catholic community (which also served as the Catholic Community Centre) and the other, the Welsh-speaking community, as Gwenffrwd Welsh Primary School.

A scheme, by Flintshire County Council's Townscape Heritage Initiative (THI), in partnership with the Heritage Lottery Fund, the Welsh Development Agency and CADW, to rebuild and extend the former school and hall into fourteen apartments was agreed upon at the turn of the twenty-first century.[73] The original exterior features of the building were incorporated in the scheme which cost around £1m. The Wales and West Housing Association carried out the work, and the new building, named Plas Gwenffrewi, was officially opened on 16 July 2004. The project was given special mention at the prestigious 2005 Civic Trust Awards.[110]

The Pedestal and Statue of Christ

The 1895 decision to have a replica of the famed marble Statue of the Sacred Heart at the Seminary Church of Saint-Sulpice, Paris, cast and installed outside the new hall and school on New Road was of significant importance, not only to the Catholic community of Holywell itself, but to the countless numbers of visiting pilgrims. Because it was sited so prominently, facing down the hill towards St Winefride's Shrine, it has become both a religious and an historic feature of the town.

A plaster cast was made of the Paris statue, from which a cast-iron, bronze-finished statue was created for Holywell. Its height is almost ten feet and its weight is just over a ton. The following report, which appeared in *Bye-Gones*, a border magazine, on 26 August 1896, indicates the importance of the statue.

> A remarkable ceremony took place on Monday afternoon at Holywell, the occasion being the removal of the gigantic bronze statue of Our Saviour (Sacred Heart) from the station [then Greenfield] to the town. There assembled at the station a vast concourse of pilgrims bearing a number of banners. The statue, which represents Our Saviour with outspread arms and the Sacred Heart affixed in gilt on the breast, was borne in a semi-recumbent position on a large lorry, which was one mass of flowers. The lorry was drawn by three horses gaily caparisoned with velvet and gold cloth and flowers. The road was lined with spectators, and flags and bunting were displayed en-route. During the passage of the procession a number of hymns were sung. The procession went as far as the top of High Street, and thence to the new St Winefride's Hall, where the statue was drawn into the yard, in which stands the pedestal on which it is to be placed. The proceedings here were brief, and were followed by benediction in the church and a Ransomer's reunion in the hall, where Father Fletcher delivered the address.[17]

In addition to the detail above, the statue shows Christ with outstretched arms displaying stigmata, standing on an orb adorned with the symbols of the Passion. By Monday, 4 September 1896, the statue had been erected on the pedestal and the unveiling ceremony was carried out by Father Towhey, S.J., of the church of St Xavier, Liverpool. Further evidence of the importance of the statue is the fact that the Ceremony of the Blessing of it was carried out on Sunday, 8 November 1896, by Bishop Dr Mostyn, the first Vicar Apostolic of Wales. The Bishop was a member of the local Mostyn family of Talacre.

As part of the refurbishment scheme for the old school and hall, it was resolved to have the statue repaired and restored to its original condition. The work was magnificently done by Euro Conservation of Telford at a cost of £12,000. The company had previously carried out projects which included the refurbishment of the Albert Memorial and the manufacture of the gates for the Princess Diana Memorial Walk in London. On 29 January 2004, the statue was returned to Holywell and replaced on the original plinth which had to be reconstructed. Now, together with the new building behind it, it is not only viewed with great admiration by travellers coming up New Road into the town, but acts as a magnificent historic religious symbol for the town's Catholic community and visitors.[73 & 110] The statue is Grade II listed.[44]

The Hospice (St Winefride's Pilgrims' Guest House), Well Hill [SJ 1849 7605]
In 1869, the old malt-kiln building was acquired and converted into the Pilgrims' Hospice which catered especially for the poor and sick pilgrims. It was officially opened and blessed by Bishop Brown on 22 June 1870. It was originally in the charge of the Sisters of Charity of St Paul (who also ran the convent and the school in High Street). The fees were kept exceptionally low. In 1895, 1,710 pilgrims stayed there and, although numbers decreased as the twentieth century unfolded, the hospice was certainly well used. After the Second World War, national poverty gradually diminished and the premises were eventually upgraded and re-titled St Winefride's Guest House.

On 1 July 2002, the Bishop of Wrexham announced that the hospice was to close and the building would possibly have to be sold. However, in June 2003, the Bishop received a proposal from the Order of the Most Holy Saviour of St Bridget, asking if he would endorse their wish to establish a new foundation at Holywell. That desire was to have the closed hospice renovated and updated for the purpose of offering accommodation to pilgrims and visitors. The nuns would be responsible for running the guest house as well as the derelict Ava Maria Hall (the first Catholic school building in Holywell) which would have to be completely rebuilt to provide living quarters for the nuns themselves. Following very lengthy discussions and applications, a scheme was devised which would involve an investment of £1.3 million which would be met by funding from the Holywell Townscape Heritage Initiative (THI), the Catholic Diocese of Wrexham, the Nazareth Trust, the Welsh Development Association, the Heritage Lottery Fund, CADW and the Wales Tourist Board. In early 2006, work commenced on the scheme — with a target date of 2008. Within the scheme, ensuite bedrooms would be provided at the hospice as well as a new dining room and kitchen.

Baron Corvo (Frederick Rolfe)
Midway through 1895, a 'shabby, pious, itinerant artist, calling himself Fr. Austin', (the 'Fr.' was subsequently found to be an abbreviation for Frederick, not Father) arrived at the Franciscan Friary in Pantasaph seeking aid and work from the fraternity. He was given work to do on the Calvary Cross but was found to be disobeying orders by using an unknown cleaning material and was not reading the

edifying book lent to him by the friars.[97] As a consequence he was dismissed. He then went to Father Beauclerk, Holywell's priest-in-charge, who said: 'I made an agreement with him that I would give him the opportunity of supporting himself by finding him lodging and board, and supplying all materials, if he would paint banners for the Shrine.'[97] In addition, he was given the facility of an unused schoolroom for use as a studio.[97] But, who was he? His full name was Frederick William Rolfe, and had been born at 61 Cheapside, on 22 July 1860. He had adopted the title 'Baron Corvo', claiming that he had been gifted some Italian estates by a Duchess of Sforzo-Caesarina.[97] In addition, he assumed the name 'Fr. Austin'. When aged twenty-six, he converted to Catholicism and, although accepted as a student to enter the priesthood, was soon expelled. During his three years in Holywell he caused confusion and was distrusted by many, but mostly by the Catholic authorities.

By early 1897, relations between William Rolfe and Father Beauclerk started to become strained. Rolfe incorrectly accusing the priest of not paying for the banners and letters were exchanged between the two. As Father Beauclerk later wrote: 'One day Rolfe asked for £100 for painting ten banners. However, it was pointed out that the agreement did not include any payment for his paintings'. Through the medium of the Catholic magazine *The Holywell Record* (which was run from 3 Bank Place), Rolfe used his writing ability to openly air his views and grievances, including hostility towards Father Beauclerk. Rolfe went further by writing letters to the Bishop and to a Superior General in Rome. This all resulted in Father Beauclerk being moved from Holywell to Malta for two years before he was appointed Priest of Accrington. By that time, the authorities had conclusively found that it was Rolfe who had caused the troubles in Holywell. It must be said, however, that Rolfe had exceptional capabilities as an artist, and the banners he produced are proof of that. Five of these still survive and can be viewed in the museum at St Winefride's Shrine.

Rolfe eventually found accommodation at Holywell Workhouse (Lluesty) but soon moved to Oxford where he took up writing. He had failed to become a priest and his time in Holywell was certainly controversial. His last career in writing was apparently the same, as the report in *The Star* newspaper of 29 October 1913 said:

> A curiously interesting and almost mysterious character has passed away in the person of Mr. Frederick Rolfe, who was found dead in his bed at Venice a few mornings ago ... he wrote verses and controversial articles on Catholic ritual and Italian politics. He used to state that he had been at one time in priest's orders, but this, we believe, was denied by the authorities of this church.[97]

Basingwerk Abbey and the Cistercian Monks [SJ 1968 7748]

To trace the beginnings of Basingwerk Abbey, we must look back as far as Ranulf de Gernon who was Earl of Chester between 1129 and 1153. By 1131 he had decided to create a chapel as a border house on the disputed lands between England and Wales, some 15–20 miles west of Chester. It was intended that it would later become an abbey. For centuries these lands had witnessed fighting for territory between the princes of Wales and the kings and barons of England. Ranulf contacted the French

Savigniac monks to open up the chapel in what was then the *cantref* (district) of Tegeingl.

King Cenwulf of Mercia died in battle in 821 AD at Dinas Basi where the Normans later created a fortification known as Hên Blas which was where the Savigniac's first chapel in this district, now generally referred to as Basingwerk Chapel, is believed to have been located. This location is now called Coed Ffrith, Coleshill [SJ 223 736]. In 1157, Henry II granted a charter to the monks at Holywell and Fulbrook for the chapel of Basingwerk in which they first dwelt.[34] In 1240, Prince Dafydd ap Llywelyn, granted the monks 'the grange at Fulbrook [i.e. by Holywell stream] … and the church at Holywell with the chapel of Coleshill'[34] which clearly ties the chapel in to Coed Ffrith. In 1147 the Savigniacs were absorbed into the Cistercian order which had been formed at Cîteaux, France, by Benedictine brethren, dismayed at the lax observance of the rule of the Savigniac Order.[68] They turned away from sources of excessive luxury and wealth and the economy of their abbeys was based on the direct exploitation of land. Because the Cistercians wore habits of undyed wool they were known as the 'White Monks'. It was when they superseded the Savigniac monks, that the move from Hên Blas to Fulbrook (Greenfield) took place. Thus, either in 1147, or shortly afterwards, the Cistercians built the first part of what was to be Basingwerk Abbey or, to give it its correct title, the Abbey of St Mary at Basingwerk.

The fast-flowing Holywell stream (Fulbrook), which ran past the west of the site, would certainly have influenced Ranulf's decision to create the abbey there and give the adjoining lands to the Cistercians. Besides the obvious advantage of a good water supply for the abbey, it proved to be of considerable help commercially to the Cistercians. They would have been the first people to generate power on any large scale from the stream when they built their wool, corn and paper mills alongside it. The first abbey building was small, but over the next four centuries, many additions and alterations were made. During the early thirteenth century, the abbey underwent major reconstruction and, by the end of the fifteenth century, was a splendid building. It had the benefits of lead roofing and fine stained-glass windows. Much of the Gwespyr-type stone used for the building is believed to have come from the Moor Quarry [SJ 180 773], on the hill about a mile to the west of the site.[58] The stone used in the late twelfth century church and chapter house was fairly massive and well squared, but other buildings, such as the frater, are thinner-bedded. Despite this variation in quality, both sets of stone seem to have come from Moor Quarry, the difference being caused by different levels in the quarry beds successions.[58] Dark limestone from near the Cistercians's Holway Grange Farm is thought to have been the source for the abbey's mortar.[62] As a result of the building changes and additions, the community became completely self contained.

The religious sections of the abbey, which included the monk's quire with adjoining north and south transepts, each had two small chapels, a sacristy and chapter house. There was a large seven-bay nave, measuring some 96 ft x 57 ft, for the lay brothers. Other buildings included a cloister, cellular's buildings, kitchen, frater and a novices' lodging. But the only room, apart from the kitchen, which provided any heat for them, was the warming house. The abbey is recorded as having a scriptoria and, in the fifteenth century, Gutun Owain, the famed Welsh scholar and herald bard, was based there with the responsibility of record keeping for north Wales. He had a manuscript book produced there which was the so-called *Black Book of Basingwerk*, the first book on armorial and heraldic devices relating to Wales.[65] There was also an infirmary where the monks tended to the sick.[68] I have never discovered where their dead were buried, but presume their graveyard was Holywell churchyard. Outer buildings included a gatehouse (at which visitors were received and alms were given), a maltery (where the monks brewed their ale), storehouses and barns.[21]

It is believed that there were about twelve French Savigniac monks at the first chapel in 1131.[68] However, the Cistercian community increased in number and also included English monks. Apart from the abbot, there were monks who had taken their vows, as well as lay brothers who received board and lodging in return for their labours.[21] They were the manual workers, not only at the abbey, but also in the grange farms and lands belonging to the order; their work was thus responsible for the abbey becoming both rich and powerful. One important person was the cellarer lay brother who saw to the comfort of visitors.[21] Stewards were at first of modest rank but later became wealthy gentry. The lay brothers were only allowed the use of the abbey nave and had their own doorway into the church which meant that they did not take a full part in the religious life of the order.[21] To become a monk proper, a prospective candidate had to take their vows and have religious education. Although life changed for them as the years passed, at first their life was spent in prayer and religious study. Worship was in the church's chancel and transept. Their meals were simple; whilst eating, a fellow brother read scripture to them. The only place they were allowed to converse with one another was in the parlour. Even that had to be for essential purposes only.

The English Crown involved the abbots of Basingwerk in carrying out duties for them — for example, when Flint castle was built in 1280, Edward I appointed one of the brethren to be chaplain there.[68] The 1285 Pipe Roll records a payment of fifty shillings for the wages and habit of a Basingwerk abbey monk who celebrated divine service at Flint Castle where he had been lodged since 1281.[21] In 1246, Henry III engaged Abbot Simon to escort Isabella, Prince Dafydd's widow, from Dyserth Castle to a nunnery at Godstow in Oxfordshire. The conflicts of the Middle Ages led to the abbey being damaged on a number of occasions and Edward I is recorded as having paid compensation to assist with restoration work.

The borderland position of the abbey placed the monks in a rather unique situation. During the twelfth and thirteenth centuries they were able to gain from the patronage of Welsh princes as well as English kings and nobility. They were granted land and buildings by both sides, with the results that their finances were helped considerably. Early grants from Earl Ranulf included the manor of Fulbrook as well as lands at West Kirby on the Wirral peninsula. The distant manor of Glossop in Derbyshire, given to the Basingwerk monks in 1157 by a charter of Henry II, was to prove to be the first of many forestry lands which they acquired in that county — as well as the manor of Chalesworth. Indeed, when the suppression of the abbey came about in the sixteenth century, Glossop manor and church were its most valuable possessions, accounting for over thirty per cent of its gross income.[21] Prince Llywelyn ab Iorwerth, who died in 1240, gave the monks property at Gelli (above Whitford) as well as Llyn Tegid and extensive grazing rights at Penllyn, near Bala.[21] The son of Prince Llywelyn, Dafydd ap Llywelyn, granted them Holywell Church and the shrine and pilgrimage chapel of St Winefride in 1240. These remained in their possession until the dissolution in 1536.[63] At the end of twelfth century, the English Crown granted the monks the right to hold a market and fair in Holywell.[74]

As time passed, income from manor rents; manorial court fines; market fairs; the brewing and sale of beer and other commodities at Holywell market; sheep farming in Flintshire, Derbyshire and the Bala area; and the sale of wool as far afield as Flanders and Florence, made Basingwerk a wealthy community by the end of the fifteenth century.[59]

Using the water from the Holywell stream, the monks also built a paper mill and the writer Thomas Pennant recorded that ancient corn mills, belonging to the abbey, had also stood on the site of the paper mill.[22]

Basingwerk, because of its geographical position between Wales and England and its proximity to St Winefride's Holy Well, was always a popular place for visitors. One famed visitor was Giraldus Cambrensis (Gerald the Welshman) who accompanied Archbishop Baldwin on his famous crusading mission in 1188.[74] In the late fifteenth century, the Abbey was given an annuity of 10 marks by Richard III for the 'Yearly sustentacione and salarie of a priest at the Chappelle of St Wynefride'.

During its lifetime Basingwerk had twenty-one abbots. The first Welshman to hold the position was Thomas Pennant (1481–1522).[21] From the fourteenth century, the abbey became beset by difficulties, both economical and political and the abbots and monks came in for criticism. The deeply religious way of life of the monks began to wane and the community no longer carried out many services, including the early morning celebrations. The frugal foods they had lived on in earlier times were replaced by richer items such as roast meats, poultry, white bread, sweet foods and fine French wines.[21] They moved to the warming house for meals.[4] Abbot Henry Wirral (1430–54) was arrested for felonies in Flint County. Abbot Thomas Pennant, the well-educated and cultured son of David Pennant ap Tudor, became a famed host to bards and gentry.[21] Gutin Owain wrote a poem that was liberal in its praise of him: that Pennant gave twice the treasure of a king in wine and, because of the numbers of guests, additional accommodation had to be built.[21] Unfortunately, Pennant, whilst still an abbot, strayed and married Angharad, daughter of the house of Penrhyn.[21] Three years after his resignation in 1522, his third child, Nicholas (born c.1495), became abbot. He was the last Basingwerk abbot before the dissolution of the monasteries. Of Thomas Pennant's other sons, the first, Edward, succeeded to fortunes (land and buildings) of the parish of Holywell; the second, another Thomas, became vicar of Holywell. Envisaging the dissolution, Nicholas gifted many of Basingwerk's outlying lands and buildings to the Pennant family. Although the Crown contested the gifts, Nicholas Pennant won, with the result that the Pennant family was able to enjoy a prosperous living for at least three centuries. During those years parcels of land were sold off, benefitting many local people.

The Rev. Dr David H. William's book, *The Welsh Cistercians*,[21] provides a detailed list of the land and buildings which were the property of Basingwerk Abbey:

The Lordship of Greenfield (alias Fulbrook)

The Abbey site [SJ 196 775], proximate 'court green' in Holywell.

In Holywell, three granges: Home Grange [possibly on the site of the later Abbey Farm], Middle Grange, Over or Higher Grange [SJ 173 762]: earlier grange names include: Fulbrook, Sovereign (1285) and Beggesburch (1291).

Woodland including: Kingswood and Great Wood [SJ 186 782].

Calcot [SJ 168 740], substantial lands here, if not the whole township.

Merton Abbot [SJ 157 778].

Tre'r Abad, Gelli Grange and Hendre Mynach: [SJ 108 768, SJ 128 782, 097 771, respectively].

Caldy Grange [SD 219 870] with Grange Wood to the east.

Property (demised in 1330) including: 'grange of Hall' [SD 223 869].

The Abbey owned the township of Grange, and, eastern border, property at Newton-cum-Larton [c.SD 236 870) and the rake House [SD 233 877]; Thornton Grange [SD 315 814]; Lache Grange.

Uncertain bounds (c.SJ 399 649), including Netherlech (SJ 407 648); Cwmtylo (SH 849 342); Gwernhefin Grange (SH 893 328); Boch-y-rhaiadr Grange (SH 847 396); Penmaen: uncertain bounds, now in estate of Plas-yn-Penmaen, including Cwm Tir-yr-mynach (c.SH 913 428).

He quotes their economic resources as being:

Grange and other chapels, Tre'r-adab (SJ 104 779) four 'capel' field-names on the tithe map; Gelli (SJ 128 782); Over Grange (SJ 173 762).

St Winefride's pilgrimage chapel, Holywell, with well (SJ 186 763).

Tithe-barn: in Coleshill.

Water-mills: in Greenfield, 'upper (SJ 186 763) and nether corn mills, close to abbey on Holywell stream; Wind-mills: Holywell (? SJ 191 758), two in Wirral (SD 222 687) and ? (SJ 242 881).

Fulling–mills: two in Greenfield, the 'lower' was two closes distant from the 'nether' corn mill.

Conyger: at Caldy Grange.

Fisheries: stank by abbey; in Denbighshire (at Rhuddlan), Dee (presumably); Llyn Tegid (Bala) and at West Kirby (Wirral).

Coal-mine: in Coleshill (leased from Crown).

Lead and silver mines: possibly worked in the carboniferous limestone west of Holywell.

Rushes: in Saltney Marsh; salt-pits: in Middlewich and Northwich (Cheshire).

Markets and fairs: Holywell, Charlesworth and Glossop (Derbyshire).

Urban property; in Chester, Flint, Holywell and Shrewsbury (1295).

After closure, Nicholas Pennant received a pension of £17. When he died (in either 1548 or 1549) he was buried, at his request, in Holywell churchyard. Although not confirmed, it is believed that he dwelt at Gelli Grange above Whitford between 1536 and 1548/9.

Following the dissolution of the abbey in 1536, some parts of it were dismantled and moved to other places. In the 1536 churchwarden's accounts of St Mary-on-the-Hill, Chester, it states the 'quere [choir] was boght at basenwerke and sett uppe with all costs and charchis [charges] belonging to the same'.[74] In 1538, lead from Basingwerk was used to repair Holt Castle,[2] the President of the Council of the Marches instructed the Lord Privy Seal to move the King for 'six fother [approximately 19.4 cwt or one cartload] of lead, from the late abbey of Basingwerk, towards repairing the castle of Holte'. A further 'sixty fother of lead' was taken from the abbey roofs in 1546 to Ireland for the covering of Dublin Castle and for the King's castles and house.[74]

The magnificent east stained-glass window in the parish church of St Asaph and St Cyndeyrn at Llanasa, was brought there from Basingwerk in 1540.[74] It is apparent, therefore, that Henry ap Harri (see below) moved very quickly to obtain the window for his parish church. The four window panes depict (1) an unknown bishop, (2) St Katherine, whose identity is unknown, but, because of a scar on the neck of the figure, it is widely believed that it is actually St Winefride, (3) St James, (4) St Lawrence, one of the seven deacons of Rome in the third century. In addition, the small vestry window also came from the abbey. It depicts Jesus on the cross with Mary and John in attendance.

Another major asset that may have come from Basingwerk is the nave roof at St Mary's Church, Cilcain. This exquisite 'rare and spectacular piece of late medieval carpentry' was most certainly not made for St Mary's, the scale of the carving and its moulding suggesting that it was meant to be seen from further away, on a higher structure. Cilcain claims that the roof was taken there from another building at the time of the Reformation. Recent scholarship, however, has cast doubt that the roof came from Basingwerk as it would not have fitted any structure in the abbey's remains.

In St Mary's, Whitford, we can view, within a small glass-topped showcase, two more objects said to be from Basingwerk. One is a fragment of stained glass; the other a roof tile of identical type to those of the abbey. They were found during building work on the old Greenfield Hall lands in 1950.

Stonework began to be taken without permission from the Abbey — this was especially so when the Greenfield Valley started to have the numerous industrial buildings erected there during the seventeenth century. A major example of this was a cotton mill, built in 1785, which was generally called the 'Yellow Mill' because of the large quantity of the Gwespyr-type stone taken from the Abbey.

On 28 April 1541, letters patent were issued under the Great Seal, granting to

Henri ap Harri and Peter Mutton 'the reversion of the house [abbey] and site of Basingwerk', in consideration of £28 11s. 8d.[75] Henri ap Harri was a member of the gentry family of Perth-y-Maen in the parish of Llanasa, and Peter Mutton was Chief Justice of North Wales; he lived in the parish of Meliden. When Henry ap Harri's daughter married one of the Mostyns of Talacre, the former Abbey site passed into that family's control. During the latter part of the sixteenth century, some of the Mostyn family actually lived in part of the former Abbey. In 1923, the then owner, Miss Clementina Mostyn, placed the Basingwerk assets into the guardianship of the Welsh Office.[74] Today, the ruins are in the care of Cadw and were Grade III listed in 1991. Miss Clementina Mostyn died on 18 September 1960 and was buried in the graveyard of St David's Church, Pantasaph.

Holywell Parish Church [SJ 185 762]

The church, which is sixty-eight feet long and fifty-six feet wide, is the focal point of so much history — both Roman Catholic and Anglican. Indeed, a study of the building reveals a great insight into the architectural changes over the centuries. In order to fully appreciate this history, a visit to the church is certainly recommended. It is beyond the remit of this book to name the many assets, memorials and items of furniture held by the Church of St James the Great. Under the chancel are the vaults of the Mostyns of Talacre, the Pennants of Bagillt and the Pantons of Bagillt.[22]

After the building work of the late fourteenth century, the next major development of the church occurred between 1769 and 1770, possibly to the designs of Thomas Meredith.[44] During the intervening four hundred years, apart from the tower, the main structure had badly fallen into decay and most of the main structure was in need of rebuilding. There was also an urgent need for extra accommodation because the population of the parish had increased tremendously due to the development of industry in the local area.

The first stage of the rebuilding work was commenced on the north side of the church on 24 July 1769; this included the provision of a gallery. Following the completion of this first phase of rebuilding, many of the local gentry subscribed to the cost of re-building the south side of the church. Upper colonnades were added to support new galleries after which the church could accommodate 1,200 people.[10] The final project, which was carried out in 1771, was the erection of a singer's gallery in the belfry, at a cost of £20.[5] It is accepted that it was in this era that the church became dedicated to St James the Apostle and the dedication to St Winefride ceased to be used.[75]

Until the parishes of Bagillt (1844) and Brynford (1851) were carved out of the parish of Holywell, the parish encompassed the townships of: Holywell, Greenfield, Calcot, Brynford, Bagillt-Fawr, Bagillt-Fechen, Welston, Coleshill-Fawr and Coleshill-Fechen.[47] After 1851, Holywell parish (including Greenfield) covered an area of 3,200 acres.

A gasometer had been installed in Greenfield in 1824 and the parish church had gas lighting installed in 1826 at a cost of £85 0s. 4d. It is widely believed that this

The interior of St James' Parish Church, c.1920 (note the gas lighting fittings).

church was, if not *the* first, then certainly one of the first to have such a facility. Electricity superceded gas in 1930.[5]

In 1884–5 a further major transformation to the church took place, to a design by Matthew Wyatt.[44] These changes included:

The east window aperture was enlarged to the size we have today.

The apse was built, thus forming a sacrarium with an altar.

Part of the nave was enclosed by a low screen, thus forming a chancel.

Both the north and the south galleries had their easternmost sections removed, thus giving the impression of a transept.

All the oak paneling of the pews was replaced by pitch pine — the panelling was used to form a dado around the church.

The belfry gallery was removed, a partitioned vestry was erected at the east, having its own entrance from outside.

Over the font a panelled ceiling was built and a lobby was erected at the south door.

Staircases were provided to give access to the galleries.

The whole of the church roof was stripped and covered with lead.

Outside the land around the church was enlarged, lowered, and a retaining wall was constructed.

The stone for the church came from Jardine's quarry in Greenfield. The total cost was almost £3,000 [2006 £162,000].[44]

Special mention much be made about the paintings in the apse as 'Few churches in the Diocese can surpass the East End of St James' for beauty and harmony of colour'. The magnificent paintings there were the work of Miss Louie Johnson Jones of Pistyll, who devoted the years 1908–22 to the project. The panels are copies of 'The Offerings of the Magi' and 'Via Dolorosa' by Paul Veronese and of 'The Last Supper' by Leonardo Da Vinci. To the underside of the santuary arch are seven panels, all originals by Miss Johnson Jones, depicting the 'Central sun as Christ, son of righteousness'.[45]

It is important to highlight the fact that the apse, protruding from the santuary at the east end of the church, not only has a dome, but is polygonal, thus there are, in fact, three independent and magnificent windows there — referred to as the 'North, Central and the South Sanctuary Windows. They were installed after the First World War by public subscription as an offering of thanks for peace and victory. The north window stands for War. From the various pictures making up the window, the main feature is that of St Michael, the warrior of heaven and defender of the Church militant, seen in golden armour. Behind him stands the dazzling glory of heaven. The main feature of the central window is symbolic of victory and triumph through suffering. It depicts the crucifixion, ascension and Christ victorious, seated on his throne. The south window stands for peace and depicts St Gabriel, the archangel of peace and goodwill. Near to this window is a memorial plaque of green granite which shows the names of those parishioners who fell in that war.

The west window of the church was originally the east window, having been moved when the apse was built in 1885. New glass was installed there after the Second World War as a further offering of thanks for peace and victory. The tracery glass depicts the shields of Belgium, England, France and Italy. Above these shields is inscribed '1914' with '1919' below. The main figures of the window represent 'Our Lord' and 'Victory and Peace'. Although in Latin, the inscription below says 'For Victory and Peace, given by the favour of God, we render thanks'.[45]

The First World War must have had a tremendous impact on the parishioners. In addition to these stained-glass windows there are, set into the chancel wall, ovals of marble which enabled those families who had had suffered the death of a relation in the war to have the name privately noted within their place of worship.

Most of the other stained- and coloured-glass windows in the church are memorials to local families and individuals. There are also a large number of memorial plaques in the church the oldest of which reads:

Resurrectio mea xtus.
Hic jacet corpus Johannis Pennant, de Holywell, Armigeri;
que obit xxx. die Augusti, 1623.
[My Resurrection Christ
Here lies the body of John Pennant, Knight, of Holywell;
who died August 30th AD 1623.]

John Pennant was second in descent from Nicholas Pennant, last abbot of Basingwerk Abbey. He married Margaret, the daughter of Hugh Mostyn, younger son of Pyers Mostyn of Talacre.[22]

In 1905, a stone-built vestry was constructed at the west end of the church; a new communion table, with raised marble foot, was provided in the chancel; the pulpit was moved to the north side of the church; a prayer desk and choir seats were added.[52] Unfortunately, in 1989, because of subsidence, the 1905 vestry was found to be unsafe and part of the north aisle was partitioned off to form a replacement vestry. The vestry has now been demolished.

During the eighteenth-century re-building work (c.1770) a mutilated, headless, stone effigy of a priest, 5 ft 7 ins long, in fine vestments was discovered.[76] He is holding the stem of a chalice with both hands. The writer, Thomas Pennant, believed it to be an effigy of Thomas Pennant, the second son of Abbot Thomas Pennant, who was vicar of Holywell during the 1520s.[75] The style of the carving is, however, remarkably similar to work done by the Purbeck marblers of the thirteenth century. Indeed, it particularly resembles an effigy of Bishop Northwold in Ely Cathedral Presbytery, dated c.1255.[45] Although it may never be known whose was the effigy, it is likely that it was created for the Basingwerk monks.

The octagonal, pyramidal font was presented to the church in 1885 by ninety people who had been baptised in the old font. Of Corsham Down stone, its sides have carved emblems of the Holy Trinity, the Cross, the Dove, as well as the wallet, staff and cockle-shell of St James. The beautiful lectern, standing on a stone base, is brass and depicts an eagle perched on an orb, ready to spread its wings in flight. It was given in memory of Major William John Williamson of Pendre and who died in Calcutta on 8 February 1883.[52] The rather unique American walnut pulpit was given on 17 March 1885 by Eliza Jones of Tower Gardens, in memory of her parents and their children.[52]

Within a glass case by the west window are a sundial (with the initials of the wardens of 1732); a bassoon (introduced in 1765 to support the singers); and the Little Bell (*Y Gloch Bach*), dating from around 1714, when it started to be used around the streets of Holywell to call people to services.[45] The bell was suspended from a man's shoulders by a strap connected to a leather pad on his knee. As he walked, the bell would hit the pad and clang. It ceased to be used in 1857 after the bell at St Peter's church took over the duty. Of particular historical interest is a rare oak chest which has the year 1679 inscribed into it, together with the initials of the two churchwardens of that time.

The church has been extremely fortunate over the centuries in gifts of communion plate; the oldest items are:

> A silver flagon with a 'Glory and IHS', inscribed: 'The Gift of Mrs Elizabeth Kaey to the Church of Holywell, 1715.
>
> A chalice inscribed: 'For use of the Parish Church of Holywell, 1727'.
>
> A silver salver inscribed: 'For the Church in Holywell'.

The organ has a fascinating history and has been moved from site to site within the church. Originally installed in 1808, it was enlarged in 1824 by Flight Robson of London. Thorold and Smith further enlarged it in 1885, but by 1920 it was in need of restoration and further enlargement. By then, the organ was twice its original size, and had twice as many pipes. In 1975 it was moved to its present position on the south side of the east-end and some new parts were utilised that were taken from an organ that had been in George Street Methodist Church, Chester. After alterations in 1993, the organ is now of three manuals, with an all-electric action.

The start of the 1980s witnessed the theft of large areas of the roof lead. This, in turn, caused problems with the insurance for the building. As a result the whole roof was replaced with stainless steel in 1985/86. That, together with other remedial work, cost around £19,500.

Since 1951 the church has been a Grade II* Listed building.

The Parish Churchyard at St James' Church
Churchyards with memorials and gravestones only really came about from about the seventeenth century. Prior to that, it was practice to bury the deceased in deep graves without gravestones. It was also common practice for a parish to own a coffin, into which a shrouded body would be placed and carried to a grave where the body, without the coffin, would be buried. Exceptions to this were nobility and gentry who were often laid to rest within the churches and plaques and memorials for such people have been retained and, provide us with some vital history of local families. In some towns, when outside graves became filled, remains were removed to a 'bone-house' (otherwise known as a 'Golgotha'). Holywell is one of the few churchyards where the remains of the Golgotha survives.

Vestry records tell us that in 1713 the churchyard was walled for the first time and that a foundation was built for the street wall in 1738.[45] The fact that the churchyard, on the steep hill down to the church, caused problems was recorded by Thomas Pennant who wrote:

> The Churchyard is the worst in the whole of the diocese, a small part is a gentle slope, but the greater almost precipitous, so that after any continuance of wet weather a fall may happen, productive of the most indecent and horrible spectacle'.[22]

That there was already a Golgotha outside the church, is borne out by a vestry minute of 1832 which stated:

> Resolved that the Golgotha (or the bone-house) be converted into a waiting room for the use of paupers applying for relief at Vestries, and that a bone-house be formed in lieu of the present one at the eastern extremity of the churchyard.[45]

Built into the wall alongside the doorway of this 'new' Golgotha was a stone which had an emblem of the skull and crossbones and an inscription dating it as 1832, along with the churchwardens names. Prior to that, in 1815, the churchyard had been enlarged, land having been donated by Sir Pyers Mostyn.[75] A hearse, purchased by the parish in 1755, was replaced by others as time went by. In 1867, the Duke of Westminster presented the church with three cottages plus a hearse-house, adjoining the west end of the churchyard. These premises were later demolished for cemetery extension.[45]

On 30 November 1864, because the graveyard was completely full, it was closed by an Order in Council. The problem had obviously been foreseen and a new graveyard had been opened at the junction of Coleshill Street and Cross Road.

St Peter's Church, Coleshill Street [SJ 1898 7570]
Lady Emma Pennant of Downing Hall and Revd Thomas Pennant of Brynbella gave land for a new graveyard opposite the junction of Coleshill Street and Cross Street. It was consecrated on 11 October 1847.[52] Public subscriptions and donations enabled a limestone and Gwespyr sandstone cemetery chapel to be built and dedicated to St Peter. The vicar, the Revd Hugh Jones, laid the first stone for it on 28 June 1848. Together with boundary walls, the chapel cost £800.[52] The pitched roof was of slate and, at the west-end, there was a belfry above the main entrance doors. Internally, the floor had a flat, stone surface, the walls were covered with plaster and there was seating for 112 people. The architect was Ambrose Poynter. The building was never consecrated. When St James' Church had a new pulpit in 1899, the old one was transferred to St Peter's. In 1905, the communion table and font were received there.

In 1916, it was decided to start holding Welsh Sunday services at St Peter's, and the interior was suitably adapted. Consequently, the building was thereafter referred to as 'St Peter's Church'. Miss Louie Johnson, who had painted pictures for both St James' Church and for Holy Trinity, generously painted two more for St Peter's; one depicted Jesus walking on the waves and the other Jesus ascending into heaven. (When St Peter's closed, these pictures were taken to St James' Church.) On 2 June 1967, a pair of wrought-iron churchyard gates were given and erected in memory of two faithful members of St Peter's, Harold A. and Gladys M. Brook.

During 1964, most of the gravestones were removed to the outer perimeter of the churchyard, but memorials which relatives wished to have left *in situ* remained so. The area was landscaped, thus enabling easier grass-cutting. Unfortunately, due to low congregations and the resulting financial problems, the church had to be closed in 1980 and it was demolished in May 1981, its assets being transferred to the Parish Church. The roadside walls were repaired, the gates re-furbished. The land is currently owned by the Representative Body of the Church in Wales.

The Additional Parish Church, combined with a Church Hall
In 2005, the Vicar of Holywell, with the support of the churchwardens and Parochial Church Council, drew up plans for the provision of a new church, with a combined church hall, to be erected on the area where St Peter's Church had stood. Access to St James' Church had presented elderly and infirm parishioners with problems and it was hoped that some services could be moved from St James' to the new church. Addionally, there had been no church hall for some time. Marriages and funeral services would continue to be held at St James'.

Despite local objections to the proposal, and the fact that some graves would have to be exhumed and reinterred, Flintshire County Council passed the plans, with certain amendments, in November 2006. There was to be car parking space for some twenty-five vehicles and the building would be able to seat up to 400 people.

Holy Trinity Church, Greenfield [SJ 1940 7762]
With the growth in the population of Greenfield a place of worship became necessary. A room near Abbey Farm, lent to the Parish Church by the Holywell Lime Company, was licensed in 1846 as a Church of England place of worship. Named 'Abbey Chapel' it could accommodate 220 people.[10] This served the community for a time but it was obvious that a purpose-built structure was needed and, following a special meeting held on 13 September 1866, an appeal was launched to build a church which would seat 500 worshippers.[7] Dr Ralph Richardson, the owner of the Greenfield Hall estate, offered to donate a site adjacent to the Holywell road but stipulated that there should be no cemetery.[52] Unfortunately, all the necessary funds needed did not materialise and on 23 August 1869 it was resolved that, for the time being, just the nave and south aisle should be built, leaving the chancel, vestry and porch to be added at a future date.[7 & 52] The designer was Ewan Christian (London), the architect Charles Lucy (Liverpool) and the builders Haigh & Co., Liverpool. Their tender was £1,962[50] but, with furnishings, the total cost was around £2,300. The bell was founded by Blews & Son.[7] There were many generous donations, including £600 from the industrialist, William Keats, and family who resided at Greenfield Hall.[75] A bazaar held in July 1869 raised a very substantial £297 10s. 0d. [2006 — £13,827].[7] The church's foundation stone was laid, in the name of HOLY TRINITY, by the Marchioness of Westminster, on 15 August 1870[75] and services commenced on 18

Holy Trinity Church, Greenfield. Sadly now the only remaining place of religious worship in Greenfield.

October 1871. Although licensed, the church was not then consecrated and came under jurisdiction of the vicar of Holywell. The main building-stone came from Tŷ Coch quarry and the dressing stone was Gwespyr sandstone. The slates were from the Dinorwig Quarry. The altar is, in the style of nineteenth century altars, divided into three bays. In 1871, the church had gas heating and lighting installed at an overall cost of £58 09s. 7d. The pulpit, richly carved with blind and trefoil tracery, flanked with ogle arches, is carried on a central hexagonal stem. The font is of octagonal stone and carried by a cluster of five columns on a square base. Miss Louie Johnson painted the pictures above the altar which depict Jesus bearing his cross (after Veronese) and twelve half-figure portraits of the Apostles. The faces are said to be those of local people.

It was not until 1909 that a decision could be made to have the second stage of construction started. In July 1910, the building contract was awarded to Williams Brothers of Holywell. The designer was John Douglas and the structure, of Early English Gothic style, included a chancel, a south aisle and a vestry at a cost of around £1,000.[44] The gabled belfry stands over the chancel, the porch was built onto the south side, the gabled organ-chamber being near the east of the aisle.[43] The church was consecrated by the Bishop of St Asaph on 25 April 1911 and named 'Holy Trinity'.[78] The exterior sill of the east window has the inscription 'AD DEI GLORIAM MCMX' (To the glory of God 1910). A Lady Chapel was built at the east end of the south aisle after the First World War and was furnished as a memorial to the local fallen of the war.[5] The names of the fallen from the Second World War were added in 1946. The War Memorial tablet from the closed Courtaulds factory in Greenfield, which was dedicated to the workers who lost their lives in the Second World War, was refurbished and placed in Holy Trinity Church on 19 February 1996. The Lady Chapel altar has Gothic tracery panels on either side of a central front pane, which has tracery surrounding a carved circle. Four exquisite strips of painting are on the riddels and dossal of that chapel. The west window has five-lights, whereas both the chancel and the organ chamber have stepped windows with three-lights.[44]

The organ, manufactured by Bishop & Co. London, was purchased in 1888.

A faculty to replace gas lighting and heating to that of electricity was granted on 30 November 1937.

The church is fortunate in having many items of plate, ornaments and monuments, mostly given by people in memory of deceased worshippers.

The church was Grade II Listed in 1991, partly because of it having been designed by architects of national significance.[44]

St Beuno's Church, Holway [SJ 1735 7680]

Once again, due to the large growth in the local population caused by residential building in the Holway, it was decided to build a wooden church to the west of Moor Lane in 1961. The cost, including interior fittings was around £1,475. The Misses Hague of Holywell donated a cross, vases, candlesticks and an alms dish for use in the church.

Unfortunately, due to the lack of worshippers, the church closed in 1980 and was destroyed by fire two years later. The items originally donated by the Misses Hague were returned to them and they most generously and graciously gave them to St John's Cathedral, Yambio, in the Sudan.

The Vicarage
Although the date of the first vicarage built in Holywell has not been established, we do know its site was at the bottom of Well Street, on the slope to the parish church [SJ 1853 7612]. However, Thomas Pennant tells us 'the vicarage house, about the middle of this century [18th] became so ruinous as to be uninhabitable'. In 1760[43] it was rebuilt by the piety of two brothers, Thomas and John Barker, of Bryn Madyn, Bagillt, agents to the great smelting company at Gadlys [Bagillt], who bequeathed £400 to the vicar of Holywell for the purpose of building a new glebe house at Holywell, for him and his successors, on the same spot as that on which the old one stood.[22] The Georgian-style, two-storey building is red brick-built, with a five–bay front and a slated roof.[44] On the land to the rear of the vicarage there originally stood the brick- and timber-built tithe barn, to which the farmers brought one-tenth of their produce as their tithe. It was only when tithes were commuted to cash payments rather than payments in kind, that church rates were established. The tithe barn was then demolished.[11]

This vicarage continued to be the residence for nine successive vicars, but there had been ever-increasing problems with the building. By 1922, the structure was over 160 years old and dampness, which was also accompanied by a general need for renovation, had rendered it almost uninhabitable. Discussions took place with the Diocesan Board but it was some two years before all the necessary work could be completed. Happily, after the Revd Rees, vicar of that time, married in Llansantffraid in July 1924, he and his wife were able to take up residence in the vicarage.

In 1978, the Parochial Church Council decided to buy a modern house on the Fron Park road as a replacement vicarage and the 1760 dwelling was subsequently sold.

Parish Buildings on Bryn y Castell [Castle Hill], Whitford Street and High Street. [SJ 1858 7625]

Castle Hill has been much used by the Parish Church authorities over many years. The *Ancient Monuments in Flintshire* provides a description of the Parish Rooms:

> The house so called[the Parish Rooms], the older part of which was built in 1704, stands immediately above Holywell Church and the old gardens have a steep fall to a dingle on the east. Some years ago, the grounds were extended northwards so as to take in the actual Castle Hill, then covered with cottages (known as Castle Hill Cottages), which were pulled down. Two dingles converge at this point and at a point of juncture is a mound having a rounded top about 27 ft across and some 30 ft above ground on the south, where there is a slight depression, marking, probably, the site of an old ditch across the neck of the promontory.[45]

In April 1918, because of the lack of a place to hold church meetings, the Black Boy

Inn, at 17 Whitford Street, was purchased for conversion into a church building. Half the purchase price of £250 (generously reduced by David Pennant, the owner) was met from the sale of Bryn Celyn School, the remainder of the cost being met by an appeal to parishioners. Later, in 1929, the Parochial Church Council voted to have a specially planned Church House erected on Castle Hill, above the church. It was officially opened by the Bishop of Menevia on Wednesday, 15 October 1930.[45]

In 1959, it was decided that a new Church Hall was needed and a special appeal was made for funds to finance it. The foundation stone for his purpose-built hall was laid by the Bishop of St Asaph, Rt Revd D. D. Bartlett, D.D., on 2 April 1960, the presiding Holywell vicar was Revd W. J. Hamer. The builders were Messrs T. H. Jones of Lloc. A second visit by the Bishop on 2 November 1960 was made to open the self-contained hall.

Sadly, due to continous vandalism and damage to the Church Hall and the curate's house at its rear, a decision was taken in 2006 to sell both, together with the adjoining land, to a developer who intends to build apartments on the site. In the meantime, the church authorities have taken a bold step to build a combined church and community hall on the site of the original St Peter's Church.

Nonconformism
Welsh Calvinistic Methodism, later Welsh Presbyterianism
In 1735, a young south Walian, and loyal Anglican, Howell Harris, started to believe that the Anglican Church was placing insufficient emphasis on the fact that the Lord Jesus should rule people's hearts. This resulted in his beginning to hold preaching meetings, which proved to be a revival in the teachings of the Church and he was followed in his beliefs by other preachers such as Mr Thomas Charles of Bala and the famed hymn writer, William Williams, Pant-y-Celyn. As a result of these teachings, Welsh Methodism was created, but, because they studied the doctrines of Protestant John Calvin, the movement became known as Welsh Calvinistic Methodism, to differentiate it from the Wesleyan Methodism advocated by John and Charles Wesley. Both movements remained friendly but had some differences in principles. In 1823 the Methodists drew up a 'Confession of Faith' which was practically the same as the thirty-nine Articles of the Church of England.

John Owen, born in Ysceifiog, married in 1762 and went to live in Y Berthen Gron, a farmhouse built in a hollow alongside the road between Lixwm and Holywell. Having converted to Welsh Calvinistic Methodism, Owen began to preach from the farm and, together with the help of his wife and his brother, encouraged like-minded preachers from far afield to come to Y Berthen Gron, which soon became the first centre for Methodists in the Holywell area. By 1776, a new chapel had been built there and Owen travelled to Llangeitho in south Wales where he persuaded an early founder of the movement, Daniel Rowland, to come to Y Berthen Gron to open the chapel. Tragically, John Owen died on the way home and thus never lived to witness the fruits of his hard labours. The chapel, however, flourished.

In Holywell itself, the first public Welsh Calvinistic Methodist prayer and preaching services were held in 1795, in a house named Pen-y-Dre in Brynford Street, alongside the King's Arms Hotel (later re-named the Hotel Victoria) which was owned by a William Jones, originally from Caerwys. During the service, the house was attacked and the preachers had to flee through a hole in the wall, then through the garden. Subsequent small meetings were held for a while at the home of a Mr and Mrs Smith, previously from Dolgellau, members of Y Berthen Gron Chapel. The group members later took a house in part of an area of the town called Tai Cochion, on the south side of what we now know as Rose Hill.[83]

Because of the growth of the congregation, the worshippers moved to a large upstairs room at the Coach & Horses Inn in Whitford Street where they remained until 1803. By then, the continuing growth in membership, together with the strong influence of Samuel Jones of Caerwys, meant the room was too small and two brothers, Hugh and James Price, obtained a ninety-nine-year lease on land called 'Y Bryn' just to the rear of the inn.[83]

Bryn Seion Chapel (Capel y Bryn) [SJ 1842 7601]
Bryn Seion Chapel, an octagonal-shaped building, erected on the site at Y Bryn in 1803, was accessed by means of two alleyways, one from alongside the Coach & Horses, the other from near the top of New Road [Well Hill]. A stone placed at the entrance read (from Ecclesiastes V, verse I) *Gwilia ar dy droed pan fyddedr yn myned i dy Dduw; a bydd barottach i wrandaw nag i roi aberth ffyliaid; canys ni wyddant hwy eu bod yn gwneuthur drwg* (Guard your steps when you go to the house of God; to draw near to listen is better than to offer the sacrifice of fools, for they do not know that they are doing evil). Thankfully, this stone has been kept and is now in Rehoboth chapel grounds. Present at the inauguration service were Mr Thomas Charles of Bala, the foremost Methodist in north Wales, and Dr Thomas Edwards of Liverpool. The chapel served the community until it closed in 1827.

Bryn Seion re-opened for worship in 1878. The elders of Rehoboth realised that many of the town's poorest and underprivileged residents failed to go to any church. At the first service of re-opening some fifty to sixty people attended. The chapel had very high backed pews which encouraged the poor to attend as they could hide the fact that they had poor and ragged clothing — some of them even had no shoes. Particular emphasis was given to the children and the local police felt that the education and discipline which they received in the chapel proved to be good for the town – statistics showing that the number of juvenile offences decreased. However, in 1894, the chapel again closed and was used as a warehouse.

Rehoboth Chapel [SJ 1832 7595]
Worship continued at Bryn Seion for twenty-four years but, because of 'Y Diwygiad' (The Revival), the premises again proved to be too small. As a result, shortly before 1827, a ninety-nine year lease was obtained from David Pennant on land higher up the left side of Whitford Street.[83] A chapel was built here which could seat 470 people

and had standing room for a further eighty.[10] This first Rehoboth Chapel was twenty yards long x seventeen yards wide, and cost £1,600 to build. The opening ceremony took place in July 1827.[83] The Religious Census of 1851 records that there was accommodation for 692 people and that the average attendance over twelve months was: 371 worshippers and 158 scholars in the morning; 370 scholars, in the afternoon; and 495 worshippers in the evening.[10] Although the building cost was high, a celebration was held on 4 August 1856 when the debt was cleared.

The Chapel Schoolroom [SJ 1832 7595] was built in 1865 within the grounds of Rehoboth, proof again of the zeal of the Holywell Welsh Calvinistic Methodists. A kitchen was later added to this building.

In 1891, Rehoboth underwent a programme of repair and restoration, followed between 1893 and 1894 by further refurbishment which included a new J. Bellamy organ (costing £400) which was quickly paid for by the congregation. By the turn of the twentieth century, however, complaints were being made, not only of the discomfort of the chapel, but also of the general unworthiness of the building itself to the Presbyterian movement. The elders thus elected that the time had arrived to have a completely new chapel building erected on the site.

The original building was replaced by a new, brick-built chapel with associated vestry at a cost of some £6,000. The architects were T. G. Williams & David Lyon of Liverpool and the builders A. B. Lloyd of Flint. The opening ceremony was spread over a few days 10–17 December 1905. It was obviously a time of much celebration.[83]

The years between 1905 and 1978 saw many changes and the chapel prospered both spiritually and financially. In April 1935, bi-centenary celebrations were organised and one important service included children from Holywell's schools.[12] Many memorial gifts were made and repairs and maintenance were always carried out as required. Structurally, however, the buildings remained basically unchanged. In November 1977, serious dry rot was discovered in the roof. A complete new roof would have been beyond the means of the chapel and it was decided to close and demolish this grand building. The final service was held on the last Sunday in August 1977. Demolition was carried out in July 1978.

Until March 1979, services were held at the English Presbyterian Church in Whitford Street, with timing arranged so that the English chapel members were able to have their own services as required. Whilst this facility was available, the Rehoboth schoolroom, which was in good structural condition, was converted into a chapel for the Welsh members. Many features of the old building, including the pulpit, were utilised in the new chapel.

The service of dedication was held there on 28 March 1979. The original two northern windows, located behind the pulpit, were renewed as memorial windows to two Elders, Mr W. E. Williams, MBE, and Captain Edward E. Roberts, who had both given many years of dedicated service to the chapel.

In 1997, disaster again struck Rehoboth when it was found that the eastern foundations of the building to the rear of the chapel were starting to sink. A few years previously flats had been built on the lower ground to the east and, it is a possibility

Rehoboth Chapel, built in 1905, demolished in 1978.

that that may have caused the problem. Underpinning was not possible and use of the chapel had to cease. The last service held there was a service of de-dedication on 3 February 1998 after which the congregation of Rehoboth had to use other chapels for worship and all their related needs. The Welsh Wesleyan Pendref Chapel in Brynford Street was the generally preferred choice.

In early 2005, however, events developed which had previously seemed an impossibility. It was found that by demolishing the rear building of the chapel and constructing a new one a short distance to the west, that secure foundations could be established. With that in mind, a decision was made to sell the plot of land to the west of the chapel (the land on which the former red-brick 1905 chapel had stood). The proceeds from this sale not only made it possible for the re-building project to go ahead, but also allowed for the interior of the chapel to be altered to make it possible for the building to be used as a community centre, not only for the use of the congregation, but also by other organisations. The project was based on the Presbyterian Church in Wales policy document 'Strategy for the Future'.

Capel Penbryn
Pendref, the only other Welsh chapel in Holywell, had to close in September 2006. Meetings between the members of Rehoboth and Pendref had been held for some time, with the outcome that a covenant was drawn up to have a joint, informal Welsh church in Holywell which would be named Capel Penbryn — 'PEN' coming from 'Pendref' and 'BRYN' from the 'Bryn Seion', the first Welsh Calvinistic Chapel in

Holywell. The resurrected Rehoboth building would in the future be the Holywell venue for Welsh chapel services and events; members from both the previous chapels would join together for such. However neither would have to separate from their representative ruling bodies — Welsh Presbyterianism and Welsh Wesleyanism. Consequently 'Rehoboth' members had a minister, the Revd Huw Powell-Davies, and 'Pendref' members would continue to have the benefit of their own circuit minister, the Revd Sue Altree.

The architect for the building project was Ken Shone of Caergwrle and the builders were Wren Construction (Buckley) Ltd. The chapel opened for its first service at 10 am on Sunday, 1 October 2006, with the Revd Huw Powell-Davies as preacher. There were over one hundred worshippers present — including the young.

Moriah Chapel, Pen-y-Maes [SJ 1939 7601]

The first religious teaching at Pen-y-Maes occurred around 1840 because Revd John Phillips, minister of Rehoboth, was concerned that the hamlet of some 300 poor people was not being recognised by other religious bodies in Holywell. He concentrated his attention on the children, and was able to find a house willing to allow him to conduct a Mission Sunday School named Pen-y-maes Ysgol Genhadol (Pen-y-Maes Missionary School) there. Its exact location has not been recorded.[81] Unfortunately, Revd Phillips left Holywell in 1843 for Anglesey and his efforts at Pen-y-Maes had to be discontinued because Rehoboth had no minister until 1866.

In 1870, Rehoboth members, and their minister, Revd John Pugh, decided to restart the Pen-y-Maes Sunday School with David Williams, a High Street butcher and member of Rehoboth as superintendent. Although there is again uncertainty as to the building which was used, it is known that they were later using part of Pen-y-Maes House. By 1888, it was decided that, because of an increase in the numbers of worshippers, a purpose-built schoolroom was needed. Land to the east of the brow of Pen-y-Maes, which had previously been the site of a silk works, was donated on 15 March 1889, by John Lloyd Price of Glyn Abbot. Besides being a member of Rehoboth, he was owner of St Winefred's Brewery, and a prominent person in the civil life of Holywell. Plans were then drawn up for a church, slate-roofed and generally of Ruabon red brick. It was built by the Holywell firm of Sibeon Brothers and was officially opened by Revd J. E. Davies, minister of Rehoboth, on 23 July 1900. Named Moriah, it thus became a daughter church to Rehoboth. Thirty-six feet long and nineteen feet wide, the new chapel cost £368, the bulk of which had been funded by donations. A loan of £100 was repaid by March 1902. There was bench-type seating for some 180 people. The harmonium, which had been in use at Ysgol Genhadol since 1896, was transferred to Moriah. Congregations grew steadily and, whereas, prior to its opening, Moriah had been somewhat financially reliant on Rehoboth, it quickly became self-sufficient.[81]

In 1952, some adjoining land was given to the trustees, thus enabling them to create a car park. An extension to the adjoining schoolroom was added, which was dedicated on 16 January 1956. A kitchen and toilet block was constructed in 1965, and, two years later, in the interests of pedestrian safety at the brow of the hill, Holywell UDC provided a footpath adjacent to the chapel on land given by the trustees. The original church entrance porch was demolished and replaced by a new, larger, one in 1978. At the same time, the six original main church windows were replaced with Flemish memorial-glass windows, each having amber glass surrounds. The schoolroom had similar glass installed in 1997.[81]

Lighting in Moriah was at first by oil lamps, but, in 1906, they were replaced by gas. Electric lighting was installed in 1931. The original heating boiler was coal, coke and wood fired, but, in 1938, an electric tubular heating system was installed. A harmonium, purchased in 1880, was replaced in 1896 by one costing £4 and this lasted well until 1951 when it had to be replaced by reconditioned two-manual and pedal bell organ with electric blower. The next organ was a Compton electric one, purchased in 1970. The 1951 organ went to Hebron chapel, Maes Pennant, Mostyn.[81]

On 5 December 1973, Moriah became established as a church in its own right, meaning, of course, that they were no longer a daughter church to Rehoboth. However, they still shared the same minister and were also still part of the Welsh Presbyterian Church in Wales. From 23 May 1985, because of the lack of Welsh-speaking members, Moriah was accepted into the English Presbyterian Church in Wales. However, this was soon to change. Due to a lack of ministers, Moriah was unable to be part of any Presbyterian joint-pastorate and in 1988 the congregation joined the United Reformed Church movement. The consequence was that Moriah became grouped with Tabernacle (Holywell), Alpha (Greenfield) and Hebron (Mostyn). All four chapels from then on had the same minister to conduct their services and affairs.[81]

The English Presbyterian Church [SJ 1848 7597]
By 1893, the Presbyterian Church of Wales decided that a church was required in Holywell for English-language services to meet the needs of the increased English-speaking population of the town and district. As a result, a plot of land was acquired in Pen-y-Ball Street, between the rear of the Feathers Inn and the Baptist Church. Here they erected a corrugated-iron building. By 1898, membership had grown and the premises were proving to be inadequate. As a result, the North Wales Presbyterian Association (Synod) decided that steps should be made to find a plot of land suitable for erecting a larger brick-built church. In April 1899, a plot of ground was procured in one of the best positions in the town for a place of worship — Whitford Street, between the Feathers Inn and the top of New Road (the Well Hill). The Association duly approved that 'a commodious edifice be erected on the site'.

Building work commenced in 1902, and by May 1903 the church had been officially opened. The cost of the site was £1,000, the church, including schoolroom and vestry cost £1,900 to build, and the heating apparatus, internal furnishings, exterior boundary wall with adjacent paving (plus architect's fees) was £315, a total cost of £3,215. At the time of opening £2,516 15s. 6d. had been received by means of subscriptions and donations; the balance of £653 14s. 6d. was soon cleared.

The original metal building was used for a number of years by the Parish Church for general meetings such as children's groups, plays and so on. After the Second World War, the premises were sold and served as a warehouse for a furniture retail company who operated their main business from Whitford Street.

The membership of the church increased over the years, and naturally ministers changed. In 1952, a staunch Evangelical minister was appointed, however, in time a split in the membership formed between those who still wished to remain traditional Presbyterians, and those who wished to follow stronger Evangelical ways. As a result, in 1971, the Evangelicals moved from the church and at first held services in the WRVS centre.

Unfortunately, during the years that followed, the traditional membership diminished to such an extent that it became necessary to close the church. The last service being held on 20 December 1992. The premises were later sold to a housing association and flats were created within the building, although the front façade has been retained.

Peniel Welsh Calvinistic Methodist Chapel, Greenfield [SJ 1999 7723]
A group of Greenfield Welsh Calvinistic Methodists started to meet in January 1862 at the home of a stalwart, opposite the site of where their chapel was later built. Two of the prime movers were William Littler (from near the Abbey) and Thomas Jones (Glan-y-Don) members, respectively, of the Llanerch-y-Môr and Bagillt chapels. By 1865, an old office belonging to the Crockford family (a spelter works site) had become vacant and the group moved there for their meetings. With twenty-four members, and sixty attending Sunday School in 1867, they were officially recognised and joined to the Holywell circuit.[83]

Although difficulties had been experienced in obtaining a plot of land for building their own chapel, James Simon, of Abbey Farm, offered land at a low price on which building work commenced in 1868. A great deal of voluntary help was forthcoming in both the supply of building materials and the provision of labour, which meant that the total cost of constructing the chapel was only about £50. The opening service was held on the second Sunday in January, 1869, the officiating ministers being the Revds William Price (Rhosesmor), William Hughes (Groes) and Dr Dickens Lewis. In 1881, the chapel was refurbished and, three years later the congregation were in a position to have their own minister, Revd Hugh Roberts. A successful effort was made in 1899 to raise monies to clear their debt. Amongst the members at this time was Urias Bromley of the Welsh Flannel Mills, and he gave the chapel an harmonium.[83]

The chapel thrived for the greater part of the twentieth century but, unfortunately, during its last two decades, membership had dropped considerably. As a consequence, financial problems developed and a decision was made to close. The final service was held on the last Sunday in December, 1996. The premises were sold in 2002 and demolished that December.

Pendref Welsh Wesleyan Methodist Chapel (Yr Eglwys Fethodistiaidd Pendref) [SJ 1868 7569]

On 24 September 1801, a Mr Bryan came to Holywell from Northop, accompanied by another zealous Wesleyan named Robert Morris, to conduct a preaching meeting in, it is thought, a room at the Antelope Inn. Despite having to overcome a great deal of antagonism from the community, it was possible to form a Society for Holywell which met for a while at the Pen-y-Ball home of Thomas Jones. Membership increased and they rented a barn for their gatherings close to the home of Thomas Jones. They then took steps to procure a site on which to build a chapel. This was difficult because landowners were generally against Nonconformists. However, an Anglican, Mr David Pennant of Downing Hall, Whitford, decided to lease them a plot of land at Pen-y-dref, Chester Street [now Brynford Street, where the chapel is now situated]. The society moved ahead quickly in the construction of the chapel (forty feet long by thirty-three feet wide). On 1 May 1808, they held their opening service there.

Although they were at first attached to the Denbigh Circuit, in 1812 they were made head of a new Holywell Circuit.[80] The efforts of all were so successful that membership grew to the extent that there was a need to extend the building. In 1830, they obtained a lease on an additional piece of land at the rear of the chapel, again from Mr Pennant, and added an extension at a cost of £660, although, at that time, the members could only raise £100 towards it.

The 1851 Religious Census records that the chapel had sufficient seating for 830 people, as well as standing room for a further 100.[10] Various activities were organised to help clear the chapel's debt, including, in 1878, the raising of an amazing sum of

Pendref Welsh Wesleyan Chapel, Holywell

£400 [2006 £18,000]. Clearance of the debt was also helped by debtors being persuaded to reduce their bills.[80 & 86]

One exceptional man was William Jacob, a very eminent and enthusiastic musician and choirmaster. His Pendref choir became one of the most famous in north Wales. In 1844, he published a book of hymn tunes and anthems, in which the tune *Huddersfield* appeared — having first been sung in Pendref, to the words '*Duw Mawr y rhyfeddodau maith*'. *Huddersfield* had actually been composed by a prominent Wesleyan, John Newton of Nottingham. Mr Jacob was also a leading personality of a thriving Sunday School at Pendref which, in 1865, after an inspection, was reported to be, of all the Sunday Schools in Wales at that time, '… the largest, the best in order, behaviour and discipline, in the Principality, the number of scholars being a thousand.'[8]

During 1892–3 the chapel underwent major renovation and the elders were able to purchase the freehold. The total cost of both exceeded £1,600.

To celebrate the centenary of the opening of the chapel, a week of special services and events were held around 1 May 1908.[80]

In 1946, an opportunity was taken to purchase a pipe-organ to replace the harmonium. During the Second World War, an English Wesleyan Chapel in Manchester had been bombed but, thankfully, the excellent organ was saved. The Pendref elders elected to purchase it and have it overhauled. It was duly installed behind the pulpit. To do this, the pulpit and the adjoining *sêt fawr* had to be moved forward. This resulted in a situation in which anyone sitting on the end of the two sides of the gallery was actually behind the vision of the preacher. A special service for the dedication of the organ was arranged and the famous London musician, Dr Tholben Ball, was the guest organist for the occasion. The organ has since been regularly serviced and has thus proved to have been a valuable asset.

When Park Lane was made a through-road to Brynford Street around 1952, two small cottages which had stood on the corner adjoining Pendref were demolished.

Around 1956 the chapel elders were faced with the prospect of two major building projects. The chapel had never had a much-needed schoolroom and the exterior of the building needed renovating. Decisions were made for both schemes to go ahead and the work for such was entrusted to Jones (Builders) of Lloc. By 1958 the new schoolroom was opened and the chapel also had an excellent new appearance.

Sadly, because of growing financial problems caused by a declining congregation, a decision was made in the summer of 2006 to close the chapel. The last service was held in Pendref on Sunday morning, 17 September 2006. The Revd Sue Altree, the minister for the circuit covering Pendref, conducted the proceedings —eighteen months short of the chapel's two hundredth anniversary.

Capel Penbryn, which included the congregation of Pendref, opened on 1 October 2006 (see above).

Bethel Baptist Chapel, (Addoldy-Bedyddwyr Bethel), Pen-y-Ball Street [SJ 1845 7589]
The Baptist movement was late starting in Flintshire, but it was in Holywell that the county's first Baptist chapel was built. It was erected on the Pen-y-Ball Street site in

1811, and the membership was accepted into the Baptist Association.[84] The site had a distinct advantage for the founders because there was a spring from which they could obtain their water supply for the baptism pool. The building could then seat 132 worshippers and there was standing room for a further 60.[10] In 1825, a successful concerted effort was made to clear their debt.[84]

The chapel was extended and refurbished in 1900. A gallery was installed, a schoolroom and vestry were added to the rear of the premises, seating arrangements were changed, and the pulpit was moved to face east from its original position of facing south. In the early 1990s, a stained-glass window was installed in the interior entrance in memory of Gomer L. Williams, who had been a faithful member of Bethel for many years.

Congregationalism, originally, the Independent Cause
Although there are no known records of the first meetings of the Independents in Holywell, as other dissenters, they would have gathered in private dwellings before 1780. This was because religious public meetings needed a licence and these were difficult to obtain without the help or involvement of an influential person within their midst. Fortunately for the Holywell Independents, a Mr Williamson came from the Midlands in 1780 as manager of a brass and copper works in the Greenfield Valley. Besides being an influential businessman, he was also a staunch Independent. Together with his works assistant, Samuel Jones, he succeeded in obtaining the necessary licence to hold public religious meetings. At first, he hired a room at the rear of the Coach & Horses Inn in Whitford Street (the Welsh Calvinistic Methodists had also used this room, possibly after the Independents vacated it, until 1803). One zealous young member of their congregations was Jonathan Catherall, the prosperous owner of the Buckley Brick, Tile & Pottery Works. He soon bought a plot of land between Well Street and New Road (Well Hill) from David Pennant for the purpose of building the first Congregational chapel in Holywell. He supplied the bricks and, possibly financed the whole project. Indeed this was the start of his dedicated life to the Congregational cause in Flintshire.

The First English Congregational Chapel in Holywell [SJ 1851 7602]
This chapel was opened in 1789 (possibly August), the first minister being an Englishman, Revd Hale. On 31 August 1789, Mr Catherall handed the deeds for the land and chapel over to trustees for the congregation. Revd Hale left in 1792 and was succeeded by a Welshman, Revd David Davies, who introduced Welsh services in addition to those in the English langauge. Importantly, he also started what is believed to be the first Sunday School in Flintshire, if not, indeed, in all of north Wales. Despite this, however, the deacons complained about his 'unorthodox views and preaching causing the congregations to decrease.' In October 1800, he left without formal resignation. By now the chapel had become known as Heol-y-Capel after the street name.

Another Welshman, Revd David Jones, was Davies's replacement, and founders

Heol y Capel, Chapel Street, Holywell.

Williamson, Catherall and Samuel Jones were still deeply involved. Revd Jones proved to be very popular and congregations grew, so much so that a gallery was added in 1806, followed by a schoolroom four years later. The population of Greenfield had by now increased and in 1814 Mr Williamson decided to build a chapel there which was named Alpha (see below).

Unfortunately, we now learn that English and Welsh language differences were the cause of much trouble at Heol-y-Capel. Revd David Jones had died tragically in Liverpool in 1830 and his ministry was followed by others who did not stay long and, in 1835, the deacons got two students, one English and one Welsh, to endeavour to sort the problem out. Alas, the opposite was the result. Following this, Revd Ellis Hughes took over, but the doors were soon locked against him. He obtained permission to hold services in the unused Bryn Seion Chapel where he was joined by the Welsh members of Heol-y-Capel. The chapel was capable of seating 170 worshippers.[10]

Tabernacle Chapel [SJ 1885 7585]
The English Wesleyans built Tabernacle Chapel in Coleshill Street in 1837. Stone-built, with outer walls plastered, it had a slate roof. Regretfully, their endeavours did not meet with success and, as soon as 1840, the Welsh Congregationalists, who had been temporarily using the Bryn Seion building, bought the premises.[82] Their alterations to the structure included the provision of an interior gallery. On 19 May 1844, they held their first service there.

The 1851 Religious Census records that there was seating for 548 people — a further 60 could stand.[10] By 1858, both Revd Ellis Hughes and Revd David Jones had resigned and both the Welsh and the English Congregationalists were without a minister in the town.[82]

Major changes were soon to follow. A Revd Jones, who was ministering at Guildford until 1860, was invited to take charge of the pastorate of the two Congregational churches. He accepted, but only on the condition that Heol-y-Capel

Tabernacle United Reformed Chapel, Coleshill Street.

would then become the Welsh chapel, and that Tabernacle would be the English church. With the condition being accepted, both chapels were run happily from a linguistic point of view from then on. It is assumed that the plaster inscription 'English Congregational Church, 1860' on the top front elevation was made because of the change in use. Outside steps lead to a basement which houses the church hall.

A very influential businessman named Thomas H. Waterhouse, who hailed from Yorkshire, had joined the management of the newly re-formed Welsh Flannel Manufacturing Company sometime after 1874. He became a member of Tabernacle in June 1878, and from then on, the family became a backbone of the chapel until the death of his son Horace in April 1965.

The congregations at Heol-y-Capel started to decline from around the 1960s but the decision in 1985 to construct the Holywell Inner Ring Road meant that the chapel, along with the adjoining Chapel Street, had to be demolished.

A national decision to change Congregationalist chapels to a newly formed United Reformed body of chapels was made in 1972. Consequently, on 5 October 1972, Tabernacle Chapel became the Tabernacle United Reformed Chapel. During the last two decades of the twentieth century, the membership of Tabernacle declined, and they were served from time to time by ministers who also had to serve other United Reformed Churches in the nearby districts. The building is Grade II listed.[44]

Alpha Congregational Chapel, Greenfield [SJ 1946 7759]
Why the name 'Alpha' was given to the church is not on record (Revelation 1:8, 'I am Alpha and Omega, the beginning and the ending, saith the Lord'.) Thus, taking the point that alpha means first, because it was certainly neither the first dissenting church or the first Congregational church in the area, the answer could well be that it was the first Christian church in Greenfield.

The first building was constructed in 1814, adjacent to the main road and in front of the present church, on land leased from Sir Pyers Mostyn. Due to the enormous industrial activity along Greenfield valley, at that time, the population in Greenfield had increased and many English people had come to reside there. There was therefore an obvious need for a church. Mr Williamson, a staunch Independent from the Midlands, had been made manager of a local brass and copper works in 1780 and he soon became active in setting up the Independent cause in Holywell. Following the building of Heol-y-Capel in 1789, Williamson provided money to build Alpha Chapel in 1814. He lived in Greenfield House but subsequently moved to Plas Morfa. In 1834 the original Alpha building was re-constructed and could seat 67 people, with room for a further 12 standing.[10] The Williamsons (father and son) continued to support the church until 1880. In 1895, the freehold of the chapel land was bought from Sir Pyers William Mostyn for £450. This cost was cleared in four years by subscriptions from local people.

By 1902, the building was in need of renovation and a project fund was opened. However, it was decided to have a completely new building and this was erected just to the rear of the original chapel. This is the red-bricked building we now see. It was formally opened in September 1907. Within a year, a lecture hall was added, the overall cost of both structures being £1,447 6s. 0d. By 1923, the last re-payment had been made, thus clearing the debt.

Towards the end of 1926, a new organ was installed at a cost of £300, replacing the existing harmonium. The next requirement was for a minister's manse and, on 10 February 1929, an offer of a gift from Mr Thomas Roberts of land alongside Mostyn Road for such a building was accepted. The overall cost of the building was £910 3s. 3d. and, over time, this was paid for by the church members. The last building addition to the church premises, a kitchen, was completed in 1956.

Alpha became a United Reformed Church on 5 October 1972, becoming part of the local circuit which included Hebron (Mostyn) and Tabernacle (Holywell). All the churches in that circuit were covered by a joint pastorate.

A decision was made in 2005 to close Alpha Chapel; once again the result of declining congregations and financial problems caused by the need for repairs to the building. Sunday, 13 November 2005, witnessed the chapel's service of de-dedication, conducted by Rev. Peter Noble, Moderator for Wales of Alpha's Synod. The final service in Alpha was on Sunday, 4 December 2005.

The Berea Baptist Chapel, Bagillt Road, Greenfield [SJ 1984 7738]
Regretfully it has not been possible to establish any history of this chapel. It was not on the 1851 census, nor on the 1871 Ordnance Survey map, although it did appear on the 1912 map. The obvious conclusion was that it was built between the latter two named dates. Unconfirmed information states that the chapel closed during the 1960s.

Ebenezer Chapel, Station Road, Greenfield [SJ 1964 7779]
Built between 1839 and 1840 as an Independent place of worship, it was brick-structured with a slate roof. According to the Religious Census of 1851, there was seating for 418 people.[10] Unfortunately, it has not been possible to trace records of the chapel's history except the fact that it had to close during the late 1950s. Subsequently the building was converted for industrial use by a welding company.

Mount Gilead Chapel, Bryn Celyn [SJ 1870 7670].
A Mr Edward Jones, who owned a smithy and foundry on part of the site of where Messrs W. Hall & Sons Ltd presently have their business, was instrumental in having this chapel built in 1830 for New Connection Methodists. The building was constructed with Gwespyr sandstone and slate-roofed. Mr Jones supplied all the necessary metal work, including the outer railings and gates.[87] There was seating space for 156 people.[10]

Sometime during the years detailed above, the Welsh Wesleyan Methodists had started to meet in a small thatch-roofed house nearby, but were soon able to have services on Sunday afternoons in Mount Gilead. However, a further decision was made to convert two lofts in Old Quay houses in order to have their own place of services. It became known as Capel y Llofft. Their small pulpit was borrowed from Pendref Chapel, Holywell.

In 1868 the Mount Gilead New Connection Methodist Movement ceased to meet and the Welsh Wesleyans bought the building for £180 — a low cost, but it needed a fair amount of renovation to bring it up to standard. Unfortunately, industrial decline

The former chapel at Lluesty Workhouse.

along the Greenfield Valley led to a decline in the membership.[10 & 47] However, the chapel continued as a place of worship until the mid twentieth century when poor attendances caused a situation whereby only occasional services were held — this caused financial problems and the chapel was eventually forced to close. The building still stands, although in a derelict condition.

The Evangelical Church, Halkyn Road
As recorded in the narration for the English Presbyterian Church, in 1971 the membership supporting Evangelicalism moved from the church and at first held services in the WRVS Centre. From there they moved to the Town Hall and then to the Drill Hall before purchasing an empty builders merchants premises in Halkyn Road. The church members completely transformed the building. The interior was decorated and furnished simply, but impressively, giving anyone who enters the church a feeling of friendliness and tranquility.

The Fron Park Christian Fellowship (The Church in the Park)
In May 1985, with the support of the pastor and elders of Sussex Street Baptist Church in Rhyl, Holywell Fron Park Christian Fellowship was established with a group of about fifteen local Christians meeting together for worship on a Sunday morning. Prior to that, some of them had been meeting midweek in homes for prayer and Bible study.

On Sundays, they met for some time in a variety of venues in Holywell and Carmel, but in 1996 were able to purchase the WRVS Centre in Fron Park. The building was completely refurbished and the interior beautifully furnished and decorated by members of the church. They have held their services and meetings there ever since.

They have always been a non-denominational, evangelical church, but in 2004 they became part of the Assemblies of God Association of Churches (Pentecostal) and currently have around seventy worshippers.

CHAPTER 4

Roads, Railways and Sea Transport

We have to go back to Roman times for traces of what could be called the first real road through the parish of Holywell, although, among the hills above there are undoubtedly tracks that were first made by pre-historic man. It is possible that a Roman road may have existed along part of Halkyn Mountain before a coastal route was created. The Romans tried to build roads that were as straight as possible, hence the line followed by their route from the Greenfield Valley to Golch [Carmel] and on to the Pen-y-Gelli area and beyond. Their roads were usually 8 ft wide, built on a foundation of heavy stone, with a finer surface material. A Roman mile was 1,680 yards; a modern British mile is 1,760 yards.

Until the sixteenth and seventeenth centuries, roads in the area bore no resemblance to those we know today. Most routes were not defined or way-marked, and did not have hedges and fences along them; they were soft, miry ways that had developed from their frequent use by people, horses, pack-animals and livestock. Even in the best weather conditions they were not really suitable for vehicular traffic and were well nigh impassable in rainy weather. By an Act of Parliament of 1555, the upkeep of main and side roads became the responsibility of each parish. Every parishioner was supposed to work on the roads for, at first, four days a year, then later, six days.

In 1510, King Henry VIII appointed a Master of the Posts to establish and control the King's Royal Messengers. These people first carried private and confidential State documents and messages to the gentry and other important people in the country. Their usual method of travel was by post horse and their journeys were made on a staged basis. At the end of each stage an appointed person, usually an innkeeper, had to ensure that fresh horses were available for the messenger to continue his journey The messenger was paid about 1s. 8d. (8p) a day.[96] At first, Holywell was not a staging place, the nearest stages being Northop and Rhuddlan. In 1635, Parliament passed an act which established the Royal Post for the population of Britain and appointed post-boys and postmasters.[92]

Until the introduction of turnpike roads, travel through north Wales was notoriously difficult. Passengers and mail destined for Ireland, had to stop off at Chester to await suitable weather conditions to allow a ship to exit the Dee before crossing Liverpool Bay and the Irish Sea. In 1756, the road from Chester to Conwy was turnpiked and, in 1776, the first regular post-chaise stage-coach service was introduced from Chester to Holyhead with Holywell as one of the designated stopping places.[88] Soon the post horses ceased to be used and general mail, together with passengers, began to be carried by Royal Mail stage-coaches which were specially styled and coloured; the driver had a black hat and scarlet coat. Certain towns were designated 'post towns', including, soon after 1807, Holywell. The first record of a post office in the town appears in *Pigot's Directory* of 1822, sited in Panton Place.[43] Mail continued to be carried through north Wales by stage-coaches until the Chester to Holyhead railway was opened in 1848.

By the mid-seventeenth century maps were becoming important and Charles II appointed John Ogilby and William Morgan to produce Britain's first official survey of roads. Ogilby's maps were completed in 1675.[88 & 90] Four of his maps included Flintshire and three of these terminated at Holywell showing the routes from St David's via Ruthin, Shrewsbury via Mold (over Halkyn Mountain) and Chester via Flint. These road maps were important because of the number of pilgrims travelling to the Holy Well.

The Turnpike system and the district's roads
The first turnpike trust (a scheme whereby local landowners and businessmen could charge a toll for using a road, using the money received to maintain the road) was created by an Act of Parliament in 1706. Originally set up in the south-east of England, the notion of trusts quickly spread and, by the late eighteenth century, were being established all over the country. Each trust employed a professional surveyor and a clerk/treasurer who kept minutes of the trust's meetings and detailed accounts which, after 1822 had to be submitted to the government. Each trust operated a route which was divided into sections, each of which had a toll-gate and a toll-house. The term turn*pike* originated from the practice of the top rails of some gates being fitted with iron spikes, or 'pikes'. Roads were measured, and distance stones or posts were installed at one mile intervals. Travellers had to pay a toll at each gate in order to continue their journey. Typical tolls were:

an unladen horse	2*d*. (1p)
a horse drawing a laden cart	10*d*. (4p)
a horse drawing a carriage	9*d*. (4p)
droves of animals	10*d*. (4p) per score (twenty animals)

Some people were exempt from the charges viz: road repairers, post horses, Royal Mail stage-coaches and passengers, soldiers and people attending religious services.

Thomas Pennant of Downing Hall endeavoured to have turnpike tolls imposed on Royal Mail stage-coaches because of the wear and tear they created on the roads they used and because of the passengers which they carried.

The first Turnpike Act relating to Flintshire was passed in 1757 and the Flint Turnpike Commissioners covered the roads around Holywell. Eventually, the area around Holywell was controlled by the Holywell District Trust, the Mostyn District Trust and the Flint District Trust.

The non-turnpike roads were still maintained by the parishes and the local population had still to provide free labour. An intolerable situation developed: the workers were dissatisfied, the quality of the work was poor and the road conditions worsened — even though the Justices of the Peace could fine parishes who failed to properly maintain their roads. To rectify this, an act of 1835 ensured that workers received pay from a 'highway rate' levied on the inhabitants.

The development of industry, particularly mining and quarrying resulted in a higher volume of traffic using the roads and horse-drawn coaches replaced individual horse riders and wagons replaced pack-horses. Gradually, cross-country communications were improved and a Parliamentary report of 1822 stated that the Holywell, Flint and Mostyn trusts controlled fifteen miles of the Chester to Holyhead road as well as sixty-three miles of branch and cross roads.[93] The trusts let out tollgates to individuals at an auction, in return for an annual fee, the value being based upon each gate's revenue for the previous year. Thus the trust did not, therefore, employ any staff to operate the toll-gates and each toll-gate keeper could fix his own charges, provided they did not exceed the maximum figure laid down by Parliament.[R104]

At the time that the Turnpike Trusts were established, the only roads from Holywell's High Street were:

- By way of Well Street to the Greenfield junction with the Flint to Mostyn road. At the junction the turnpike was named Greenfield Gate (note: there was a second gate yards way to toll the road, left, to Mostyn).

- By way of Bagillt Street and Pen-y-Maes to the Walwen Gate on the Flint to Greenfield road.

- From Bagillt Street another road turned right along Rose Hill and descended past Garth-y-foel (the road to Riverbank, Bagillt now crosses this) into the dingle then up and along the road past Panton Hall (no tollgate).

- By way of Chester Street (now named Brynford Street) where, half way up there was a gate named Stagg's Gate. The road continued up the present Old Chester Road to the Stamford Gate turnpike. From here it went via Pistyll, Pen-y-pyllau, Pentre Halkyn, Middle Mill, Northop, for Chester.

- A branch went off the side of Old Chester Road up to the Brynford Gate turnpike (cottage still there) and then on the hill up to Brynford.

- From the bottom left of High Street steeply up Pen-y-Ball Street and the hill to Pen-y-Ball top, turning right for Pantasaph. At the junction with Babell Road was the Bryn-y-Gaseg turnpike. The cottage is still there, but now has the higher approach road to the bridge over the new A55 Holywell by-pass to the west of it.

- By way of Whitford Street to Brynffynnon, just after which, where the Holway Road levels out, the turnpike, named Brognallt, was sited. The road continued through Carmel and Gorsedd to the Brickhill area (present Travellers Inn area) for St Asaph and beyond.

Other nearby turnpike gates were located at: the Boot Gate, at Bagillt; the Llygan-y-Wern Gate at the bottom of Church Hill, Halkyn; the Springfield Hill Gate by the Hare & Hounds public house, below Pentre Halkyn.

In 1808, Thomas Telford created a road from Shrewsbury, via Betws-y-Coed, to

The Turnpike Gate at Greenfield, leading to Mostyn.

The Brognallt Gate on the brow of the Holway Road from Holywell.

Bangor, which reduced the number of travellers using the Holywell route. The distance from London to Holyhead was cut by seventeen miles and the dangerous ferry at Conwy could be avoided.

The Highways Act of 1862 established Highway Boards throughout the country with responsibilities for many of the roads. Locally, the Holywell District Highway Board operated from offices in Well Street.

Transport improvements

Thomas Pennant describes how, when travelling by carriage from his home at Downing to Holywell in the early eighteenth century, the Holloway was unsuitable for carriages and carts. He had to go up Pen-y-fford-waen (now named Gorsedd) and then over the mountain to descend, with locked wheels and at great peril, down the precipitous Pen-y-Ball Hill.[22]

It was after the 1769 Highway Act was passed that four-in-hand coaches began to run, carrying both passengers and mail. The first such route with Holywell as a staging station was from Mold via Pentre Halkyn. From Holywell, the coach travelled via Gorsedd for St Asaph.[95]

The only conveyances for travelling in the early 1800s were horse-drawn: the poor journeyed in cumbrous broad-wheeled wagons; those who could afford it would use four wheeled post-chaises; those in a hurry travelled by mail coach. As coaches approached Holywell from the west, a horn was blown near Gerddi Beuno (Whitford Street) and mothers would be seen pulling their children out of the way. Hens, dogs, etc. would be run over as the foaming horses, with coach swaying, would speed along to the yard of the King's Arms (now the Hotel Victoria). There the passengers would have a twenty-minute break for refreshments while the horses were changed before the *High Flyer* drew off at full gallop to the sound of the horn up Chester Street, for the onward journey to Chester.[11] It was 278 miles from London to Holyhead via Holywell and coaches averaged just over $9^{1}/_{2}$ miles per hour over the whole journey.

Pigot's Directory of 1835 lists both the King's Arms and the White Horse Hotel (now the HSBC bank) as posting houses and details the following coaches:

- to Bangor, the *Hawk-Forward* (from Chester) calls at the White Horse every Monday, Wednesday and Friday afternoon at 1 p.m., goes through St Asaph, Abergele, Conwy and Aber.

- to Chester, the Royal Mail (from Holyhead) calls at the King's Arms every morning at half-past two.

- the *Hawk-Forward* (from Bangor) calls at the White Horse every Monday, Wednesday and Saturday afternoon at half past two.

- to Holyhead, the Royal Mail (from Chester) calls at the King's Arms every night at half-past ten, goes through St Asaph, Abergele, Conwy and Bangor.

- to Liverpool, *The Lord Mostyn* from the King's Head every morning (Sunday excepted) at seven, and the *Lady Mostyn*, every Monday, Wednesday and Friday, to the King's Ferry and Neston.[43]

The carriers listed transported goods to Chester, Flint, Liverpool and Wrexham.[43] Besides the hotels mentioned above, the King's Head, and possibly the Cross Keys and Red Lion, also benefitted from being stopping places; besides having income from stabling and providing a change of horses, they also provided passengers with food and drink as well as accommodation when required. Due to the poor roads and lack of wheel suspension shock-absorbers, one can well imagine how welcome a stop would be!

The 1820s saw an improvement in the post roads. Most notable locally was a new road from Stamford Gate to Middle Mill (Northop) which was completed by the summer of 1827 at a cost of £4,521 [2006 £211,300].

The town's first post office was in Panton Place and coach route letter postage charges, such as 4*d.* to Mold and 11*d.* to London, were maintained until the introduction of the 'Penny Post' in 1840.

The 1833 Flintshire Roads Bill planned many improved and new roads for the county[R105] including: 'a new line of road commencing at, or near, a public house called The Boot by, or near, a farmhouse called Twll — to terminate on the east side of the Kings Arms Holywell'. This became the main road [now A5026] from The Boot in Bagillt and created Coleshill Street. Another road improvement was the widening and altering of the Holway:

> … a part of the present road at or near to a shop in Whitford Street, Holywell, in the occupation of Wm. Vickers, to termination at about 300 yards alongside the home and premises of Richard Addison and from thence a division, or new line of road, by or near Golch, to, or near to, a farmhouse called Merllyn and to terminate at, or near, a plantation nursery belonging to Wm. Vickers adjoining the turnpike road leading from Holywell to St Asaph.[R101]

The original road, which had gone from the front of St James Place, behind Sea View Cottages, and on to what is now the rear of the Holway Garage to the Carmel road, was replaced by a new road in front of Sea View Cottages. A new curved branch was built to the Carmel road. The new road cut through the old buildings of Holway Farm, continuing past Golch (by the Half-way House), creating the Celyn bends. Old maps show that there had previously been a track near this latter section. This new road then continued across both the Waen crossroads and the present Rock Inn crossroads, before joining up with the turnpike road from Gorsedd, at a point near the present Nerse Farm Smithy (where there is still a stone benchmark nearby). This road was completed in 1845 and later became part of the original A55 trunk road. When the Holywell by-pass from Pentre Halkyn to Lloc was opened in 1984, the road was re-numbered as the A5026.

Halkyn Street and Halkyn Road to the Stamford Gate were constructed in 1833, and the section of road from Perth-y-Terfyn Cottage to the turnpike on Brynford Hill was constructed in 1863. Fron Park Road was constructed in 1931–2 at a cost of just over £20,000 (excluding land purchase) [2006 £729,000]. It was opened in June 1932, becoming the first Holywell by-pass, relieving the town centre of considerable traffic congestion.⁴⁹ At Greenfield, the road from the A548 coast road, over the main railway to the dock, was constructed and opened in 1898.

The three local turnpike trusts ceased to operate on 1 November 1884 and the Holywell District Highway Board handed over control of local roads to the newly formed Flintshire County Council in 1888. A few minor roads remained under the control of Holywell UDC until the Local Government Act of 1930 transferred the responsibility for them to the County Council.⁴

Over a period of many years, the whole of the A55 trunk road across north Wales was upgraded to dual-carriageway and, as part of this project, a new Holywell by-pass was constructed in 1983–4, at a cost of some £13 million. It was built from the Pentre Halkyn area (Springfield/Old Casino) for seven miles, through the lands of Brynford and Pantasaph, to the junction of the Caerwys road by the old Singing Kettle Restaurant. As a consequence great volumes of traffic ceased to use the original by-pass along Fron Park Road.

Holywell road improvements
In a lecture given in 1912, J. Lloyd Price, of Glyn Abbot, described the High Street in the early part of the nineteenth century as 'a town plan, devoid of either regularity or design, but with a broad and good avenue, approached at both ends by very narrow and crooked lanes.'⁹³

During the first half of the twentieth century, both sides of High Street, in front of the Town Hall, were used as the bus terminus. At around the time of the Second World War, this was moved to the roads on either side of the Hotel Victoria. Western-bound buses used Coleshill Street while eastern-bound buses used Halkyn Street.

In May 1956, a road connection was made between Halkyn Street and Coleshill Street, at the rear of the Hotel Victoria and a new bus station was constructed along it with passenger shelters on each side, together with an office for the inspector.

When Holywell's Inner Ring Road was opened in 1985, the bus station was transferred to the northern side of that road until a new purpose-built terminus was constructed in 1993 on the northern side of the Hotel Victoria.

The Inner Ring Road was constructed to the north and east of Holywell between Halkyn Street and Whitford Street, in order to take through traffic away from the High Street, which was being used by some 8,500 vehicles on a normal working day. The new road was officially opened on 25 October 1985 by the Chairman of Clwyd County Council, Councillor Edgar Jones. Built by Messrs McFaddon & Co. Ltd. of Deeside, the final cost of this short length of road was around £1 million. The project caused the demolition of a great many properties and the disappearance of Chapel Street. The top of the New Road (Well Hill) was re-aligned and the new route also cut through Station Road, Well Street and Bank Place. From Tower Gardens, a pedestrian underpass was constructed which led to a large new car and coach park at lower Bank Place. The two walls of the forty-five feet-long underpass have local historical themes depicted on them in large mosaics; the design of which had been the subject of a competition organised by the Welsh Arts Council. The winner was Brenda Oakes, who was assisted in the work by others during 1986/87. This car park then had a new walkway link to the Greenfield Valley, under the old railway station bridge. Four more new car parks were constructed alongside the road. In all, with associated side roads, about 600 yards of road was constructed. A one-way traffic system was introduced around the junctions in front of, and behind, the Hotel Victoria.

High Street, and some approach roads, were pedestrianised in 1992. For most of each working day, designated areas are traffic free. At the same time, the old footpaths and roads were taken up and replaced by brick paving.

Road buses and coaches

The first public motorised bus service in the Holywell area was established on 11 October 1905, by the London & North-Western Railway for the conveyance of passengers, freight and mail between Holywell High Street and Holywell Railway Station at Greenfield. This service lasted until 1 July 1912, when the new railway link to the town was opened. The first bus was a Milnes-Daimler, powered by a 24-horse-power Mercedes engine. It had seating for twenty-one passengers. A Foden steam lorry was introduced for the carriage of freight.

In 1906, at Crane Wharf in Chester, Crosland Taylor Brothers started a motor car business which, three years later, they expanded to include buses, with the first service running from Chester to Ellesmere Port. Crosville became the company name and the business rapidly extended in Cheshire and beyond. Bus services had to be granted local authority licences, which were difficult to obtain (in the early 1930s the National Traffic Commissioners Licensing Laws replaced these original licences). In 1919, Flintshire County Council granted Crosville licences to operate some services in the county. On 27 August 1919, Holywell experienced the start of a Crosville service which ran to Mold, via Greenfield, Flint and Northop. In 1921, a Holywell to Chester service (via the coast road) was established followed by many others shortly

L&NWR bus service from Holywell to Holywell Station (Greenfield) which started in October 1905.

The L&NW double-decker service from Holywell via Halkyn to Mold travelling along lower High Street, Holywell. The portico on the left is the main entrance to the White Horse Hotel (now the HSBC Bank). The Town Hall with its black-face clock can be seen behind the bus. This wide section of High Street used to house the old market fairs.

afterwards, including one to Afonwen Station for the Mold and Denbigh rail connection. Crosville could not, however, expand its services towards Rhyl from Greenfield because the Rhyl firm of Brooks Brothers had their White Rose services firmly entrenched in the western part of the county. The early 1930s witnessed the start of a rural circular service from Holywell, serving Brynford, Pantasaph, Gorsedd and Carmel. Local bus passenger trade was by then very much in prominence and Crosville was acquiring firms throughout north Wales and Cheshire. By 1930, they had bought out Brookes Brothers and opened a small depot on the site of Roberts' Garage in Bagillt Street, Holywell. In 1936, they built a new bus depot at Holywell Road, Flint, capable of holding up to forty-seven vehicles, and the Holywell depot was closed with the staff and vehicles being transferred to Flint.

After the Evans flourmill closed down in the early 1900s, a Greenfield man, Edward Phillips, together with his son Robert, started a general haulage and bus company from the mill site. They converted a steam-powered traction haulage vehicle into a bus by adding a redundant rail goods truck to it. The bus soon earned the nickname the 'Monkey House' and it was put into service to convey workers to the Courtaulds factory in Flint. As time passed, at least one bus was added to the company fleet and the whole business prospered. One major project Robert later became involved in was that of carrying stone from the Halkyn quarries to the Courtaulds Greenfield factory when its foundations were being laid between 1934 and 1936.

In 1921, Edward Henry Phillips, a nephew of Edward Phillips, started a bus service from a site in Brynford Street. One of his first services was from Holywell to Mold, via Halkyn and Rhosesmor, an operation which has continued uninterrupted ever since. The business later operated private hire coaches, day tours and a schools service. As well as the depot in Holywell, they also had a garage built alongside the coast road in Greenfield, opposite Basingwerk Abbey. Since 2003, the business has been run from the Greenfield site.

In 1927, another operator, Pryce Lloyd, bought a bus which he operated from an outbuilding of The Plough at Walwen. His cousin, Owen, joined him within two years and they then jointly ran the firm of P. & O. Lloyd, Bagillt, purchasing land over the road, where they built the Rhydwen Garage. This company has also given invaluable service to the district and became well known in the long-distance coach tour business.

George Oare, of Ffrith Lane, Brynford, started a private car hire business in 1976, which included the hiring out of cars to funeral directors. Soon the business extended into mini-buses. The natural development was then into main bus and coach hire, thus making them the third such firm to operate in the Holywell district.

Crosville had been involved in mergers and takeovers as far back as 1929 and the company name was maintained until 1998. After the Transport Act of 1985, British Bus acquired the company and most of the buses in the Holywell area were run by Crosville Wales. In August 1996 the company was acquired by Cowies which, from 1 January 1998 changed its name to Arriva and the name Crosville disappeared.

During the 1960s bus companies nationally were experiencing financial problems due to the growth in private car ownership. The Transport Act of 1967 enabled companies to claim financial support from local government – in this locality from Flintshire County Council — enabling the bus companies to operate services on routes which would not otherwise be financially viable. This system means that the County Council put routes up for tender to the bus companies, and, after vetting each application, the successful company is awarded the route for a period of two years, before re-appraisal. Buses used on such routes are operated in a different livery, making the population aware that the route is financially supported by the County Council. In addition, buses used on school services are now starting to have a special yellow livery and 2006 witnessed the gradual introduction of a special fleet of buses and it is intended that all double-decker buses on school services will be phased out by 2010.

Railways
On May Day 1848, the Chester to Holyhead Railway (CHR) was opened which included a station for Holywell at Greenfield [SJ 1970 7788]. This was renamed Holywell Junction in 1912 when the branch line to the new Holywell Town station was opened. The two-storey brick and stone station building at Greenfield was built in the Italianate style to a design by Francis Thompson. The builder was Thomas

Hughes of Liverpool.[44] Built at the same time was the two-storey signal-box which has five bays and a slated roof. To the east of the station the lines crossed the existing Holywell Limestone Company's rail which ran from beyond the Greenfield Valley to the Greenfield Dock. The CHR promoted industrial growth further east along Deeside, and the trade at Greenfield Dock declined.

An Act of 29 July 1864 authorised the Holywell Railway Company to extend their line from the dock to a new pier reaching out into the river, with a bridge planned to cross the CHR in lieu of the level crossing. This was completed by June 1867. From the King's Head Hotel yard in Holywell a horse drawn service started to take passengers and goods by road between the town and the station at Greenfield.

The Holywell Railway & Limestone Company, (HR&L) was formed in August 1856. In 1863, the Holywell Railway Company (HR) was formed and an Act of Parliament was passed on 29 July 1864 for the construction of a line from Greenfield to Holywell town, up the eastern side of Greenfield Valley. It was intended first for freight, with a passenger service later. Included in that project was the grand railway bridge, thankfully still in being, carrying the line over the main A548 road — it was made a Grade II listed structure in 1991.[44] Work on the project began on 27 April 1867, which involved cutting into the hillside, especially along the length nearer to Crescent siding, and moving a great deal of earth down the valley for levelling and building up hollows. Although the line did carry freight to the Crescent siding for a while, it never reached the town, nor did it carry passengers as, by July 1871, the company had run into financial trouble and was wound up. The section of line from the Parys Mine Company to the harbour continued to be used. Although the LNWR agreed in 1868 to allow a platform to be built adjacent to the main line station, the HR merely continued to use their railway for the transportation of lime and cement stone for a short while longer and it became derelict during the 1870s.

The London & North Western Railway's (LNWR) Holywell Town Branch Line.
Following the closure of the old Holywell Railway line in the 1870s, the track became choked by undergrowth and, in 1891, was bought by the LNWR with a view to it being converted to an electric tramway but the scheme was subsequently abandoned.

On 11 October, 1905 the LNWR started a motorised bus service between Holywell High Street and the station at Greenfield. The vehicles were garaged under the bridge arches by the station. This proved to be extremely well used and, as a result, the LNWR drew up plans for a line with a station and sidings in the town itself. Acts of 20 July 1906 and 26 July 1907 duly authorised the new line which opened on 1 July 1912. A new bay platform was built on the south side of the junction station with a curve leading to a new line, $1^3/_4$ miles long with a 1 in 27 gradient, leading to Holywell Town Station. This was said to be the steepest standard-gauge passenger line in the UK. Holywell Town Station had a waiting room and freight sidings and a fine two-arched bridge carried Station Road over the railway.

On the way up from Greenfield, just by the Crescent siding, a special halt, called 'St Winefride's', was erected for visitors to the famous well. The Crescent siding

Holywell Town Station on the opening day, 1 July 1912.

served the needs of the Upper and Crescent cotton mills. The engine first used on the service was an ex-LNWR, 0-6-2 side-tank coal engine which was always on the lower end of the one passenger coach, i.e. pushing uphill. The journey time took eight minutes up to the town and ten minutes down to Greenfield. A great deal of freight was also carried to the town, in particular, coal which was stored alongside the town's sidings. The line was a busy one and, by the late 1930s sixteen trains operated in each direction on weekdays, with twenty-nine on Saturdays and seventeen on Sundays. One renowned person who travelled daily on the 'little train' on his way to and from Holywell County School was the actor and playwright, Emlyn Williams, when he lived in Connah's Quay. A few years after the town station opened, a freight lift was installed from its station platform to the road above; today, a close look at the bridge wall shows the replacement stonework from when the lift was discontinued.

After 1848, the Holywell Junction Station underwent many changes, including the quadrupling of the main line which necessitated the building of two extra platforms along with further buildings. A subway, with inclined footways, was created for access to each platform, thus avoiding the need for an overhead footbridge. Goods sheds were built and a freight siding was provided on the south side which was particularly useful to the nearby Greenfield Abbey Paper Works with facilities for their incoming supplies of coal, esparto grass and woodpulp. During the Second World War, the Junction station handled bombs and ammunition which were being transported to and from the Holway Grange Caverns.

After 1945, the ever-increasing numbers of private cars meant that the line to the town declined. Buses also became more popular, as did the movement of freight by road and as a result services to the town ceased on 6 September 1954, although the freight service to the Crescent siding continued until 11 August 1957. From 1935, the Courtaulds factory at Greenfield had brought a tremendous volume of rail freight traffic to the junction and extra sidings had been added, with branch lines to each of the two factory units. However, by the early 1960s, road haulage proved to be more advantageous. The final blow to the railways in the area came on 14 February 1966 when Holywell Junction Station was closed. The main station building was rightly made the subject of a preservation order, the first railway station in north Wales to be so designated, and it was given a Grade II Listing in 1970. The signal box and bridge were similarly graded in 1991.[44]

The River Dee and Greenfield Harbour
Greenfield Harbour (wharf/dock)
This natural inlet off the River Dee at Greenfield was formed by the steep sides of the Greenfield Valley creating a natural course for the Holywell Stream to gain outlet to the river. The River Dee was used extensively by the Romans when they built their legionary fortress at Chester and they may well have been the first people to create a harbour at Greenfield, when the inlet came up to the bluff to the north of what is now a car park by the Abbey. During the Middle Ages, trade at Chester increased

St Winefride's Halt, with Crescent Siding to Holywell Textile Mill on the right-hand side. The Level, a track leading to the Level leadworks, can be seen on the valley side above the houses centre right of the photograph.

Holywell Junction Station, 1963. Note Courtaulds Nº 2 Unit Factory in the background.

significantly and the Dee was a busy river for shipping. However, by the end of the thirteenth century, the river was silting up and large vessels could no longer reach Chester. As a consequence, Parkgate became a significant port. Eventually, however, Liverpool developed into the most important port in the region and the harbours on both sides of the Dee suffered.

The monks of Basingwerk Abbey would most certainly have gone out from the inlet to the river to fish and it is also a distinct possibility that they crossed the Dee to the grange they had established at Caldy and to other holdings on the Wirral.

Chester was responsible for the passing of an Act for the canalisation of the Dee during 1735–6, on the Flintshire side from Golftyn to Chester, and shipbuilding was established between Connah's Quay and Sandycroft. Thomas Pennant wrote in 1778, of shoals of herrings being fished in the winter months by 'multitudes of small vessels'. In 1740, the River Dee Company was created to help preserve navigation on the river and Greenfield harbour was being increasingly used following the industrialisation of the Greenfield Valley. Problems with silting and marshland resulted in the passing of an Act of Parliament on 8 May 1788 whereby a canal was to be constructed along the marshland from Greenfield to Pentre Rock, Flint, where a lock would have been capable of receiving vessels of up to 100 tons. Unfortunately, nothing developed from this and it was left to the industrialists to finance and further expand Greenfield harbour. Because the land and the stream outlet near the river were low-lying there was constant flooding at the harbour. A problem was overcome to some extent by the construction of a flushing reservoir with sluice gates which could quickly release any build-up of water and thereby flush out the silt deposits. The harbour mouth was also widened and the channel deepened.

During the boom years of the copper industry, ingots for use in the valley's factories to manufacture copper items, were conveyed into the dock in about forty small ships.[88] The bulk of this ore came from Ravenshead, near St Helens. The dock was also used for shipping various finished products to both the home and overseas markets, the latter being transferred to ocean-going vessels in Liverpool.[88]

Apart from cargo vessels using the harbour, passenger ferry services were also inaugurated from time to time. In 1802, regular sailings were introduced from the harbour to both Parkgate and Chester.[87] However, no services were recorded from Greenfield in the 1835 *Pigot's Directory*, which only listed:

> To Liverpool, a steam packet from Mostyn Quay, every Tuesday and Friday, according to tides.
> To Parkgate, boats from Bagillt daily.[91]

An iron steamer called *Fanny* started a passenger service to Liverpool from Greenfield in 1851. The journey took $1^1/_2$ hours and cost 3s.(15p) or 4s.(20p) for deck and cabin. By 1865, the facility had ceased. Around 1868 a consortium of businessmen set up the St Winefred's Packet Company with the rather ambitious aim of establishing a steamship service, for both passengers and goods, between Greenfield and Liverpool. They had a paddle-steamer purpose built on Merseyside, the designers having to bear in mind not only the small size of the port at Greenfield, but also the dangerous and ever-changing channels of the Dee. Their end product was a vessel 130 ft long by 18 ft wide with a draught of only 8 ft. Powered by a 60 h.p. engine, it could carry up to 400 passengers. Amidst jubilant celebrations, the steamer was launched in Liverpool on 16 April 1870 and, following satisfactory trial trips, came to Greenfield and the first passenger-carrying sailing was organised to Llandudno for 15 August 1870. After sailing gracefully out to the river, it soon became apparent that the vessel suited the port and not the open sea. After a difficult journey with the ship rolling and plunging, some passengers decided to return home by train. For those who decided to return to Greenfield by sea, there was worse to come and the vessel ran aground on a sandbank in the Dee estuary. The passengers had to be transferred to small boats and then rowed to land. Subsequently, the company had very little commercial success and it went into liquidation on 30 September 1873.[11]

Worrall's Directory of 1874 records that two steam packets operated between Greenfield, Llanerch-y-môr and Mostyn Quays, and Prince's Landing Stage, Liverpool were used by large numbers of excursionists in summer.[43]

Despite the public interest and the numbers of passengers and companies wishing to use Greenfield Harbour, problems were caused by the shifting sands and the silting up of the harbour which were not so prevalent at Bagillt and Mostyn. Consequently, the use of the harbour diminished during the latter years of the nineteenth century. Even so, some schooners were able to pass by and get as far as Chester until 1906, and other trading vessels used Connah's Quay until the middle of the twentieth century. The Newton Keates company leased most of the wharf by 1890 but, when the firm closed down, the harbour was no longer viable and the wharves, buildings and plant were put up for sale on 3 September 1901. The sale details included:

- The main wharf, with a 198 ft frontage onto the Dee, had two cranes (3-tons and 2-tons) each with timber jibs and cast iron posts.

- The brick built, slated roofed, warehouse was 32½ ft x 15 ft, with stone paving, sliding doors, loading stage and a smith's shop.
- The office, which was brick-built, with a slated roof, and measured 18 ft x 15 ft.
- Inland from the wharf, the reservoir, which was described as 'extensive', having sluice gates for use in scouring out the silt deposited by incoming tides on the wharf frontage.
- The whole covered an area of 2½ acres and, on a spring tide, the wharf had a depth of 12 ft.
- Two additional wharves with a 2-ton crane sited out into the Dee. These had a water frontage of some 470 ft, and occupied a ground area of 1½ acres.

As the twentieth century progressed, use of the harbour, which became known as Greenfield Dock, diminished and only used by local fishermen with small vessels. In 1935, Courtaulds built a strong bridge over the dock to gain road access to their No. 2 Unit factory. The dock gradually fell into disrepair but the County Council renovated it in the mid 1990s. At last the local fishermen had better berthing facilities, with adjacent land from which to carry out their hobby.

CHAPTER 5

Industry

After the dissolution of Basingwerk Abbey in 1536, the Mostyns of Talacre and the Pennants owned most of the land in the Greenfield Valley. Although the Mostyns granted leases on their land, they were generally opposed to the establishment of industries which caused pollution (at one time, the oldest lead-smelting works caused them to take legal action because of 'the smoke doing injury to their fine woods').[22] The Pennants were just the opposite and had interests in lead-mining.

Until 1917, the water of the Holywell stream, which issued from St Winefride's Well at a rate of 25,000 gallons per minute, at a fairly constant temperature of 40°F, was what attracted industry to the Greenfield Valley. The close proximity of coal, as well as calamine from the lead mines, were additional attractions for the industrialists. After a visit in 1774, Dr Samuel Johnson recorded that there were nineteen factories of various types in the valley.

It would be quite impossible to write a full history of the many and varied industries which, over centuries, have been established in the Greenfield Valley. This chapter therefore concentrates on the larger and longest established businesses — brass, copper, wire, cotton, wool and paper, and also gives a brief outline of many of the other businesses carried out in the valley over the years. Dams were built to create reservoirs which enabled water-wheels to be built to provide power for the larger factories. By 1853, steam engines were replacing the water-wheels.

Large numbers of children were employed in the valley, especially in the cotton industry, but an Act of 1835 decreed that children under the age of twelve were not to be employed and youths between the ages of twelve and eighteen could only work for a maximum of sixty-nine hours a week.

Early Industries
The Romans were possibly the first people to make use of the waters of the Holywell stream and the monks of Basingwerk Abbey harnessed the waters for their two corn mills, two nether mills and a paper mill. After the dissolution, a lead-smelting works is known to have existed in 1589. By 1733, another lead-smelting works had been built, followed in 1758 by a zinc-spelter works, erected by Warmley & Company.[120] Calamine, a by-product of lead, was being produced as near as the Holway Level and in Carmel, hence the creation of the smelters and spelters. Used in brass-making, calamine was the main reason why leading brass manufacturers were attracted to the

valley.⁹⁹ By 1750, the valley also had a white-lead works, a red-lead works, a tilting mill, three corn mills, two fulling mills, two snuff mills and two iron-wire mills.

*Paper Making**
Of all the many industries established in the Greenfield Valley, paper-making has the longest history. During the fifteenth century, a famous Welsh scholar and herald bard named Gutin Owain was based for a while at Basingwerk Abbey working in the abbey scriptorium and one of his responsibilities was that of keeping a record of events for north Wales. Whilst he was there, the first Welsh book on armorial and heraldic devices, *The Black Book of Basingwerk*, was produced on parchment. It is quite probable that a lesser work was produced on paper as the monks had their own paper mill.²³ In 1764, a pin mill [SJ 1955 7765] was built for James Eden on the site where the Abbey Paper Mill was later built.¹⁰⁰ It appears that Eden was only in business for two years before a Mrs Chambers converted the mill to produce coarse paper and, shortly afterwards, she opened a second paper mill on the site later occupied by Hall's mineral water works. In 1783, the mill passed into the hands of the nearby Cotton Company.¹⁰⁰ Clarke's *Tour through Wales in 1791* and Aitkin's *England, described in 1818*, both make reference to the Chambers works and, in 1821, the excise authorities identified the mill as N⁰· 193 (in a numeric index of all the mills in England and Wales). At the same time, William Hill of Greenfield was granted a licence to erect a fourdriner paper manufacturing machine (which could produce paper in a continuous roll) on the site of the Parys Mine large copper forge, alongside the main coast road, which had been closed in 1814.⁸⁷ Until then, the mill, equipped with two vats, had been making paper by hand. In 1824, Richard Unsworth worked the mill, using machinery to manufacture both paper and millboard. Charles Stevens bought the mill in 1844.⁸⁷ A Parliamentary Return of 1851 showed the mill, then the largest paper mill in Wales, as having five beating machines.

A major turning point in the mill's history and fortunes came in 1854 when Britain's oldest paper manufacturing company, Grosvenor, Chater & Co. of London, acquired the mill from Stevens. Their experience in the industry went back to 1690 and the earliest *London Directory* (1736) confirms that Robert Grosvenor was a supplier of paper to the Bank of England. The company had acquired the works because, in addition to the plentiful supply of water, there was an abundance of coal available from the nearby Englefield Colliery, bleaching powder and other chemicals were readily obtainable from the Flint chemical works of Muspratt Bros & Huntley and all liquid waste could be discharged into the stream which entered the nearby River Dee. Six years earlier, the main line Greenfield railway station had opened a quarter-of-a-mile away, providing an efficient means of transporting raw materials and finished products. The company paid an annual rent of £260 for the mill site to the Mostyns of Talacre until 1916, when it was raised to £283. In 1920, the company bought the freehold from Sir Pyers Mostyn for £5,750.

* Much of the background information for this section was obtained from the books *Abbey Mills* (Grosvenor Chater Ltd, 1930) and *Family Business — a history of Grosvenor Chater* (Michael Chater).

The new proprietors changed to the manufacture of engine-sized writing, envelope, news and printing papers. Raw materials for paper making at that time were old linen, cotton rags, jute and hessian. There was no esparto grass or woodpulp available then but, in 1861, Thomas Rutledge introduced the grass into Britain and it was not long before Grosvenor Chater used it at Greenfield. Wood pulp, ground from trees, was also introduced as an alternative raw material but its impurities meant that the paper produced did not have as long a life and it was therefore used for newsprint.

From 1871 production at the mill increased with the introduction of better machinery. In 1882, a Scotsman named John Petrie joined the company as a foreman. His abilities were soon recognised and he was appointed mill manager in 1897. A substantial residence, named Abbey House, was built for him on land to the rear of Alpha Chapel.

A near disastrous fire broke out in the corrugated-iron buildings housing the esparto grass and rags stocks at 6.30 a.m. on 30 November 1894 but desperate fire fighting by employees prevented it spreading to adjacent areas of the mill. In 1897, some £3,000 was spent on a new 60-inch paper machine which was replaced with a 90-inch machine in 1904 when a new soda recovery building was also built.

The company's logo, a chariot, was adopted around 1900 and was used as a watermark in their manufactured paper, as well as being used on their letterheads, vans, buildings and so on.

The water supply from the holy well was interrupted on 5 January 1917, due to the construction of a tunnel from Bagillt to the Halkyn mines, which resulted in the paper mill suffering a drop in its main source of water. The new, but much reduced supply of water to the well that was connected on 22 September 1917 meant that the water supply was a constant problem from then on. In 1928, the company purchased three properties from Holywell Textile Mills to try to alleviate the problem.

In the early 1920s, under the guidance of the Sales Director, A. D. Chater, the company concentrated on the production of fine quality paper with names such as Basingwerk Parchment, Glastonbury Antique, Royal Cornwall Cover.

In 1922, the company bought land between the mill and Basingwerk Abbey where, by 1925, they had built a very imposing house, named Basingwerk House, for the assistant mill manager.

The 1930s witnessed much modernisation, including the installation of a bleach-making chlorine plant, a new dye plant, a conditioner plant and a fibre recovery plant. During the Second World War, fine paper production received a set back as, due to import restrictions on raw materials, home produced straw had to be used which caused the paper to become brittle and yellowish in colour. It was 1951 before production returned to its former level.

By 1964 a decision was made to stop importing raw esparto grass in lieu of pre-manufactured esparto pulp. This material did not use as much water in the manufacturing process, reduced the freight charges incurred by the company and did not require chemical treatment with caustic soda (thereby eliminating many of the effluent problems).

Grosvenor Chater & Co. Ltd. also manufactured stationery in London. On 10 May 1941, a German incendiary bomb destroyed the warehouse in Old Street. In 1947, the stationery business was revived at Greenfield where the company purchased a site across the main coast road where they built a purpose-designed, brick building known as the Park Works. In 1975 the work was transferred to the Abbey Mill where sufficient space had become available to cope with orders. The Park Works were then sold to Shotblast Engineering Ltd, a welding and plating firm.

The Grosvenor Chater Fire Brigade formed in 1939, became part of the Auxiliary Fire Service during the Second World War. Besides serving their own mill, they were called out to local fires, including bomb damaged sites. In addition, from time to time during the war, members were sent to major cities, including Liverpool and the Midlands, to help with the huge fires caused by bombing.

In the early 1970s, Abbey Mill's paper-making business started to hit hard times. Not only was there an economic recession in Britain but the European Federal Trades Association removed protective tariffs which resulted in a dramatic increase in the volume of imports from other European countries. This caused many British paper mills to close but Grosvenor Chater, with its renowned quality papers, was able to keep going. Investment in modernisation led to the opening of a new laboratory and power house, and the installation of a computer-controlled paper-making machine. A new metal chimney was also erected, but the historic brick chimney, a local landmark,

Abbey Paper Mill, Greenfield. The road which runs L–R across the centre of the photograph is the present-day A548. The road lower right is Gasworks Road and, on the far centre right, is Dock Road. The building at the bottom right is Gasworks House.

was left standing until 1983 when it was finally demolished. Despite these efforts the battle to survive was lost in 1982 when the receivers had to be called in and paper-making on the site ceased after an unbroken period of 212 years. The site was then altered beyond recognition and re-named the Greenfield Business Centre, where a variety of small business units operate. Basingwerk House was absorbed into the Greenfield Valley Heritage Park. The large iron entrance gates of the paper mill, originally located off the Holywell road, have been have been moved to just beyond the Flour Mill Pool.

Copper, brass and wire
Dr Samuel Johnson, writing during his 1774 tour of north Wales recorded:

> We then saw a brass work, where the lapis calaminaris [calamine] is gathered, broken, washed from the earth and the lead … then calcined, afterwards ground fine, and then mixed by fire with the copper. At a copper-work … we saw a plate of copper put hot between steel rollers, and spread thin: I know not whether the upper roller was set to a certain distance, as I suppose, or acted only by its weight. At an iron work I saw round bars formed by a knotched hammer and anvil. There I saw a bar of about half an inch, or more, square cut with shears worked by the water, and then beaten hot into a thinner bar. The hammers all worked, as they were, by water, acting upon small bodies, moved very quick, as quick as by hand. I then saw wire drawn, and gave a shilling.[26]

Thomas Williams, born in Anglesey on 31 May 1737, qualified as a solicitor and, in 1769, was asked to act for a family in a lawsuit concerning the ownership and revenues of what was to become the Parys Copper Mine near Amlwch. The case proceeded slowly, and in 1778, Williams emerged as managing partner in the company. In 1779, he set up copper ore smelting works in Swansea and Ravenshead in Lancashire and in 1785 acquired a holding in Mona Copper Mine.[120] Copper ore was exported from Anglesey to Ravenshead where it was smelted into copper cake and ingots before being shipped to Greenfield.

Eventually, Williams also owned copper works at Marlow and Wraysbury (on the Thames), which he ran independently of his other interests and he became Member of Parliament for Marlow in 1790. Known as *Twm Chware Teg* (Tom Fair Play), Williams ended up virtually controlling the British copper industry for two decades — and gaining the nickname of the 'Copper King'.

The Copper Works Parys Mine Site, Greenfield
The Battery Copper Works was first established in the Greenfield Valley in 1765. In 1780, Thomas Williams leased all the land up from the main coast road to Abbey Lane from Sir Pyers Mostyn; the eastern boundary ran adjacent to Basingwerk Abbey and Abbey Farm. Thomas Pennant wrote:

> Thomas Williams, that useful and active character, with unparalleled speed, covered the lower part of the stream, or that next to the sea, with buildings stupendous in expense,

Two views of the Greenfield Brass Works. Late eighteenth century illustrations by Ingleby. Above: The view looking south showing the water flowing out of the Copper Works Pool. Below: The view looking north from the Battery Mill Pool, across the Flour Mill Pool, with the Dee estuary and the Wirral in the distance.

extent, and ingenuity of contrivance. There great works are under the firm of Parys Mine Company.[22]

This complex comprised: a copper rolling mill (sited by the present-day Heritage Park lower car park, alongside the Holywell road), with a reservoir to its upper, southern side; a large copper forge (adjacent to the coast road); and a copper-wire mill (alongside Abbey Lane). The rolling mill created sheets of copper which were used for lining ship's hulls to prevent teredo worms eating into the wood. It was then discovered that the worms bored holes in the hulls alongside the iron bolts which secured the sheets to the ships. To resolve this problem, Thomas Williams began to produced copper bolts by 1784 to replace the iron bolts. Rudder bands and braces, weighing up to $1^3/_4$ tons were also manufactured here. All these products were supplied to not only the Royal Navy, but also the East Indian Company, the French Navy, and numerous merchant shipping companies.[120] After 1785, some of these products were also manufactured at the Battery Works. Thomas Williams died in 1802.

The Abbey Wire Works [SJ 1945 7735]
This was sited on the south side of the lane leading into the valley from what is now the junction of School Lane. Water was fed to the site by launders (iron chutes) leading to two water-wheels which drove the machines making the copper and brass wire for Thomas Williams' Parys Mine Company. Rods of the metals were drawn through numerous holes, decreasing in size, thus reducing the diameter of the wire. A pit for one of the water-wheels and a launder are still visible, as are, to the east of the adjacent road, the ruins of some worker's cottages named Tai Coed. After the wire works closed, St Winefride's Soap Works took over the site.

The Battery Copper Works [SJ 1895 767]
These works were the first to produce copper items in major quantities from the Greenfield Valley (i.e., before The Parys Mine Works). Thomas Patten's firm, the Warrington Company, leased land from Edward Pennant in 1765 and built a reservoir with four water-powered copper and brass battery mills. The water-driven tilt hammers 'battered' (shaped) brass into pans, bowls, ingots and rods, which were exported, via Liverpool, to West Africa as part of the 'triangular trade' — the copper goods being exchanged for slaves who were then transported to America where they were exchanged for cotton.[87 & 100] By 1785, Patten and his associates had decided to concentrate their business interests in Cheadle in Cheshire, where they concentrated on the production of brass wire. Thomas Williams then took the Greenfield premises over for the Greenfield Copper and Brass Company.[87] He raised the height of the dam and increased the area of the pool so that it covered the site of a former snuff mill to the south. The factory was enlarged considerably, the existing water-wheels were repalced by cast-iron wheels, and the company's trade increased dramatically.

* A second snuff mill had also existed for a while below the brass works.

Two views of the Meadow Cotton Mill, Greenfield Valley. Late eighteenth century illustrations by Inglby.
Above: The view looking south.
Below: The view looking north, across the Dee estuary towards the Wirral.

Thomas Pennant recorded:

> Since January 1786 … the firm of The Greenfield Copper and Brass Co., who have very much improved them [the works] by various erections, so as to enable them to finish goods for Africa, America, and most other markets, viz. brass Neptunes, or large pans, in which the negroes make salt; pans for getting the gold out of their rivers, and for various other purposes; kettles; brass and copper rods; bright and black manilas — the first are rings for ornaments to the arms and legs, the last for the current money of the country. The last are not unlike the golden bracelets of the antient.[22]

Prior to this, the copper and brass manufacturing industry had been dominated by merchants from Bristol and Birmingham who had also provided the Royal Navy with its requirements.

Williams also produced vitriol with sulphur (a type of sulphuric acid) which aided the local chemical industry and entered into agreements with industrialist Matthew Boulton of Birmingham, as well as some Cornish copper companies, to open warehouses in London, Birmingham and Liverpool.

The Meadow Mills [SJ 1907 7698]
In 1787, Thomas Williams's Greenfield Copper & Brass Company built a copper and rolling mill complex on the site below the Battery Works. This new plant was named Meadow Mills and its main building was eighty-six feet long by sixty-nine feet wide, with a copper-sheet roof, supported by two iron pillars. According to Pennant, 'their chimneys discharged tremendous volumes of thick black smoke'. The fall of water from the dam to the south was some twenty-one feet, and it fed three eighteen feet diameter cast-iron water-wheels, which provided the factory with its power. Copper sheets and wire, were manufactured there before being forwarded on to the

Flour Mill Pool, c.1906.

A view of the Upper Textile Mill (lower right), Inkerman Mineral Railway Bridge crossing the main road, Crescent Mill (large building centre), Battery Pool with the Copper Works beyond.

company's battery works and wire mills. Brass plates, utensils and wire were also manufactured and sold on to other foundry companies.[23, 87 & 119]

A smaller mill was also built alongside the Meadow Mills to manufacture copper rollers for the printing trade.[87]

Battery Row Cottages [SJ 1883 7662]
These forty-two cottages were built to the west of Battery Pool, between 1785 and 1790, for the workers of the Greenfield Copper & Brass Company. They were of a generally high standard for their era. Most were two up and two down cottages but some had a cellar. For many years, part of one cottage was used as a shop. After falling into disrepair, the cottages were demolished during May and June 1965.[118] Close to the Royal Oak public house were two other dwellings which had been built for the works manager and time-keeper. These were pulled down, c.1970.

The latter days of the Greenfield Valley copper industry
The copper industry, which covered an area from the Battery Works [SJ 1895 767] at Bryn Celyn (the first buildings of which were erected in 1765), to the main coast road. Beginning in 1780, Thomas Williams had gradually taken control of all the sites.

From about 1797, a number of factors combined to gradually cause the demise of the valley's copper industry. Firstly, copper prices nationally were falling, partially because of cheaper imports of copper ore which led to the decline of mining in Anglesey mines. By 1802, there was insufficient Anglesey ore to supply the Lancashire smelters. Locally, the silting up of the River Dee was beginning to cause difficulties for the larger ships using Greenfield Harbour. On 29 November 1802,

Thomas Williams, the driving force behind the industry in the region, died and the business was taken over by his sons. One son, Owen Williams, went into partnership with Pascoe Grenfell and and gradually bought out the previous partners. Their first acquisition was the site of the Greenfield Copper & Brass Company[120] and they bought the Meadow Mill and Abbey Wire Mill in about 1814. Ten years later, Williams, Pascoe & Company closed down production in the Greenfield Valley. After protracted negotiations of the lease, the firm of Newton, Lyon & Company re-opened the copper works, removed the battery works, and built new rolling and shearing mills to produce and trim copper sheets. New foundries and a pattern workshop enabled the company to manufacture copper castings and they became the first company to use gas from the local gas works which had been built on the coast road. In 1839, the company built a red lead mill and shot tower to enable them to produce rolled lead sheet and pipes. The raw materials were supplied by their own smelting works at Bagillt.[121]

Joseph Lyon (of Newton Lyon & Company) died around 1845 and William Keates, who had been with the firm since 1833, became managing director and took up residence at Greenfield Hall. The re-named company, Newton, Keates & Company, took over two other valley sites, namely the Meadow Mills and the Abbey Wire Mill where they produced items such as plate and pipes for the industrial and marine trades, and steam-engine fittings.[121] After the death of Keates' son in 1866, some of the company's Greenfield interests were sold. A tinplate works was built east of the Meadow Mill site in 1868, but this only traded until 1874. Old pictures of Meadow Mill show four very tall, and wide chimney stacks, beneath which ran four water culverts, which discharged into the next reservoir. In 1872, the company demolished the red lead mill and the shot tower, replacing them with a large wire mill. Over the next twenty years, trade became increasingly difficult and production had ceased by 1895.

The closure of the works naturally caused a great deal of distress, and a special committee was set up in late January 1895, which resulted in the Greenfield Relief Fund being formed to raise funds and food for the families affected.

No further business was carried out at the works before the company's property, comprising a copper foundry, a rolling mill, two brass foundries with purifiers, a shearing shop and a wire mill, was sold in 1901.[87] Although one or two small companies rented some of the buildings (one operating a rubber grinding business), it was the Gwalia Hosiery Company which took over some of the site and built the brick clock tower which (minus its clock) is still a local landmark.[87]

The large copper forge, sited alongside the coast road, at the Parys Mine site, had fallen into disrepair and was sold to a paper company by Owen Williams, Pascoe Grenfell & Partners sometime before 1824. The bulk of the Parys Mine site, however, had been abandoned and there was no activity there for a number of years. The company's main interests lay in the copper industry in Swansea, which was better positioned to take advantage of the ore from Cornwall. In 1840, the Admiralty built its own copper works in Portsmouth which meant that the Greenfield copper works

A History of Holywell and Greenfield   135

lost their best customer.[105] Around 1846, the Holywell Lime Company took out a lease on the higher part of the Parys Mine site, as part of a scheme to crush and burn limestone that was brought down from Pantasaph.

Zinc Smelting Works [SJ 197 776]
In 1842, William Crockford of London purchased land on the northern side of the coast road at Greenfield, just to the east of the gas works, where he built a zinc speltering works, where calamine was smelted to produce zinc. Railway sidings were laid from the works to the nearby wharf. He died in May 1844, and the running of the business was taken over by his

The Zinc Smelting Works, to the riverside of the Coast Road (opposite today's car park).

wife, Sarah. She sold some of the land to the LNWR in 1847 to enable them to build their main line railway across her site. She managed to include a clause in the sale which gave her the 'use & enjoyment of her company's continued right of way across the new lines', which included the free movement of her livestock, carts and carriages by level crossing — as, and when, she thought fit![R106] Her brother-in-law, Charles Crockford, later had a limestone mineral railway laid from Pantasaph to her factory, and converted the old Parys Mine works into a limestone crushing plant. The company also ran a cement works at Bryn Celyn.[43]

Although Charles Crockford's mineral railway and its related limestone works at the Grange and Parys Mine site were successful in their own right, the spelter works was beset by management problems and, after a number of changes in ownership, the works closed towards the end of the nineteenth century. The buildings remained in a derelict condition until the 1920s. The chimney was demolished in 1928.

Cotton and the Woollen Industries
The Cotton Industry
John Smalley, a native of Preston, moved to Holywell in the mid 1770s and, within two years, built the first cotton-spinning mill in the Greenfield Valley. He was a former associate of Richard Arkwright, inventor of the cotton spinning frame, and pioneer of the enclosed factory method of production.[113] It is believed that Smalley had no real capital for constructing his mill and therefore used Gwespyr stone taken from the ruins of the Basingwerk Abbey which could account for it being known as the 'Yellow Mill' (otherwise known as the Old Mill) [SJ 1864 7646]; sited to the east of

the main Holywell road, below the later Upper Mill, it was built on the site of a former paper and wire mill.[104] Being three storeys high, it was 100 ft long by 25 ft wide; power was supplied by a 15-inch high water-wheel which had a fall of water of 11$\frac{1}{2}$ ft.[23] John Smalley died, aged 53, on 28 January 1782, and is buried in Whitford churchyard. His business, the Cotton Twist Company, was continued by his mother and his eldest brother, Christopher, who became a very influential figure in the district.

The 1780s were boom years for cotton and Christopher Smalley built further cotton spinning mills. The first took only six weeks to erect in 1783, and was named the Upper Mill [latterly the Holywell Textile Mill] [SJ 1857 7638]. Sited north of St Winefride's Well, and opposite the Holway Level, it was originally six storeys high with measurements of 120 ft long by 30 ft wide. It was powered by a water-wheel 20 ft high and 7 ft wide, with a twenty feet fall of water. The ten storey-high Lower Mill [SJ 1912 7741] (described by Thomas Pennant as 'rising up like the Tower of Babel') was built in ten weeks during 1785. It was sited below the pool now called the Flour Mill Pool and measured 100 ft x 25 ft. It was powered by a centrally sited 18 ft high and 7 ft wide water wheel.[22] This large wheel provided sufficient energy to drive not only the shafts, belting and gears, but also to turn the spinning frames which processed the raw cotton into thread. The company, at that stage, was named the Holywell Twist Company.[22] The Lower Mill closed in 1840 and the main building was converted into a flour mill around 1850.

Christopher Smalley then set up a partnership with John Douglas of Manchester, re-naming the company Messrs Douglas & Smalley,[104] and they built the valley's fourth cotton mill in the spring of 1790 and named it Crescent Mill [SJ 1872 7655].[104] It was sited in what is today the rear storage yard of W. Hall & Co. Ltd [SJ 1865 7658]. Having six storeys, this mill measured 78 ft x 30 ft.[104]

The Upper Mill operated 12,218 spindles, the Lower Mill 7,492 and the Crescent Mill 8,286.[106] A most enlightening insight to the method of cotton production in the valley was written by Revd Richard Warner in 1798:

> ... the raw cotton, being first cleansed and picked, is spun into a thread of a texture superior to all other brought to the market ... In this work the cotton after having been previously picked by the poor of the town, is reduced to thread, being thrice carded, thrice roven, and once spun. The process is performed by the improved cotton machine, a stupendous piece of mechanism, the first view of which irresistibly impresses the mind with the idea of magic; here thirty or forty thousand wheels and spindles are seen moving in the most rapid manner, without any perceptible cause, spontaneously performing operations of the most curious nature, and in the most systematic manner.[154]

By the early 1830s, there were well over 1,200 people employed at the mills.[139] A building, named The Barracks, erected opposite the Upper Mill, served as a place of accommodation for the young female workers. While some believe that the young male employees slept in the mills themselves, Thomas Pennant wrote that:

> the cotton-twist company have between three hundred and four hundred apprentices,

which they clothe and feed themselves, in commodious houses built for that purpose, the boys and girls in separate houses.[22]

John Douglas became very involved in other business ventures in the district, including the Holway Level Leadmining Company. In 1817, he purchased the Gyrn estate at Llanasa built Gyrn Castle.[87] In about 1820, Douglas, Smalley & Company set up the Holywell Bank and issued their own bank notes and opened a branch in Mold. Christopher Smalley died in 1829, but Douglas and his family carried on the business. The cotton industry suffered a slump in trade in 1837 and, after the death of John Douglas the following year, his family found it difficult to continue. Although steam power had been introduced to the mills by 1835,[9] Douglas, Smalley & Company could not compete with the Lancashire mills. Also, very many of the employees of the mills were young 'parish apprentices', some of them orphans and the Factory Act of 1833 had restricted the use of such cheap labour, causing employment costs to increase. The bank business collapsed in 1839 and, in 1841 the cotton business went into liquidation[100 & 139] and the cotton mills were closed which was a disaster, not only for the employees, but for the town of Holywell. The Yellow Mill stood empty until the 1870s when it was taken over for use as a cement works by the Holywell Lime Company whose mineral railway virtually passed the premises.[43 & 87]

The Woollen Industry

Flannel manufacture had been active in south and mid Wales from the first half of the seventeenth century, but it was 1840 before Holywell became involved in the industry. Flannel (the name originates from the Welsh word *gwlanen*) was a fine woollen cloth for which the weavers of Wales became famous.[111]

John Jones, a Newtown man, took over the disused Crescent Cotton Mill building in 1840 and formed a new company, the Welsh Flannel Manufacturing Company,[111] which operated the first practicable power loom in Wales to produce flannel. Replacing handloom weaving, this loom doubled the output. However, as a result of the lack of capital, his business failed around 1850. Richard Baldwin, another Newtown man, obtained leases on both the Crescent and the Upper Mills, but, despite obtaining a great deal of investment, he too went bankrupt by 1874.[106]

The Welsh Flannel Manufacturing Company Ltd was formed in 1874 and obtained leases for the Crescent and Upper Mills. The two company directors were William Brown (of Brown's of Chester) and a Urias Bromley. Whilst Brown provided the capital, the technical knowledge was supplied by Bromley. Thomas H. Waterhouse, a Yorkshireman, joined the company, first as secretary, but later as a manager. There was by then a huge demand for Welsh flannel and the company invested in modern machinery and a 28 ft diameter water-wheel which developed 24 h-p.[106] The Holywell stream provided the mills with some seven million gallons of water each day which was augmented by an additional supply which they had laid on by pipe from the Holway Level.[111] One major factor contributing to their initial success was the fact that Welsh wool had properties which limited the cloth shrinkage and readily absorbed perspiration, making it very suitable for such items as underwear and nightgowns. In all, they operated eighty looms.[111] In the six-storey, brick-built Upper Mill, wool sorting, carding and spinning was carried out, whilst in the Crescent Mill the weaving and finishing was done.[111] This business brought renewed prosperity to Holywell at a time when so many industries had closed down. Its importance to the local economy was highlighted by a major fire which broke out at the Upper Mill on 19 February 1883. This resulted in the cessation of production and 170 employees being put out of work,[106] causing serious trouble to the town's economy. The Town Council immediately voted to house the machinery that had been saved in the market section of the Town Hall, causing disruption to some market traders, but only temporarily, until a new three storey mill was built, utilising bricks manufactured by the local Victoria Brickworks.[106] Production, with 5,200 spindles, started in the new mill in September 1884. The opening event was celebrated in the town by a public holiday.[106]

Within a few years, however, the Lancashire woollen manufacturers had started to produce imitation Welsh flannel. That, coupled with changes in women's underwear, brought about a drop in production at Holywell. As a consequence, in 1901, the company decided to set up a new business, the Gwalia Hosiery Company [SJ 1893 7673] on the site of the Battery Copper & Brass Company, below the Battery Pool of the old Greenfield Mill, where they planned to produce machine-knitted items such as shirts, underwear and pyjamas. Production commenced the following April and, with modern machinery, sales quickly rose. They were boosted by the Boer War of 1900 when shirts in particular were in great demand. For over sixty years the manufacture of such items continued on the site until, on Saturday 30 October 1965, a disastrous fire completely destroyed the factory. It was an impossible task to rebuild the works, and consequently the thirty female employees were made redundant. The clock tower, which still stands by the old entrance, had been constructed by this company.

When Thomas H. Waterhouse died in 1902, his son, also named Thomas Waterhouse, succeeded him as General Manager.[111] Under his guidance the mill underwent major modernisation, additional machinery was installed and electricity was utilised as a source of power in 1913. Due to the declining demand for flannel, the name of the company was changed to the Holywell Textile Mills Ltd. and the company traded under this name until it closed in 1991. Thomas Waterhouse's son, Horace, joined the company around the time of the Second World War.

The 1913 changes resulted in increased production and the introduction of new products such as tweeds and shirting. The First World War created an increased demand for flannel for both the British and French armies.[106] The business fought its way through the general slump of the early 1920s, and invested in newer, electrically-driven, machinery, resulting in the operation of 200 looms in 1925.[111]

Despite the economic depression of the 1930s, the business survived and exports of their textiles increased. New products were manufactured, perhaps the most notable being Welsh tweed, which included blankets. However, because competition was so fierce, profits went into decline. Yet again, war reversed the decline and the mill could not cope with demand. After the war, demand for their goods was high, not surprisingly, perhaps when one considers that the British people had gone through six years without being able to buy clothing and other textiles. The company erected additional buildings, more new plant was installed and the production of flannel was abandoned and, in its place, cloth was produced for women's coats. Export demand was high and the company hit its highest peak of production in 1951.[111] Unfortunately, the following year, the British textile industry went into reverse, partly because the post-war boom came to an end, and partly because of increasing imports from aboard. The Holywell company fought back and exported an increasing quantity of its production. Of note at this time were orders from the Cunard White Star liners for luxury fabrics for liners such as the *Queen Mary*.[111] The Crescent rail siding from the Holywell rail line served the Holywell Textile Mill from 1912 until the closure of the siding on 11 August 1957.

Horace Waterhouse retired from the company in 1957, and a private investment company, headed by Lord Davies of Llandinam, acquired the business with Paul Dudek as the Managing Director. He proved to be a tower of strength in the new firm as it adapted to the changing fashions and specialised in the production of yarns from natural fibres, in natural colours. These high-quality products included honeycomb bedspreads, blankets and travel rugs. Finished goods were exported as far afield as Japan.[100] Despite these developments, trading became increasingly difficult and, although the oldest surviving woollen manufacturing company in England and Wales, the company eventually went into receivership and closed in 1991, bringing to an end the production of textiles in the Greenfield Valley after 214 years.*

The site and premises then came under the control of Flintshire County Council, but fell into decay. In 2002, most of the factory was demolished for safety reasons, leaving only the section which had housed the shop standing. In October 2006 Flintshire County Council announced that a project had been agreed upon to restore and re-use the remaining building through the Holywell Townscape Heritage Initiative. Once completed, the site would be used as an arts and crafts centre with a new car park which could also be used by visitors to the St Winefride's Well site. The appointed architects were Ainsley Gommon, of Hawarden and the contract for the work was awarded to R. L. Davies of Colwyn Bay. The £850,000 project would be funded by the Heritage Lottery, the Welsh Assembly Government and Flintshire County Council. It is envisaged that, when completed, it will attract visitors to the area and reflect the legacy of the Greenfield Valley.

The Victoria Corn Mill (Flour Mill)
Around 1850, with the Lower Cotton Mill closed, a Caerwys man, William Evans, purchased the premises and carried out major alterations which turned the building into a flour mill.[109] This new business produced Evans' Patent, Extra & Superfine Flour which sold well throughout north Wales. William died in 1840, and his wife, Ellen (née Kerfoot of Bodhafod), together with other business partners, continued the

---

* The Crescent Mill building, which had been used for storage, was demolished in 1958.

E. Evans & Co's traction engine delivering flour in Denbigh.

business until her death in 1897, when she too died. Her business partners were able to continue operating the mill until c.1908.

Other businesses, including wheelwrights and general engineers, later operated from the site and Phillips of Holywell garaged their buses there for some years around 1920.

In the late 1970s, the two-storey warehouse underwent restoration and it now houses a museum and a reconstructed steam-powered bottling plant.[109]

Breweries and Mineral Water Manufacturers
St Winefred's Brewery [SJ 1861 7635]
On the grassed area between St Winefride's Well and the Upper Cotton Mill (later Holywell Textile Mill) there once stood a brewery, which had been built around 1820 by a local man, Joseph Vickers. By 1870, Philip Dykins of Greenhill, Bryn Celyn, who, by learning the art of brewing over some years, was able to call himself a master brewer and retailer of beer. He was joined by his son, Llewellyn, and took out a lease on the Vickers brewery and corn mill. Llewellyn died in 1871, and his brother-in-law, John Lloyd Price, took his place in the business. Within a year or two, Pryce took control of it from Phillip Dykins. From that time, there are no further records of the corn mill, but it would be safe to assume that the brewery took over its site for expan-

Mr Lloyd Price's motor car and chauffeur. He was the first Holywell resident to own a motor car.

sion. Known as the 'St Winefred's Brewery', the premises had a 185 ft frontage to the main road.

John Lloyd Price, who lived at Glyn Abbot from about 1900, in addition to the brewery, acquired a number of local inns and beer-houses. He was a very influential figure, not only in Holywell, but in Flintshire where, he became High Sheriff in 1910 and an Alderman on Flintshire County Council for over twenty years. He was a member of the Holywell Local Board, the Urban District Council and the School Board. He died, aged 67, on 24 December 1923, and one of the windows of St James Parish Church bears a memorial to himself and his wife. He was buried in St Peter's Churchyard.

The forty-four licensed premises owned by Mr Price were put up for auction in 1928, followed by the brewery, the old malt house and associated land on 7 October 1929. They were bought by the Roman Catholic authorities who demolished the buildings and cleared the land to provide much needed open space to the north of St Winefride's Well.

W. Hall & Son Ltd. [SJ 187 766]
In 1872, a mineral water manufacturing and bottling company was started by William Hall & Son in adapted premises alongside the Holywell–Greenfield road and the old foundry yard at Bryn Celyn. In later years, the business also bottled beers. Hall's 'pop' became a household name for miles around, not only because of the superior quality of the mineral water, but also because of the delivery service they provided to small businesses and the licensed trade. On a personal note I well remember as a child two favourites: Dandelion and Burdock and American Cream Soda.

From the mid twentieth century, the company expanded further and concentrated more on the licensed trade; opening their own off-licence outlet from their premises. After Crescent Mill closed down in 1958, the company acquired the land that backed onto their premises – much of which is now used as an outdoor storage area. Thankfully, one of the old mill chimneys still stands as a landmark and reminder of the old cotton trade.

The latter years of the twentieth century witnessed great expansion and by 2005 the company was offering a wholesale service through seven depots in north Wales and north-western England. That service includes the manufacture, distribution and sale of soft drinks; the wholesale distribution and retail of beers (keg and cask), wines (specially imported from all over the world) and spirits; and the distribution of bar supplies and bar snacks.[150]

The company, which is still in the control of the same family after 134 years, is now the sole industrial survivor in the historic Greenfield Valley.

Rope works
Rope was needed in the Greenfield Valley industries, as well as in the local lead and coal mines. *Pigot's Directory* of 1835 records a ropemaker in Whitford Street, Holywell, but the entry does not appear in later directories.

142   *A History of Holywell and Greenfield*

Soap Works [SJ 1945 7735]
The St Winefride's Soap Company went into production around 1909 on the site of the old Parys Mine Company's wire works. The company did a great deal to advertise the fact that the soap was manufactured using the pure water from St Winefride's Well. The *Catholic Times* of 2 April 1910 stated:

> Recently a company has started soap making at the historic Basenwerke Abbey Mills at Holywell. In the manufacture of the soap, the water from the well is used and combined with the purest materials, a fragrant antiseptic toilet soap is the result, which is sure to become popular as it becomes known.[66]

The first soap produced was sent to the Pope, who was also sent fifty boxes every year for the feast of St Winefride.[66]

A photograph of the works shows a fairly large premises about which very little else is known.

Iron Foundry
In 1783, the premises at Bryn Celyn (previously used as a pin mill, and later, a paper mill) were leased by the Smalley family, who adapted them to enable a smithy and foundry business to operate there.[87] When the Smalleys stopped trading has not been established, but an Edward Jones was trading there as 'an iron and brass founder' in the mid nineteenth century. Between *c.*1870 and 1928, these premises were leased to the St Winefred's Brewery, who converted them into a malt kiln.

Between 1870 and *c.*1900, Charles and Samuel Jones operated a foundry in premises on the other side of the main road at Bryn Celyn.

The Pen-y-Maes district, and the road leading from Holywell to Riverbank, Bagillt (A5056).
Groes Onnen Windmill, Pen-y-Maes [SJ 1905 7587].
The name Groes Onnen can be translated into Ash Cross. The Basingwerk monks had a windmill site in Holywell, and, although the actual site has never been confirmed, it is generally accepted that it would have been here. Basingwerk Abbey certainly held the land in this area of Holywell and it was passed on by Nicholas Pennant, the last abbot, to Edward Pennant who, in turn, sold it to Thomas Pennant. Early windmills would have been wooden structures and therefore would have had to be replaced as the years went by. This site, on the brow of a hill, was ideal for catching the wind and would have been an obvious location for such a building.

The present windmill building, built of Holywell shale, was constructed around 1805 by the Sankey family and is a rare example in Wales of a full height windmill.[87] It remained in operation until 1894, after which it gradually fell into disrepair. When it was active, people used to take their corn there to be ground into flour and the miller took one-tenth of the grain as payment. A wooden walkway connected the mill to the granary which stood alongside.

During the 1980s considerable work was carried out on the derelict mill and it was converted into a remarkable private dwelling, retaining its original shape. The top was replaced with a weather-boarded boat-shaped cap which has a timber balcony. The building was given Grade II listed status in 1951.[44]

The Groes Onnen Granary and Malt Kiln [SJ 1905 7587]
These premises stood next door to the windmill, although, for many years they had been derelict. Thomas Pennant wrote that in 1796 the kiln and granary were the property of 'the generous business-man', Richard Sankey.[22] Now demolished, a modern house has been built on the site.

The derelict windmill, with granary building to its left, c1910.

The Vitriol Works [SJ 1939 7607]
To the left of the brow of Pen-y-Maes a vitriol manufacturing plant was built by the Pen-y-Maes Company in about 1785.[120] The company had had capital from Thomas Williams's Garston Vitriol Company. Thomas Pennant wrote that it was the property of a 'Mr Donbavand, placed under the care of Mr John Jones, of Holywell, an able chemist'. His operations are directed to three articles: blue vitriol, or vitriol of copper, which is made by dissolving copper in oil of vitriol or acid of sulphur. After the solution has taken place, the product is dissolved in boiling water, evaporated down to a given weight, and put in coolers to evaporate. This type of vitriol is used to dye cottons a green or olive colour, and hats and woollen cloths black.[22] The Garston Vitriol Company ran into trouble and, after 1796, the Pen-y-Maes Company was re established as The Holywell Vitriol Company.* Pennant also wrote that sugar of lead was also manufactured at the Pen-y-Maes plant for a short time. This was obtained by dissolving lead in distilled vinegar. Barley or malt was also used in the process, but a shortage of raw materials caused the operation to cease.[22]

It is not known when the vitriol works closed down, but it is likely to have been around 1810, when the old works at Garston were sold.

---

* The Meadow Mill Copper and Brass Works were under Donbavand's directorship.

The Silk Works [SJ 1939 7605]

An Act of Parliament in 1793 had regulated the wages of silk weavers in London, but it did not apply to places such as Holywell, where lower wages could be paid. As a result of this legislation, a silk works (Ribbon Weaver's Colony) was built in October 1794, by Hugh Roberts, from Little Moorfields, London. His brother was a chemist and druggist in Holywell and it was at his suggestion that the move was made to Flintshire. A ninety-nine year lease was negotiated with Thomas Pennant on land, not only for the factory site, but also to enable Hugh Roberts to erect cottages for his employees. One building erected here was the Weavers Arms public house.[81]

The site (opposite the vitriol works) was well chosen as it had its own spring. The two-storey factory was 74 ft long and 17 ft 6 ins wide, with a boiler house and chimney.[81] In 1796, there were sixteen looms in operation there[23] and, by 1821, sixty. An economic depression in the early 1830s caused the business financial problems, and female workers had to be employed at 9s. (45p) per week, instead of male labour force workers who had received 12s. (60p) per week.

There is no record of when the works closed down, but it does appear on the Ordnance Survey map of 1871.

Cement Works [SJ 197 758]

There was a cement works in the Greenfield Valley and opposite Victoria Cottages alongside the A5026 Holywell to Bagillt main road. Named the Halkin Cement Works, this was in operation for some years from the mid nineteenth century.

The Coal, Leadmining, Limestone and Quarrying Industries

Coalmining

Coal was first mined at Mostyn during the thirteenth century. By the eighteenth century, several mines had been opened along the coastal strip, including Llanerch-y-Môr, Greenfield and Bagillt which were of great importance to the industry in the Greenfield Valley. Traditionally, the Holywell Stream had provided the power for the various industries, but the introduction of steam power made coal essential during the nineteenth century. The Englefield Colliery [SJ 188 782], west of the Greenfield crossroads, was the nearest colliery to the valley. In 1790 it was owned by Richard Sankey (senior). By 1874 it was owned by William Jones & Son of Mertyn Hall.[43] Mining ceased in 1931 when it was owned by the Englefield Collieries Ltd.[49]

Trade directories mention two collieries in the Greenfield Valley, however, they were small and of short duration. Abbey Colliery was listed in *Robson's Directory* of 1840, with Hugh Jones as its agent. It is believed that this colliery was worked until 1858.[87] *Slater's Directory* of 1844 lists Dingle Colliery, which was owned by Harry Crockford.

Leadmining

Lead mining and smelting took place at Pen-y-Ball, Brynford, in the lordship of Holywell, in the fourteenth century. At that time, special privileges, including

A History of Holywell and Greenfield 145

A view of The Upper Textile Mill and the lane leading up to The Level, where a Lead Mining Winding House and Chimney can be seen. To the right of that is the outline of where Crockford's Mineral Tramway ran towards Inkerman's Bridge.

freedom from some tolls and taxes, were granted to miners in the Holywell area. There is no translation for the name Pen-y-Ball but, according to the book *The Archaeology of Clwyd*, 'Ball' is almost certainly a distortion of the medieval word 'Bole', which was an early type of lead smelter.[6]

The lead market was conducted in Holywell in a particular way. Notices of the quantity and the quality of the metal offered for sale were forwarded to the managers of the leadworks where samples were taken and tested. The prospective buyers then met in Holywell on an agreed Thursday every month. The samples were ticketed, the prices offered were written on pieces of paper and placed in a glass from which the highest bidders were identified and the procedure ended with a friendly lunch. These are called ticketings.[115]

Within the boundaries of Holywell, the lead-mining was particularly important in the Level and the Holway. The Great Holloway Vein commenced at the Level before running west, under the Holway and through Carmel, Gorsedd, Pant-y-Wacco and Pen-y-Gelli, before it ceased north-east of the Travellers Inn. Whilst mining at the Level is only known to have commenced in 1773, there is no doubt that the Romans sank shafts down to the Great Holloway Vein in the Carmel area. The land was owned by Sir Pyers Mostyn and he granted leases for mining to the Holywell Level Company whose agent was Thomas Edwards of Saithaelwyd. One of the partners in this venture was Thomas Pennant, who owned the adjacent land. In his 1796 book *The History of the Parishes of Whiteford and Holywell*, he gives graphic details of a journey he made up the level waters by punt. At the eastern entrance [SJ 184 764] to the mine, water flows out from the subterranean streams. Pennant wrote of water cascading down from higher underground streams.

For a short distance Pennant travelled through passages cut into Holywell shale before reaching an area of chert. Several shafts had been sunk to allow air to flow down to the tunnel. When they were below the Holway Brognallt turnpike they entered a cave, in which there was a table and benches – apparently it was practice to take people up to view the tunnel. Arthur Aiken, a mineralogist, visited the mine in 1796:

> We entered it through a water-level which is cut from the bottom of the lowest shaft, and is a long subterranean archway that opens in a valley about 1,300 yards from the bottom of the shaft, the top of which in on the brow of a hill. This canal is navigated by long narrow boats that are pushed along by hand against the sides of the arch. The whole passage is perfectly straight, and at the extremity of the level is built a mill that is turned by the waste water from the mine. We got into the boat at the open part of the level, and soon lost sight of day-light. The first 600 yards of this canal are cut through [Holywell] shale and chertz, the remaining 700 through hard limestone; the whole passage is blasted by gunpowder. When we had got nearly to the end of the level, we quitted the boat, and clambered up through the narrow winding passages to the ore. The veins in this mine are uncommonly rich, the chief seam being from five to six feet thick, it is the property of fifteen owners, who employ about sixty miners ... The great bank of ore is found about forty yards from the surface dipping down gradually almost as low as the level. The ore is chiefly galena, and steel ore, which last contain also silver; considerable quantities of

calamine too are procured. 152 Working conditions endured by the level miners in 1798 was written by Rev. Richard Warner on his second walk in Wales: Here these laborious beings, who are content to sacrifice health and safety for the scanty gain of about twenty-pence per day, are seen busied in their terrible employ, shut out from the blessed light of day, and tearing down from the heart of the mountain, amidst dust and noise [including blasting by gunpowder], and confusion, the fatal mineral, the instrument of fate, and messenger of death to thousands.[154]

Even from the beginning of the Holloway vein other veins, running south were being mined.[22] These latter veins generally came from the Brynford/Calcot area and some terminated on the hillsides around the Holway road. By 1795, the Holywell Level Company prospectors had lost some £5,000 but, from around 1800, as mining tunnels lengthened, and shafts deepened, large profits began to be made – partly due to the rather high percentage of silver and calamine that was being extracted from the ore.[116] In 1818, the company was bringing in about £130,000 each year [2006, £4,912,700].[116] In 1830, when the main tunnel extended generally westerly over 1,800 yards, a rail system was laid to replace the punts. There was a great deal of mining activity westwards along the Holway, with many shafts being sunk over the years by several companies. The shaft names included: Holway Level, Great Holway, Holway District, Holway United, Holway Consuls, Holway East, and Holway West Peak. Output from the Great Holway Mine averaged between 1881 and 1885: ore, 643 tons; lead, 507 tons; silver, 7,312 ounces. At that time the mine employed eighty-two underground and fifty surface workers.[123]

Above ground, some 500 yards east of the level tunnel entrance, two large shafts had been driven down [SJ 181 764] to the main tunnel, which acted, not only as ventilation shafts, but also had steam-driven winding gear and machinery fitted to bring up the mined ore. There was another winding house just east of Hillside Road. Although the mine owners derived great profits from leadmining, the miners themselves were poorly paid, and had to work hard in atrocious wet and cold conditions, breathing foul air. The latter gave them severe stomach and bowel problems, as well as breathing troubles.[22] Few lead miners lived beyond the age of fifty.[25]

Further extensive lead-mining also developed in Carmel and Gorsedd in the eighteenth and nineteenth centuries.

The ore taken from the underground veins is a lead sulphide named galena from which eighty per cent lead could be obtained. In places, the silver content could be as high as twelve ounces per ton. Calamine, used extensively in the production of zinc, copper and brass, was another important product. According to Pennant:

> Of calamine, which figures in the making of brass from Roman to modern times, our county abounds with it; but, till within these sixty years, we were so ignorant of the value, as to mend our roads with it; which have of late years been turned up in a hundred places most successfully to recover lost wealth.[22]

The smelting houses, to which the ore was taken, were sited near the coast, at

148   *A History of Holywell and Greenfield*

Llanerch-y-Môr, Siop Gôch, and Pen Rho. But the largest refineries were sited around Bagillt. The extensive Gadlys smeltery had been in operation from 1704, the Riverbank Refinery opened in 1785, and Deebanks in 1794.

The Gadlys Works was owned by the London Lead Company, which sent 430,604 ounces of silver to the Royal Mint. The company had been granted the right to have a motif (the Prince of Wales's feathers) shown on all coins produced which contained their silver. This appeared on the florins (2s./10p), the 1s. (5p) and the 6d. (2.5p) coins of both Queen Anne and King George I.[124]

Quarrying
Within the Holywell and Greenfield district, the three main types of stone were available for quarrying: Gwespyr stone, Holywell shale and limestone. The largest quantity of Gwespyr Stone came from Moor Quarry [SJ 181 773]. It was used in the building of Basingwerk Abbey, St Winefride's Wellhouse and Chapel and the tower of Holywell Parish Church. One of the main sources of Holywell Shale was the Level. It was used extensively for building houses and roadside walls. Carboniferous limestone has been used to an even greater degree in the building of dwellings and walls. The quarries were and are mainly in the hills above the Holywell.

Crockford's Tramway
A mineral line was built by the Holywell Lime Company around 1848, to carry limestone for a distance of some four miles from quarries on the hills above and to the west of Holywell, down to the Greenfield Spelter Works. The instigator of the project was Charles Crockford, whose brother, William, had built the spelter works in 1842. The project manager was a William Parry. The line was laid on land owned by Sir Pyers Mostyn. Positive confirmation of the track gauge cannot be established, but whilst 3 ft $8^{1}/_{2}$ ins was most likely, it may well have been 4 ft as this was considered the best gauge for horse-drawn trams. The tramway was worked by both horse and gravity.

One branch line started at the large Pantasaph White Quarries (otherwise known as the Crecas or Grange Quarries) where encrinital white limestone was obtained. A second branch started to the east of this, nearer Pen-y-Ball, at the Coetia-Butler Quarry, where the product was common black limestone. The two branches joined to form one line which went through a small tunnel into a quarry above Grange Farm where it served the underground Aberdo Quarry (otherwise known as the 'Grange Cavern') where the line had a passing loop (there were several loops further along the route). The Aberdo limestone was particularly important because, when burned, it could be used to create hydraulic cement which was capable of setting under water. This important Grange area had branches serving six limekilns which had their own waste-tipping areas and sidings.

The main track then ran down from this busy area, to the west of the present Holway Garage (the edge of the bend up to Carmel), dropping through a stoned-lined tunnel under the Holloway road. After some fifty yards, the track bore right and then ran parallel to the Holloway road, until it reached what is now Hillside Road where it took a steep run down before turning right to run along the north side of the Level. There was a branch-off along here which served the busy Great Holloway Mine and its associated lime kiln. The route of the tramway left the Level and crossed the Holywell/Greenfield road, north of the textile mill, by means of a stone pillared wooden trestle bridge, known as Inkerman's Bridge. After this it turned left at what became the Crescent siding before continuing through the Greenfield Valley, down almost the same route as the Greenfield–Holywell passenger train line. Before reaching Basingwerk Abbey, there was a branch (which is now the subway leading to the children's play area of the Heritage Park) which led west to the Parys Mine site, where a stone crushing and processing plant had been built by the company. This plant included two limestone crushers, limestone grinders and lime-kilns (the ruin of one is still in existence, behind the Environment Centre above what is now Parys Mine Pool) which dealt with the White Quarry and Coetia Quarry stone (the Aberdo stone having been processed at the Grange site). Other sidings here enabled filled wagons to be held ready for transporting down to the spelter works, Greenfield Dock and, after 1848, Holywell (Junction) Station. The route from Parys Mine sidings went to the west of Basingwerk Abbey, crossing the coast road by means of a wooden bridge, with a branch to the Spelter Works.

Some of the ruins of the Parys Mine plant can be seen today, some twenty feet below the car park.

The Grange Quarries were used during the Second World War for the storage of bombs which were transported by lorry from Holywell Junction Station. Amongst these bombs were the famous 'bouncing bombs' designed by Dr Barnes Wallis.

Courtaulds
Rayon Staple Artificial Silk and Sulphuric Acid Manufacture
Because of the immense impact that the Courtaulds factory at Greenfield had on the local economy, from 1935 to 1985, a brief background on the company's earlier history is first given thus:

The Courtaulds company was established in 1825. Until 1904, they concentrated on the manufacture and sale of silk fabrics, especially crêpes. In 1905, they started to manufacture and sell, from their factory in Coventry, a new artificial silk product named rayon, using the viscose method of production. In 1916, they acquired the Aber Works in Flint from Glanzstoff & Co. who had been producing artificial silk by a different process. Six years later, Courtaulds bought the Flint premises of the United Alkali Company which they rebuilt and extended and re-named as the Castle Works.

Vast quantities of water were needed for the manufacture of rayon and the carboniferous limestone Halkyn Mountain range provided a reliable source. The Aber Works at first drew water from the Swinchard Brook which had its natural source up in the hills, but was supplemented by waters emerging above Flint [SJ 230 711] from a man-made drainage tunnel completed in 1875. In 1897, the Holywell – Halkyn

Mining and Tunnel Company started to drive a second underground tunnel from Deebanks [SJ 213 760] at Bagillt, up to the Halkyn area to try an alleviate the problem of mines being flooded. Courtaulds later built a water pumping station alongside this drainage tunnel's portal at Deebanks, and, from there, constructed a thirty-inch pipeline to Flint which supplied both the Castle and Aber Works.

In the early 1920s, the company began to experiment with the possibility of manufacturing viscose staple fibre as a result of which they realised that there was a potentially large market for the product. By 1933, they were in a position to proceed with plans for a new factory to manufacture the new product, viscose fibro, which differed from the continous filament yarn because, at the spinning stage, it was cut up into short staple lengths. A really large factory was needed for this venture. The company's success at Flint had been helped by the reliable and low-cost water supply and the close proximity of coal. To these factors were added good road and rail links and the fact that the majority of their customers were located in Lancashire and Yorkshire, led to the decision to locate the new factory in Flintshire.

Courtaulds duly found some 600 hectares (around 1,500 acres) at Greenfield, between the A548 main road and the River Dee [main entrance SJ 201 772]. The contract for building the factory was awarded to Melville, Dundas & Whitson in May 1934. The only major obstacle that the site had was that the soft, sandy soil was not very suitable for heavy buildings and piles had to be driven down through the topsoil into firm clay. Many thousands of tons of limestone from the Halkyn Mountain quarries were laid on the site and, onto this, especially for the larger, heavier, buildings, concrete rafts were laid. The main Chester to Holyhead railway ran through the centre of the site and two independent manufacturing units, N°s 1 and 2, were built on either side of the tracks. North of N$^{o.}$ 1 Unit they erected service buildings, including a boiler house, with eight coal-fired boilers, and a power house with three turbines to generate electric power. There were also facilities to switch essential services into the national grid in the event of an internal breakdown. At each end of the boiler house were 220 ft-tall brick chimneys which took up the smoke from the boilers as well as the fumes from the two manufacturing units (in 1952–3, two specially-lined 210 ft-high concrete chimneys were erected for the extraction of fumes). From the boiler house and the power house both high pressure and low pressure steam was piped into the factories. A compressor house provided a vacuum and air of different types for use in the factory. Each manufacturing unit was initially set up with ten production finishing lines.

Construction of the N$^{o.}$ 1 Unit commenced in April 1935. Although Greenfield needed a far greater quantity of water than the Flint works, the Bagillt pump-house could more than adequately meet the demand. Additional pumping facilities were installed there and a thirty-inches (seventy-six centimetres) diameter water-supply pipeline (along what is known as the Cob) was laid alongside the foreshore, between the factory and the Dee, to a large water reservoir which was built in N$^{o.}$ 2 Unit. Because of the complexity of the production requirements, water had to be treated in order to produce such types as soft water, neutralized water, hard water and raw

Courtaulds Greenfield Factory c.1969.

water. To do this water treatment plants were installed in each of the production units. In the main, the raw, untreated water was used for the boiler and power houses. This water became heated, and was then pumped to the two wooden water-cooling towers. From these the cooled water was returned to the service plant. Service units (including a soda farm), an acid recovery and wash re-agent departments were built for each of the production plants. Chemical storage areas with vessels and tanks for such commodities as caustic soda, carbon disulphide and sulphuric acid were also set up close to each production plant.

Each factory unit had its own effluent pump house, from which waste waters and other waste liquids were piped to two large impounding tanks sited adjacent to the reservoir by the river foreshore. Within these impounding tanks, sulphur bacteria broke up impurities before the waste was discharged into the river on an ebb tide. The company also used the cob as a site for their waste tipping.

Because of the large volume of rail freight traffic created by the new works, Holywell Junction Station witnessed considerable expansion. The rail system was used for the importing of coal as well as raw materials such as caustic soda and wood pulp. Sidings were laid for each factory unit and there was a total of some thirteen miles of railway track in the whole site. A subway, built beneath the mainline railway, connected the two production units and small, battery-operated trucks with trailers, used it for light internal transport. A unique, specially built, low height railway engine was used to transport heavier goods and factory waste between each unit. Service pipelines ran alongside the subway, but also crossed over the main railway by means of a specially built bridge.

By 26 January 1937, N$^{o.}$ 1 Unit was in full use and building work on N$^{o.}$ 2 Unit was underway (production of fibro began there in September 1938).

The first manager of the factory was James A. Johnson who remained in post until his retirement in 1968, having been made a member of the board in 1963. Throughout his business life at Greenfield, he resided at Plas Morfa, but later moved to Perth-y-Terfyn Cottage in Holywell.

Production of Viscose Rayon Staple Fibro was a very complex chemical process, taking approximately seventy-two hours from start to finish. Firstly, caustic soda was added to sheet-form cellulose woodpulp (which was imported in bales from South Africa, Canada and Scandinavia). The woodpulp was then shredded into crumbs, which, in turn, had carbon disulphide added. A diluted caustic soda was then mixed into the crumbs to produce viscose. The viscose had then to be filtered twice before it was ready for spinning.

In the beginning, each factory unit had twenty double-sided chemical spinning machines. This was not the traditional type of spinning as carried out in cotton and woollen mills. Each machine was fed by a viscose main pipe which had up to 120 branches leading from it. Each of these had a small pump to which was attached a costly, circular platinum jet. A jet could have anything from 3,500 to 20,000 minute holes in it — the greater the number of holes, the finer the ensuing fibre. The jets were immersed in a lead bath of running sulphuric acid. When the viscose came into contact with the acid, a chemical reaction occurred, creating a fibre. The fibres were then combined into a length of fibro, which was cut into staple lengths at the end of the spinning machines.

The fibro then fell through a chute onto a wash machine conveyor-belt of each of the ten machines. At first the fibro was conveyed along by numerous wooden, waxed, bleach rails. When new wash machines were installed as part of the modernisation scheme in the mid 1960s, the bleach rails were replaced by continuous lengths of stainless steel conveyor belts which proved to be of enormous benefit, not only for production, but also to employees. As the fibro was conveyed along the machine, it was subjected to some six or seven different types of washing, including an acid section, a hot wash section, a sulphide section, a neutralising section and, finally, soap washing. Heavy stainless steel mangles squeezed out most of the liquid before an inclined conveyor took the product to each one of the ten dryers.

A dryer was really a special type of oven in which the fibro went under two beaters, which opened up the thousands of fibres and facilitated the drying process. From there the fibro was transferred to the baling machines, falling first into a deep pit until the required weight was available to make a bale when it was pressed and compacted and wrapped with hessian before being bound, wired and sealed and transferred to the warehouses for storage.

The Main Services Departments for Production included Caustic Soda Farms; Carbon Disulphide Storage and Recovery; (later) Fume Scrubbing; Sulphuric Acid Storage, Recovery and Circulation; Water Storage, Softening, Cooling and Circulation; Effluent; Coal Storage and (later) Oil Storage.

The works had several major additions and improvements over the years including the fume scrubbing units that were installed in 1954–5, the 180-ft high carbon disulphide plant (otherwise known as Landmark) built in 1958 and, in 1964 the boilers were converted to oil. In the same year, a massive three-year modernisation project was commenced for both factory units when the old spinning department buildings were replaced by new, taller, buildings.

The 1960s were the boom years for the factory. From a production of twenty million pounds of fibro before the Second World War, the site was producing 200 million pounds by 1960. Amongst the various new fibros was the strong Evlan which was used by carpet manufacturers.

At the end of the 1960s, the Lancashire and Yorkshire textile mills went into terminal decline and there was a great deal of competition from abroad, where some country's companies received subsidies and grants from their governments. As a consequence, the N° 1 Unit closed down in 1976. With further types of fibro being invented, an ultra-modern viscose-making plant was built in N° 2 Unit in 1980–1 which reduced the amount of labour required. Trade, however, continued to be difficult and, in May 1985, production ceased and the factory closed. Apart from warehouses, the main office block and a few other buildings, most of what had been the largest factory in the Courtaulds Group was gutted and buildings demolished.

The site was sold to Delyn Borough Council for a token £1 and subsequently a variety of individual business units were erected, serving companies, of various sizes and the whole site was named Greenfield Industrial Park (not to be confused with the Greenfield Business Centre which is situated on the site of the old Abbey Paper Mill).

CHAPTER 6

Education

Between the Reformation and the seventeenth century, the Church of England had been almost entirely responsible for education and in Holywell, the vicar and church authorities established two schools in St Winefride's Chapel building. In 1811, the Church of England National Society set up National Schools and the school at Bryn Celyn was the local example of this. From 1808, the Nonconformists opened their own schools which were known as British Schools and the Roman Catholics began to set up schools for their communities.

It soon became obvious that Parliament had to take more positive steps to have education provided and controlled nationally. They gave £30,000 to the National Schools which can be viewed as the beginning of state-aided education in England and Wales. In Holywell, the desire to have more educational facilities for local children resulted in many small schools being opened – some of these were operated privately, others were funded by religious groups and individuals. School inspections commenced in 1839 and the use of pupil teachers began in 1847. Forster's Elementary Education Act of 1870 made it compulsory for all children to have a basic education through the establishment of Local School Boards. The Holywell School Board was established on 14 November 1878, with an office in Chapel Street[43] — their first achievement was the building of Spring Gardens School off Well Street.[12] The Intermediate Education Act of 1889 enabled the newly-formed County Councils to create County Schools for pupils aged eleven plus and Holywell County School was opened in 1898. The Education Act of 1902 abolished the Local School Boards and the administration of the Board and the County Schools became the responsibility of the County Council.[4 & 135] These developments led to the closure of many small private schools.

The 1944 Education Act was very important in that it set up free secondary education for children between the ages of eleven and fifteen, according to their aptitudes and abilities. Pupils had to sit the eleven plus examination in their primary school and those that passed were able to go to Holywell Grammar School (until then named Holywell County School) and those pupils who failed the examination were educated at Flint Secondary Modern School (generally known as Flint Central School). In 1965 the eleven plus examinations were abolished in Flintshire and Comprehensive Schools replaced both the Grammar and Secondary Modern Schools.

The Holywell Local School Board decided, in March 1893, that Welsh should be taught in their schools for the first time as a specific subject.[17] In the years immediately after the Second World War, not only was there a wish to have more Welsh taught in schools throughout Wales, but there was also a call for Welsh language schools. Holywell was no exception and Ysgol Gwenffrwd was opened on 30 May 1949.

In 2006, there were about 1,950 pupils being taught in the schools of Holywell and Greenfield. Some of these children travelled from nearby villages, whilst others travelled to schools out of the district.

Holywell Parish Church Schools [SJ 185 762].
St Winefride's Chapel, adjacent to the Parish Church, was converted into a charity school in 1723.[19 & 52] On 11 January 1728, Mr Ellice Price was appointed as schoolmaster; in Browne Willis's 'Survey of Saint Asaph', he was described as the most eminent schoolmaster in north Wales.[52] Thomas Pennant records that this school provided free education for sixteen boys, and that the master received a salary of £10 p.a. 'The vicar appoints the master, which, as far as I recollect, has been a clergyman, excepting one instance'.[22] By 1762 the school had became a day school known as the Holywell Grammar School at St Winefride's Chapel.[137]

Pennant also wrote that:

> Besides the Sunday School, where the cotton-company's apprentices are instructed, there is another parochial one kept in the chapel over the well. This is supported by a general subscription through the parish, and about seventy poor children are instructed by proper masters, in reading, writing and arithmetick. The copper and brass companies are

St Winefride's Chapel, where the first school in Holywell was established.

handsome subscribers, but they send only a few adults, to be instructed in matters, their more advanced years make them capable of learning.[22]

This closed in 1819 when the National School opened Bryn Celyn.

By 1847, Holywell Grammar School was educating eight boys, all over the age of ten. As with other schools run by religious authorities, the catechism was an important subject. The church still appointed and paid the master.[137] When this school closed has not been established, but it is possible that the pupils were transferred first to a new school opened on Castle Hill just before 1835.

The National School, Bryn Celyn [SJ 1885 768]
A National School was built at Bryn Celyn, opposite the heart of the Greenfield Valley industrial belt, in 1819. The land was obtained from Sir Pyers Mostyn, the builder being Thomas Orme. The project cost £1,160, which included a heating stove and all fixtures and fittings. Its first year's income was derived from donations amounting to £679 17s. 0d., with a further £126 11s. 6s. coming from annual subscriptions.[75] In the first year the school taught 192 boys and 125 girls.[R101] The President was the Earl Grosvenor, the secretary was the Vicar of Holywell and the treasurer was Christopher Smalley. Amongst the committee were the David Pennants (senior and junior), Richard Sankey (senior) and Thomas Harrison. The infamous 1845 *Report on the State of Education in Wales* (known as *Brad y Llyfrau Gleision,* the Treason of the Blue Books) provides a great deal of information about the teachers, pupils and the education provided. As was typical in other schools, the two main teachers (a husband and wife) had only received the most basic of training in a very short period of time — two weeks in this case — but around 100 infants were being taught in a separate room by a mistress who was only seventeen-years old. Her own training had been provided by the other female mistress of the school. When the children attained certain standards, they were transferred to the upper-school in the same building.[137] The first headmaster of this school was Mr J. A. Hope who was appointed in 1889 and stayed there for about ten years. He left Holywell to become ordained and was subsequently rector of Llandegla and vicar of Bodelwyddan. Mr Hope had been the parish church organist and, when he left, his successor as headteacher as well as organist, was Mr Gwilym Morris. After the school closed in 1910, he became head of Greenfield's new school which had been built in School Lane. Bryn Celyn School remained in constant use for ninety-one years. The Parish Council sold the premises for £125; they were later demolished.

Other nineteenth century schools
It would be impossible to provide details of many of the smaller schools which operated in Holywell during the nineteenth century as no records have survived. The various trade directories provide some details as did the 1845 *Report on the State of Education in Wales* which recorded that there were fifteen day-schools, in which children were instructed at the expense of their parents; two boarding-schools, where forty males and ten females were privately educated; eleven Sunday schools,

conducted by volunteer teachers, and in which 2,000 scholars (adults as well as children) received instruction; and a school for Catholics in Well Hill.[117]

Gents Boarding School, Castle Hill
The first record of this appears in *Pigot's Directory* for 1835, naming it as William Skelton's School.[43] By 1844, the premises were listed as Mr Cole's School who, by 1858, had moved to the Collegiate School in Brynford Street.[47] It is possible that this latter school superseded the Castle Hill School, and that there was a link between it and the original grammar school. The land for Castle Hill School being owned by the Parish Church.

The Collegiate Grammar School, Brynford Street
No date has been traced for the opening of this establishment, thus, it is unclear whether or not Mr Cole (who moved there from the Castle Hill School) was the first master. In 1887, the school was listed and advertised in *The Flintshire and Denbighshire Postal Directory*.[43]

Dr Williams's School, Chapel Street, Chapel Schoolroom
Trustees of the Dr Williams Charity were responsible for the administration of this school which, in 1847, had sixty-five pupils. The trustees paid the master, an Independent Minister, £7 p.a. Books and equipment were provided from a fund administered by the trustees. Typical quarterly fees for pupils were between 4s. and 10s. 6d., although some children received a free education which was funded from a £25 endowment.[137]

Pendref Chapel School, Brynford Street
This school had been established by a lady of the district to provide an education for some of the very poor children of the town. Rather uniquely, subscriptions to fund the school were given by people who, in return, received needlework carried out by the pupils. Although the school-mistress was dedicated to teaching, she had had no training.[137]

Hope Cottage School, Pen-y-Maes
This was a private school for about nine young ladies which opened in the early 1830s.[43, 81, & 135]

The Jesuit Seminary, High Street
This seminary was established around 1870, on the site of today's Post Office. Its main purpose was the training of Catholic priests. It remained in use until the early 1930s.

Holywell Union (Lluesty) Workhouse School
This school was for the education of children resident at the Lluesty Workhouse only. Pupil numbers varied from time to time, averaging about sixty children. The

workhouse authorities were at liberty to send children on errands, or to perform duties in the workhouse, during school time.[137]

> Other nineteenth century schools and teachers (list not exhaustive) were:[43]
> Panton Place (Thomas Croft, then Elizabeth Hughes)
> Panton Place (Martha A. Stevens, then Jane Hughes)
> Mount Street (Edward Davies)
> Mount Street/Mount Zion (Daniel Pritchard)
> New Road (Daniel Pritchard)
> Well Street (James Williams then Thomas Croft, then Miss Roleston)
> Well Street, Spring Vale Academy boarding and day school
> New Road Catholic School (James Cavanagh, first Thomas Muldoone, then James Kinder)
> 43 New Road (Mary Jones)
> Bank Court/Place (Ann Edwards, then Susanna Roberts, then Ellen Roberts)
> Whitford Street (Thomas Bagshaw)
> Whitford Street, Fair View House Ladies day and boarding school
> Bagillt Street (Eliza Turner)
> High Street (The Misses Whitehouse)
> The Grove High School (see, also, more detail below)
> Brynford House Collegiate School, first headmaster — Revd Edward Thomas, MA
> Holywell Board School, Brynford Street, headmaster Dan Pierce
> Grammar School in Tower Gardens off High Street, headmaster William Thomas.

Holywell Board School, Halkyn Street [SJ 188 756]
The school building now forms the western part of Ysgol-y-Fron. The original entrance was on Brynford Street, but was later moved to Halkyn Street. The school was run by Mr and Mrs Daniel Pierce. The school-house is now a private residence.

The British School, Halkyn Street [SJ 188 756]
I have not been able to establish exactly when this school was built. However, from various trade directories, it would appear to have been built in the early 1870s. The building was a brick-built, slate-roofed structure, designed by R. Scrivener. The first headteachers were H. M. Nichols and Ellen Nichols.

Holywell Council School/Ysgol-y-Fron [SJ 188 756]
At the beginning of the twentieth century, the County Council had plans prepared for the erection of a new elementary school just to the east of the Holywell Board School. It would appear that the British School building was demolished to make way for the new school. This school, named Holywell Council School, was of red brick with a slated roof, and was built by the Holywell building firm of T. W. Sibeon, and opened in 1904. Although all classes were mixed, separate entrances, cloakrooms and toilets were provided for boys and girls. There are two Second World War brick Air Raid Shelters, with a reinforced concrete roof, to the east and rear of the boy's playground.

During the 1970s the school was renamed Ysgol-y-Fron.

In 2003, a major scheme was undertaken to update and modernise the two buildings in this school. The original British School structure and the later 1904

The original British School (right), part of the 2003 extension to Ysgol-y-Fron and, to the left, is part of the 1904 school.

The Original Spring Gardens School, now re-erected in the Greenfield Valley Heritage Centre.

building were linked by a new modern entrance, reception area and staff room. The closure of the old 1904 entrances meant that a new kitchen could be built with access to the school hall. The hall is now used as an assembly hall, a dining room and a gym. The head teacher's former office, together with the former girls' cloakroom, were converted into storage, toilet areas and a new cloakroom.

The old Board School building now accommodates a modern classroom, a computer room, a special needs classroom, a library and the head teacher's office. All the windows of both former schools were fitted with double glazing and the remaining doorways were modernised. The school now educates approximately 150 pupils.

Spring Gardens Infant School, Well Street [SJ 1855 7605]

This school, with two classrooms and outside toilets, was built off Well Street during 1876/77 on behalf of the Holywell School Board. It was officially opened on Monday, 9 April 1877, when the the first headmistress was Miss Emma Parry who remained in post until her retirement in 1918.[33] In about 1942, the Greyhound Inn, located alongside the school, was demolished and the land converted into use as a school playground. In 1953, due to a severe shortage of space, the school were granted use of the St John Ambulance Headquarters next door which was used as an additional classroom.[12] The school gave service to the younger children of the town until it was closed on 29 September 1961.[12] A new infants' school, Perth-y-Terfyn, had been built on Halkyn Road. For a while after closure, the premises were used for Welsh education, and later as an Adjustment Centre. The building, however, became unusable and it was eventually abandoned. In 1993 it was carefully dismantled and subsequently re-built 'brick-by-brick' in the Greenfield Valley Heritage Park to serve as a valued historic building. It was opened as an additional attraction to visitors on 1 April 1995. The interior retains the old desks and furniture from the original school.

Perth-y-Terfyn Infants School, Halkyn Road [SJ 1885 7552]

Due to the need for a new infants school in Holywell, the County Council purchased Perth y Terfyn House and grounds (meaning 'boundary between town and country') and adjoining land between Halkyn Road and Fron Park Road in the late 1950s. Building work began on the school on 2 May 1960. The school was occupied by 1 October 1961 when the children transferred from Spring Gardens School. All the staff of the old school moved with the children. The official opening ceremony was carried out by Alderman Horace Waterhouse, JP, MBE, with other dignitaries present. The Vicar of Holywell, Revd J. Jenkin Jones, conducted the service.[12] Almost immediately,

Perth-y-Terfyn Infants School.

the school buildings proved to be too small and two classes had to be taken in the main hall. In January 1968, this problem was resolved temporarily by the provision of a mobile classroom. In 1971, work commenced on a two-storey extension which created two new classrooms. This was opened in early 1972. The ground floor room was used as a nursery unit from September 1977.[12]

Roman Catholic Convent School
A decision to establish a convent in Holywell was made in 1859, and on 15 August that year, some of the Sisters of Charity of St Paul came to the town and set up a convent in two dwellings named Loyola Cottages. In 1869, a large house was bought which had been built on the site of the Cross Keys in Well Street [SJ 1855 760]. This was converted into a private convent and boarding school for Catholic children.[47] The convent became the only fee-paying school in Holywell and continued to provide a very high standard of education for both Catholic and non-Catholic female children for over ninety years until a new purpose-built convent was built behind Gerddi Beuno in Whitford Street. The establishments were always run by the Catholic authorities and not the County Council. During its latter years, the old convent began to admit male pupils. The move to the new convent took place during 1965 and the Well Street building was subsequently pulled down.

The second convent school served the Holywell district until the early 1980s when, because of the reduced number of pupils attending, it was forced to close and the County Council bought the premises and site. In January 1985, Ysgol Gwenffrwd moved from the building which they shared with St Winefride's School in Whitford Street to the convent building where they have remained ever since.

New Road Catholic School (Ava Maria Hall) [SJ 1847 7610]
When erected around 1830, this school was known as the New Road Catholic School. Its first headmaster was Mr James Cavanagh.[43] Although it continued to provide

Holywell Convent, c.1909.

education until a replacement school was built in 1895, no other details of it have survived. After its closure, the building served as a Catholic youth centre and, in later years, was the home of a thriving scout group.

In early 2006, major reconstruction work started on the premises in order to convert it into a residence for the Bridgettine Nuns of the Most Holy Saviour of St Bridget, who are responsible for running the modernised hospice just further up New Road.

St Winefride's Catholic School, New Road [SJ 1846 7613]
The building was erected 'by Rev. Father Charles Beauclerk, S.J. , in 1895'. Built when Catholicism in Holywell was experiencing great advancement, including visiting pilgrims, the premises were intended to serve as a parish room as well as a Catholic children's school. A Catholic School, which had existed in New Road since at least 1830, may have been the forerunner of this school.

The primary school was very active until it closed in early 1975.

St Winefride's Roman Catholic Primary School and Ysgol Gwenffrwd [SJ 183 761]
A new dual-purpose school was opened off Whitford Street on 3 March 1975, built partially on the grounds of the former residence named Pendre. It was quite unique for Holywell in that it catered for the primary education of two sets of children: those of St Winefride's Catholic School, as well as those from Ysgol Gwenffrwd, the Welsh medium school. The official opening was performed by Councillor David Schwarz, JP, on 17 September 1975.

The respective schools were, as far as possible, run independently of each other, however, from the start, it was obvious that the open-plan building was too small for the number of children and mobile classrooms had to be provided. Sharing the hall and dining facilities caused additional problems.

Outside school hours, the building acts as a community centre mainly for Catholics. In January 1985, the pupils and staff of Ysgol Gwenffrwd moved to the empty convent building adjoining its grounds.

St Winefride's School now has seven classrooms — one is an early year's unit, two are for infants and the other four are for the juniors. Besides the hall, which also doubles up as a dining room, there is a kitchen, rooms for the head-teacher and secretary, and a staff-room.

Ysgol Gwenffrwd
Holywell's first Welsh school was opened on 30 May 1949. A nursery school, with just eight pupils, it met in the vestry of Rehoboth Chapel under the auspices of Mr W. E. Williams, head teacher of [then] Halkyn Street Council School. It was named after the Holywell born poet, Thomas Lloyd Jones, who used 'Gwenffrwd' as his *nom-de-plume*.

Within three years, the number of pupils had increased significantly and accommodation was found for them in the old Halkyn Road School building until

Ysgol Gwenffrwd.

1958 when they moved for two years to a concrete-structured building adjacent to the Grammar School. Pupil numbers continued to increase and, because the Spring Gardens school had became vacant, Ysgol Gwenffrwd moved into the building; they remained there until a brand new school campus was opened off Whitford Street on 3 March 1975. This housed two distinct schools; the Catholic St Winefride's Primary School, the other was the Welsh Ysgol Gwenffrwd. Whilst the 'open plan' structure had some advantages, there proved to be difficulties with two schools sharing. The Welsh pupil intake continued to grow and, eventually, in January 1985, Ysgol Gwenffrwd moved into the premises of the old Catholic Convent at the top of Whitford Street.[136] Six moves into different buildings in thirty-six years — some record! Happily, Ysgol Gwenffrwd has now become firmly established in its present environment and there are some 200 children aged between four and eleven being educated there. The school has latterly been classified as a Welsh Medium Community Primary School.

Holywell County School, later Holywell Grammar School latterly Holywell (Lower) High School, Pen-y-Maes [SJ 189 759]
As a result of the 1889 Act, Flintshire County Council voted to establish a new county school in Holywell for pupils aged eleven and over. A subscription list, to which the Duke of Westminster was a generous benefactor, was opened in 1890. In 1895, a site was acquired from the Earl of Denbigh to the north-east of Pen-y-Maes Road. From the four tenders submitted, the building contract was given to T. W. Sibeon of Holywell, at a price not exceeding £3,283. The building, when completed, consisted of a main hall, two classrooms, a teachers' room and toilet facilties. However, because of the urgent need for such an education facility, the Town Council agreed to a request to lease out the Town Hall from 15 September 1896 at a rent of £35 p.a. Boys only were taught at first, at an annual fee of £6. The new school was opened in 1898, when there were mixed classes. The first headmaster was Mr J. C. Davies (of London) who was later appointed Director of Education for Denbighshire. From the start, the

Holywell County School, early 1900s, before any extensions.

school proved to be too small and new wings were added which were officially opened in 1927. Further major extensions, which included a new school-hall, gymnasium and dining hall, were made in the middle 1930s at a cost of £26,500.[4]

During the Second World War years, a group of Belgian children were evacuated to the district and school facilities were provided for them in the County School gym and the adjoining corridor.

As a result of the 1944 Education Act, those children who passed the eleven plus examination were able to go to a Grammar School free of charge. The title of Holywell County School was changed to Holywell Grammar School in September 1945 and the catchment area covered Oakenholt, along the coast to Ffynnongroew as well as all the country areas between Trelogan, Caerwys, Lixwm and Halkyn.

From September 1967, further changes meant that no distinction should be made between children's ability — which had, since 1945, split secondary education into Grammar and Secondary Modern schools. As the years passed, extensions were made to the Basingwerk School, resulting in all pupils being taught there [see below], and the old Lower High School was closed and it was demolished during the spring of 1994 and the site sold for housing development. The County Council retained the playing fields for the recreational purposes of the High School, as well as the public in general.

Holywell (Basingwerk) Secondary Modern School, the Strand [SJ 190 763]
Construction work for this school started in 1949 by builders Alun Edwards & Co of Cefn-y-Bedd. Because of the gradient of the land, the building has five levels, and, in one block, two storeys. There were twenty classrooms, plus a gymnasium, central

Holywell High School

hall, canteen, staff rooms and toilet blocks. The building cost was £204,843.[48] The school was opened for pupils, aged eleven and over on 5 January 1954. Due to the introduction of comprehensive education in September 1967, Basingwerk School was renamed Holywell Upper High School and all pupils, between the ages of eleven and thirteen were taught here, before being transferred to Holywell Upper High School (the former Grammar School). Additions were made to the school in:

    1976 — three science laboratories.
    1982 — a chemistry laboratory.
    1990 — an additional block of classrooms.

After the 1990 extensions, all pupils aged eleven and over were educated in the Upper High School and the Lower High School closed and the name of the school was again changed, this time to Holywell High School. The catchment area also changed and pupils living in Ffynnongroew and Flint went to the schools in Prestatyn and Flint. New Welsh-medium high schools in Mold and St Asaph, and the Roman Catholic Blessed Richard Gwyn School in Flint also reduced the intake of Holywell High School.

Flintshire Technical College
This was opened in September 1954 at Kelsterton, Connah's Quay, having been built on a forty-acre green-field site at a cost of £600,000, with the aim of providing technical and commercial education for pupils who had completed their education at the county's grammar and secondary schools, and who would not be staying on at such schools to try to attain admission into universities. This naturally included pupils from Holywell and Greenfield. As time passed, pupils also went to Llandrillo and Wrexham Technical Colleges.

Greenfield School.

The County Primary School, Greenfield. [SJ 191 774]
Construction of this school commenced in 1909 to replace the old Abbey Schoolroom as well as the Bryn Celyn National School. It was opened on 5 September 1910.

The school provided Greenfield with continuous primary education for children between the ages of four and eleven. After the Second World War, the expansion in local housing meant that the school became overcrowed and an additional separate building for the younger pupils had to be provided lower down School Lane. This also acted as a school canteen. In addition, to promote outdoor sporting activities, a field was used opposite Fulbrook Avenue, which meant that the school was split over three sites. Naturally, by the end of the twentieth century, it became obvious that Greenfield needed a new school. On 18 July 2003, the old school closed, and the new school, Ysgol Maes Glas, opened on 2 September 2003.

Ysgol Maes Glas, Community Primary School, Greenfield [SJ 192 777]
Work on the building of a new primary school at the northern end of the large School Lane housing estate commenced during 2002 and it was opened on 2 September 2003 at an overall cost of £3,200,000. Flintshire County Council architect Andrew Garner, designed the school and the builders were Felton Construction of New Ferry.[46]

It was officially opened on Monday, 22 September 2003 by Mr John Clutton, Flintshire's Director of Education, Children's Services and Recreation, who also unveiled a commemorative plaque. The head teacher of the old primary school, Mr Peter Roach, held the same post at Ysgol Maes Glas. Accommodating 200 pupils, it has ten classrooms, an early years unit, a stand-alone computer suite, a library, a dual purpose school hall/dining room, a kitchen, toilet facilities and staff accommodation. Externally, the play areas are split into three – one each for nursery, infant and junior children. Car parking areas are included in the grounds for staff and visitors, as well as parents bringing their children to school by car.

Chapter 7

Businesses, Licensed Premises, Residences

A walk along Holywell's High Street and its adjoining streets will quickly reveal numerous old buildings, most of them being either two or three storeyed structures, some of which date back to at least the seventeenth century. The Holywell Townscape Heritage Initiative (THI), which has been run by Flintshire County Council since September 2001, has revealed a great deal of new evidence about the history of Holywell e.g.

- there is evidence of medieval origins in more than one structure.
- stonework, old brickwork, hidden window frames and wooden features have been uncovered which give us a far better understanding of what the town was like during the last five centuries.
- at least one of Holywell's surviving buildings is of a wooden structure.

Whilst it is far beyond the remit of this book to give detail of all finds and work done by the THI some of the more significant discoveries made by the THI project are given later in this chapter.

The eighteenth century witnessed a growth in leadmining, quarrying and coalmining in the districts adjacent to Holywell which led to the development of shops and business premises in the town. Additionally, there was an increased demand for accommodation for the growing numbers of pilgrims visiting St Winefride's Well. It would not be possible to detail the history of all the buildings in the town but an effort is made to record the history of those premises which housed significant businesses such as banking, hotels and inns, as well as the older shop buildings.

Many large residences have been built in the Holywell and Greenfield area, some dating back to at least the fifteenth century. Some were built by local gentry families such as the Mostyns, the Pennants and the Pantons, whilst others were built by the owners of industrial premises, especially from the Greenfield Valley. Some of the surviving houses have been adapted for other use. Again it would not be possible to write about all of these, but a selection follows.

Banks

The North Wales Bank
This was the first bank established in Holywell and an entry for it appears in the *Universal Directory* of 1790 when its main business involved receiving monies in and the settling of bills for local industrialists and traders. Richard Sankey (senior), the owner of the Englefield Colliery, was one of the partners, others being members of the Oldfield and Oakley families (who were involved in coal and lead mining) and Thomas Jones, a local ironmonger.[126] By the late 1790s, the bank had changed its name to the Flintshire Bank. In 1811, because of the shortage of notes and coins caused by the Napoleonic Wars, token coins were issued by the bank. By the early 1820s, Richard Sankey was the sole proprietor. The bank was sited in Bank Court [SJ 1863 757590], later re-named Bank Place, where further buildings were subsequently added.

The North & South Wales Bank (later the Wales Bank)
This was established in Liverpool in 1836 and acquired a number of established country banks. In July 1837, Richard Sankey agreed to the take-over of the Flintshire Bank by the Wales Bank for which he received 200 shares (then worth about £1,000) plus an annuity of £500. He also carried out the work of local bank director for them.

The Holywell Savings Bank [SJ 1878 7571], later named the Actuary Saving Bank
This was established at Maes-y-Dre, Coleshill Street, on 30 January 1818 with Christopher Smalley as the treasurer. Smalley died in 1829 but the Savings Bank continued, and whilst the date of closure has not been established, it was still in being in 1886 when the treasurer was the Earl of Denbigh. At that time, it opened every Friday between 12.00 noon and 3.00 p.m. Note that this was not the National Savings Bank which was operated by the General Post Office.

The Holywell Bank [SJ 1862 7588]
Notable in the rapid growth of the area's textile industry were two families, named Douglas and Smalley, who had come to Holywell from Manchester and Preston. Around 1820, Douglas, Smalley & Company set up the Holywell Bank and issued

A £5 banknote issued by the Holywell Bank.

their own bank notes, which were signed by John Smalley's son, Christopher. They also set up a branch in Mold. Smalley died in 1829 and the business collapsed in 1839.

The 1833 map of Holywell by John Woods shows the Holywell Bank sited at 20 High Street (one of two buildings joined, in recent years, to form Iceland Frozen Foods). John Douglas died in 1838, and his surviving partners went into bankruptcy in 1840. The Wales Bank then acquired the business and moved their existing business from Bank Court to the premises at 20 High Street, becoming tenants of Philip Pennant. For the next seventy years the Wales Bank prospered and was a very important and familiar feature of the Holywell business scene. Major customers included the Holywell Level Silver & Lead Mining Co., the Talacre Mining Company and Adam Eyton, lead miner, of Llanerch-y-Môr (who was also one of the bank's directors). As for the Holywell Level Company, A. H. Dodd in his book *The Industrial Revolution in North Wales* reported that, in 1818, the company were turning over about £130,000 per annum. [2006, £4,912,700] – a massive figure for those days, and evidence of the important role that local banks were playing. By 1870, the Holywell branch of the Wales Bank was listed in the top ten branches outside Liverpool.

In April 1871, the White Horse Inn, over the road at 17 High Street, was put up for sale and the Wales Bank bought the building at a cost of £700. Local builder, Thomas Hughes of Brynford Street, converted the building into a bank and office for £890. The bank then moved there in 1872. In 1892, they purchased additional land at the rear of the premises.

The Midland Bank Company [SJ 1858 7592]
In 1836, the Birmingham & Midland Bank Company had been founded in Birmingham. From the beginning, the company used the title the Midland Bank and, despite mergers, continued to be known as such for many years. They extended their network of branches throughout Britain, coming to Holywell in 1908 as the London City & Midland Bank, buying out the Wales Bank. Although the business has remained there ever since, there have been many changes. In 1923, the building underwent major refurbishment and extension, which included removing the original ornate stone porch entrance from the centre of the building's frontage and erecting a new stone entrance porch to the right of the front. Part of the additional land to the rear was utilized to enlarge the premises.

Within the building, the passing years have also witnessed many changes and, on the two floors above, many other companies have rented office space (accessed from a side-entrance on old Station Road. In 1951, the premises was given a Grade II listing.[44] Although the Midland Bank group was acquired by the International Banking concern HSBC in 1992, the title Midland Bank was retained until 1999. In 1995, the interior was transformed with further changes being made in 2002. Outside, the original familiar railings and wall were dismantled and a ramp installed to allow access for disabled people to the exterior cash dispenser unit.

From 1936 until 1980 there was a sub-branch of the Midland Bank in Greenfield [SJ 1997 7721] opposite Peniel Chapel.

The National Provincial Bank of England
This bank opened a branch in Holywell in December 1839. Their Rotation Committee minutes of 12 December 1839 stated that Mr Griffiths of Bangor 'desired to arrange a house at Holywell and make it known that a branch of the Company will be opened there'. The branch must have opened almost immediately because the board minutes of 24 December 1839 recorded that the manager of Holywell should take action on a certain matter. From their records it appears that they first occupied 19 Panton Place (note that the numbering of the houses in Panton Place has changed over the years). In the Ordnance Survey map of 1870, the bank site is shown as being 44 High Street [SJ 1864 7583] when the adjoining Panton Place premises housed the Post Office. It is believed that 44 High Street has its origins from 1816 when Paul Panton (junior) established Panton Place – it being the corner building on the west side, opposite Panton House on the eastern corner. Later records show that, in 1897, the bank was still leasing 19 Panton Place. In 1905, they also leased 20 Panton Place.

In 1921, the National Provincial Bank obtained the freehold of both those premises and, together with 44 High Street, the buildings were referred to as the United Bank & Bank House. A photograph, taken between 1900 and 1910, shows that besides the front entrance in High Street, the bank also had an imposing side entrance with a porch in Panton Place. The doors and windows of 19 & 20 Panton Place were still in being at this time but, at some later date, they were bricked up and the bank utilised the interiors as part of the 44 High Street premises. The side entrance from Panton Place is now non-existent. Certainly, in the twentieth century, the entrance to Bank House was from the west side of the building, although the managers ceased to live in it from the early 1970s. In 1918, the merging of banks led to the name being changed to the National Provincial & Union Bank of England but, in 1924, the name was shortened to the National Provincial Bank. This title remained until 1968 when the Westminster Bank, the National Provincial Bank and the District Bank merged on 1 January 1970 to form the National Westminster Bank. From 2 December 1996, the branch lost its own site-resident manager but the business continued to operate with a customer service manager. In 1982, the building was listed as Grade II.[44]

The National Provincial Bank, c.1900–10 (note the manager's original entrance and bay-window on the Panton Place side; also the cobble stones and the gas light).

The National Provincial Bank had a sub-branch in Greenfield [SJ 1852 7770], opposite the Holywell road junction, for many years until its closure around 1975.

Barclays Bank
This bank opened its first branch in Holywell on 7 November 1921 in Hyfrydle, Victoria Square [SJ 1871 7579]. The building was the first on the right-hand side of Brynford Street, and extended for forty-two feet up the street from the corner of Victoria Square (i.e. the two premises currently used by St Kentigern's Hospice Charity Shop and the Clifton Dry Cleaners). Interestingly, when the bank took occupation, the outline plan of the building showed a front brick boundary wall with railings and the manager's office with a bay-window jutting out to the pavement. The manager's living accommodation was on the first floor. The actual lease for the premises had been taken out on 24 June 1921 from local builder George Pierce. His company, George Pierce & Sons, carried out the structural alterations to enable the bank to commence business there.

On 3 June 1925, Barclays decided to purchase the freehold of the Post Office premises at 48 High Street, [SJ 1866 7581], for the sum of £2,000, from M. Ll. Price. Alterations to the building were necessary and, again, George Pierce & Sons carried out the work. The cost was £2,700. With work complete, Barclays moved in on 30 September 1927, and have traded there ever since. For many years, the first floor was used as offices by an accountancy firm. The bank later utilised the whole building themselves, until the mid 1990s when they reverted to carrying out customer business and their own office work on the ground floor only. Over the years, various internal alterations have been made. Perhaps the most significant development in the bank's operations was the change in the management structure during the 1990s which meant that the branch no longer had its own site manager. There is, however, a branch customers service manager.

Friendly Societies
Really a very early form of modern insurance companies, friendly societies were established to protect members from debts caused through illness, death or old age. To be able to receive any benefit, a person would have to join the society and pay a fee, usually weekly or monthly. The popularity of friendly societies became more widespread during the nineteenth century. In Holywell, the first friendly society office opened at Maes-y-Dre, Coleshill Street, just before 1840. Other branches in the town soon followed.

Building Societies
Nationally, the 1930s was the era when building societies really came into prominence. The prime reason for their existance was to lend money to people for house purchase by way of a mortgage. To enable the system to work, people were invited to invest money with a society and, in return, an investor would receive a competitive rate of interest. In the late 1930s, the first society to open a branch in

Holywell was the Bradford Permanent Building Society under the control of local estate agent, Arthur Roberts. Many other societies have since opened (and closed) in the town. In recent years, building societies have entered into direct competition with banks and insurance companies by offering the public an increased number of financial incentives and services.

The Holywell Credit Union
The definition of a credit union is 'a co-operative organisation that makes loans to its members at low interest rates'. The basis of how much a member can borrow naturally depends on how much they have paid in. Such monies are invested elsewhere by the credit union, thus the fund attracts interest and consequently funds build up and larger loans can be made.

Holywell became the first town in Flintshire to open a credit union branch when, in 1989, the Holywell Council of Churches realised that such a facility would be helpful to people who were not in the habit of opening either a bank or building society savings account. A local committee of fifteen people was formed and rules were set up in accordance with national guidelines. That July, collection centres were opened in the schoolrooms of Tabernacle Church, Coleshill Street and Alpha Chapel, Greenfield. Soon, the popularity of the system meant that it was possible to convert an empty shop in Cross Street into a suitable office. In latter years, the branch has moved to a site opposite the old Town Hall.

By the late 1990s, other credit union branches had opened in Flintshire and it was decided to create the All Flintshire Credit Union, which had representatives on its committee from each branch.

Hotels, Inns and Beer Houses
During the nineteenth century, the town and surrounding district had a great many licensed premises — in 1874 there were thirty-one recorded as being in business in the High Street and the adjoining roads.

White Horse Hotel, 17 High Street [was SJ 1858 7592]
Over time, these premises have also been known as the Golden Lion and the Royal. It is believed that the premises were built around 1750. Three storeys high, it was a large hotel for those days, providing accommodation for local industrialists and their visitors. The 1800s also saw the hotel develop as one of the main posting houses on the London to Holyhead stage-coach route, where horses could be changed and travellers refreshed. Perhaps the most important person to visit the White Horse was the thirteen-year-old Princess Victoria, who stopped here in 1830, accompanied by the Duke of Sussex, en-route from Anglesey to Chester. Edward Parry's *Royal Visits & Progresses to Wales* (1850) gives a vivid description of the tumultuous welcome conveyed to her in the town.

Until it was outlawed in 1822, the annual county cockfight took place here as well as many dances and social functions, such as those for the annual Holywell Hunt

Society during the weeks of the Holywell Races at Pantasaph and the annual fund-raising ball for the Holywell Dispensary.

In April 1871, the hotel was put up for sale and the Wales Bank bought the building. The building was given a Grade II listing in 1951.[44]

The Feathers Inn, Whitford Street [SJ 1847 7593]
Built in 1796, this three-storey inn is now the oldest surviving licensed premises in Holywell. The date, 1796, is a notable feature in darker brick on its side wall in Pen-y-Ball Street. The present side-entrance is believed to have been the first main entrance, and the western part of the building would have had other uses – as John Wood's 1833 map indicates. During the first half of the twentieth century there was an independent business unit to the west side (in Whitford Street) where a gents' hairdressing and umbrella business (later a shop) was run. Behind that, part of the building provided rented accommodation. The inn was listed Grade II in 1991.[44]

The Hotel Victoria, Victoria Square [SJ 1871 758]
Built in 1837, these premises have a dominant position at the east end of High Street.[44] Originally named The King's Arms Posting House the hotel had extensive coaching facilities and served as a stage-coach changing station for many years. Cottages which originally flanked it on either side were demolished when Coleshill Street and Halkyn Street were constructed. The hotel itself is three storey, with a slated roof and a five-bay front elevation with quoins and decorative features, as well as an almost full front stone porch, above which is a first-storey balcony.

In 1897, to celebrate Queen Victoria's Diamond Jubilee, the premises were renamed the Hotel Victoria. The old stables were demolished in 1956 and the site, along with associated land, was used for a new bus-station, complete with a road connecting Coleshill Street and Halkyn Street. During 1986, extensive alterations and modernisations were carried out to the interior of the premises. The hotel was listed Grade II in 1991.[44]

The King's Head Hotel, High Street [SJ 1870 758]
Built in the early part of the nineteenth century, this three-storey hotel also served as a coaching house, having stables and a coach house to the rear (behind which there was for many years a bowling green). The front of the hotel has a central porch with a first-floor balcony above. In the twentieth century, the Cyclist's Touring Club appointed the premises as a Holywell venue and, in later years, the AA and the RAC gave it a two-star grading. After the opening of the railway station at Greenfield in 1848, a horse-drawn coach passenger service ran there from the hotel. When motor vehicles replaced horse transport, the stables were converted and used as a motor garage and service centre. The building was listed Grade II in 1991.[44] In 1989, the hotel closed for business and, together with the buildings and land at the rear, a building developer purchased them and rebuilt the hotel interior, converting it into flats. A new block of flats was also constructed to the rear.

The King's Head Hotel taken from an 1873 billhead.

The Cross Keys Hotel, 26 High Street [SJ 1887 7586]
Whilst the date of the original hotel has not been established, it does appear on John Wood's 1833 map of Holywell. It was rebuilt in 1871 and had a coaching entrance to its rear from the western side. Four years later, the town's free-standing clock was erected on the adjoining pavement. The hotel closed in 1958 and estate agent, S. H. Brown, purchased the premises. In January 1983, the estate agents Molyneux bought the premises and closed the wide side-entrance, thus enlarging the ground floor business area.[128] On the front east side, they created a separate shop which was rented out to florists.

The Red Lion, 28 High Street [SJ 1887 7586]
This three-storey late-Georgian building was erected in the early nineteenth century and has been in constant use as licensed premises. It had a one-storey entrance porch and, until the middle of the twentieth century, had a figure of a red lion standing upon it (this was replaced by a new one in 2006). To the left of the building is an entry which originally led to the rear of the dwellings on the west side of Panton Place and which was used by the mail coaches.[44] It would seem likely that the passengers from the coaches would have used the facilities of the Red Lion. The premises were Grade II listed in 1951.[44]

Ye Olde Boar's Head Inn, 19 High Street, now Disraeli's Inn [SJ 1859 7591]
This inn could possibly be the oldest surviving licensed premises in the town. During major renovation in 2003 under the auspices of the Holywell THI scheme, it was discovered that the inn could have originally been of wooden construction and was substantially reconstructed sometime in the mid eighteenth century; further refurbishment took place in the late nineteenth century. Between 1912 and 1914, the premises were extended to take in part of the next door premises.

In 2003, the property was completely refurbished by the owners, Burtonwood Brewery, to the tune of £300,000 and with the aid of the THI. On re-opening in December 2003, the name was changed to Disraeli's Inn.

The Royal Oak, Bryn Celyn [SJ 1875 7562]
Listed Grade II in 1976, this building has a cruck-frame which is believed to date back to the sixteenth century.[44] It was enlarged, possibly in two stages, in the late Georgian period when a long, red-brick transverse-range was added. The structure has two-storeys and is slate roofed.[44] This may originally have been a private dwelling, but became a public house in 1776. By the early 1920s, it had closed as a licensed house and reverted to being a private dwelling until 1980, when it was left vacant. W. Hall & Son (Holywell) Ltd, whose mineral works are next door to it, purchased the dilapidated building and, after a three-year restoration programme, it re-opened as a public house in April 1987.[127]

Hotels and Inns in Greenfield
The oldest surviving inn in Greenfield is the Ship (known locally as the Gletch after a nearby stream, possibly the one which flows under the main road between what was Peniel Chapel and Courtaulds N°. 1 Unit canteen), sited off the main A548 road to Bagillt. This is believed to date back to the early nineteenth century.

Until the mid 1930s, the Crown & Anchor stood on the Mostyn side of the junction of the road from Holywell and the main coast road. It had been a two-storeyed establishment and had four bedrooms.

At the eastern side of the junction of Station Road and the A548 stood the three-storeyed Royal Hotel which had been built in the early eighteenth century. The premises are believed to have closed c.1910.

Of the smaller inns, another four served Greenfield and Bryn Celyn, namely the Swan & Station, the Liverpool Arms, the Plough Inn and the Alexandra Inn.

Today, the only licensed premises in Greenfield are the Packet House and the Queens Head.

General Businesses and Shops
Printing and newspapers
Master-printers became prominent in Wales during the latter part of the eighteenth century and the first to establish himself in Holywell was Edward Carnes in early 1796. His first publications were a Welsh periodical series entitled *Y Geirgrawn*. He became well known and his 1823 publication *Blodeu-Gerdd Cymry ... Treffynnon* was hailed as a credit to the craft. In 1811, he printed *A Selection of the New Version of the Psalms of David* for use in the parish church. *Pigot's Directory* for 1828 showed his office as being in Whitford Street. The same directory also stated that a William Carnes worked in Well Street as a bookbinder — perhaps he was either a brother or son? Edward Carnes died of typhus fever on 25 May 1828, aged 56.[125]

The *Flintshire Observer, Mining Journal & General Advertiser* was the first newspaper to be printed in Holywell having been established in January 1855, by a Mr Davies. It was prepared and printed from a long building at the back of 8 High Street [SJ 1853

7592] with a general newsagents and stationery shop operating at the front. Like *The County Herald*, it was published every Friday morning. In 1913, one of their reporters, Frederick Eyton Morris, purchased the shop and printing business stock with goodwill for £27 and, with the help of his sister, carried on the business until he died in 1918. Although his nephew, William Catherwood, inherited the business, he did not continue printing the *Flintshire Observer*.[43 & 127] The shop continued to trade in the ownership of Mr & Mrs Catherwood until their retirement in 1963.

The F*lintshire County Herald*. Because of the important role, and the length of time that this newspaper was published, the following deliberately detailed history of it is given:

Peter Maelor Evans was born near Adwy'r Clawdd (Coedpoeth, near Wrexham) on 10 April 1817. After his final schooling at Ruthin Grammar School, he planned to make a career for himself in law but, instead joined a Mold printing and publishing firm which became Lloyd & Evans. In 1838, the business set up an office in London House Yard, just off the High Street in Holywell and Peter moved to Holywell to live. He immediately became a staunch member of Rehoboth Welsh Calvinistic Methodist Chapel in Whitford Street and, in 1844, was appointed a deacon there. In 1848, John Lloyd left the business and moved to Liverpool causing the closure of the Mold office. In the same year, Evans married Mary Kerfoot, the third daughter of the notable James Kerfoot of Faenol Bach, near Abergele. Peter and Mary had four sons and one daughter. Their family home was Strand House.[131]

His business flourished and he published the Welsh commentary on the Old Testament by James Hughes, and he began publishing *Y Drysorfa*, as well as *Y Traethodydd* and he was given printing work to do for the Calvinistic Methodist Association of North Wales. Needing an apprentice, he employed John Lloyd, of Pen-y-Maes Road.[81] In the early 1850s, James Kerfoot Evans, Peter's second son, joined him in the business and the company title changed to P. M. Evans & Son. The company prospered, but, unfortunately, Peter died on 29 May 1878, following an accident in Aberystwyth, were he was attending the General Assembly of the Presbytery as representative of the Flintshire *Cyfarfod Misol*[81] and James continued the business.[43]

In the early 1880s, a decision was made to launch a newspaper, named *The County Herald*, in opposition to *The Flintshire Observer, Mining Journal & General Advertiser*. P. M. Evans & Son acquired a two-storey building in Spring Gardens, between the rear of the Midland Bank and Well Street which housed the printing presses and served to house the staff directly involved in the paper's production. At first, the type was laboriously set by hand for every edition. The company took over 15 High Street at the rear of the printing works, using the ground floor as a shop from where they sold *The County Herald*, as well as general stationery. The first and second floors housed their offices.

The first edition of the weekly *County Herald* went on sale on the first Friday of January 1883, with eight large pages, it was priced at 1*d*. In those days there were few national daily newspapers, thus both the *County Herald* and the *Flintshire Observer* carried not only local news covering a wide area of Flintshire, but also items of news relating to national and international events. James Kerfoot Evans was politically a Liberal while Mr Davies of the *Observer* was Conservative and their political views were reflected in their advertising posters which were yellow and blue respectively.[129] Supplies of the newspaper to outlying districts were usually made by pony and trap.

On 1 March 1915, the company became P. M. Evans & Son Ltd, with James serving as the managing director.[129] and the senior compositor, John Lloyd, as a director. Also around this time, the company moved from High Street to 4 Well Street, from where the retail sales and office work were carried out. The initial financing of the new paper was a problem which was overcome by the sale of shares to the public — especially by Liberals.

On 10 June 1917, James Kerfoot Evans died and was buried in Brynford Parish Churchyard, alongside his wife Ethel Jemina, who had died on her thirty-first birthday in 1887.[130] Tom Stillings, who hailed from Pudsey, Yorkshire, became the new controlling shareholder. However, whilst he paid visits to Holywell, it was his son, George, who moved to the town and was appointed manager of the business. The first improvement they made in the printing of the paper was to introduce linotype machines whereby lines of type were put into column form in a metal frame, which made up the page size. This change speeded up the production of the paper considerably. George Stillings died in 1935, and his son, Thomas moved to live in Holywell and assumed overall control of the business until his death in 1940.[129] The following years were difficult because of the Second World War and the paper had to be reduced to just four pages. Production, however, still went ahead every week, and the paper proved to be more popular than ever.

In 1950, the title of the paper was changed to *The Flintshire County Herald*, and demand for the paper was still strong. Mr Stillings sold the printing side of the business to *The Chester Chronicle* and Associated Newspapers Ltd in July 1960. The new owners retained all the staff, under the supervision of Mr Stillings, until he retired in 1962. The Thompson organisation purchased the capital of the *Chester Chronicle*, including *The Flintshire County Herald*, in March 1965.[129] Unfortunately for the Holywell printing staff, a decision was made to print the paper in Chester from November 1965. The office staff, reporters and editorial staff remained based in Holywell in the old printing building until May 1967 when they transferred to Well Street and the old Spring Gardens building was demolished.

The move to Chester brought about immediate changes. The first edition from there was on a rotary press, and the number of pages was increased from eight to twelve. The following February witnessed yet another change when the front page, which had always been full of adverts, was turned over to news.[129] In July 1966 the newspaper was produced on a new web-offset press which gave the paper better picture reproduction.[129]

The day eventually came when the company decided to merge *The Flintshire County Herald* into the Flint and Denbigh edition of *The Chester Chronicle*; the last issue of the *County Herald* being produced on 1 March 1968. The paper had been printed weekly without a break for eighty-five years — including the difficult times of two world wars. Indeed, if the opening years of the P. M. Evans printing business in 1838 are added, there had been just over 130 years of service to the public.

The Flint and Denbigh edition of *The Chester Chronicle* had varying district editions printed each week until August 2006 when it was renamed *The Flintshire Chronicle*, encompassing all the Flintshire districts.

The Holywell Record was another paper published and printed in the town. The editor was a Mr Hochheimer who ran the business from 3 Bank Place. It commenced business in the May 1896 and its content concentrated on the events of the Catholic Community. As mentioned in the chapter dealing with religion, 'Baron Corvo' became involved in its business, with the unfortunate sequel that the magazine had to close down during the summer of 1898.[97]

A. Schwarz & Sons, 4 & 6 Whitford Street
This jewellery and clock-making business was established in 1864 by Antony Schwarz, who had come to live in Holywell from Baden Baden in the Black Forest of Germany. The family has served the local population continuously ever since from the same premises. Although they now provide an optometrist service, over the years they have also concentrated on the sale of fancy goods and jewellery. In addition they became renowned for their sales and service of clocks and watches (when Carmel Welsh C.M. Chapel opened in 1900 they had their wall mounted clock supplied by the company — and it has been in continuous use to the present day). In the latter part of the twentieth century, the family ceased to trade in retail goods and concentrated solely on the optician side of the business.

John Sibeon & Sons
This is a very well-known and respected business in the Holywell area and can be traced back to a Thomas Sibeon who lived at Calcot, Brynford, from *c.*1768 to 1822. Thomas Whitefoot Sibeon founded a joinery business in Holywell. Although born in Liverpool on 19 January 1834, where his father had moved following his marriage, Thomas came to work in Holywell as a self-employed joiner around the age of twenty and, on 24 April 1860, married Sarah Stephenson, a Holywell lady from another well-known local family. Although married in Liverpool they lived in Holywell. One of their four children, John Joseph Sibeon, was born in Holywell in 1864 and joined his father in what was proving to be a fast expanding building and contracting business. He had built his own residence, Aughton House, alongside his business workshop, near the top of Brynford Street. They were fortunate to secure a number of good contracts in the town, the earliest being awarded by the Board of Guardians of the Union Workhouse for an extension to Lluesty Workhouse. That contract also included the building of a chapel there. In the mid 1890s, they won the contract to build the first part of Holywell County School. Thomas died in 1898 and his son, John, took control of the business and some of the building contracts awarded to the firm included: Holywell Council School, Halkyn Street; the extension to St Winefride's

Church, Well Street; Holywell Cottage Hospital; the Territorial Drill Hall, Halkyn Street, and possibly the Masonic Hall, Coleshill Street.

William, John Sibeon's son, served a joinery apprenticeship at the Holywell Textile Mill and then joined his father in the family business which became J. Sibeon & Son As general bulding and contracting declined, the firm concentrated more on joinery work and became funeral directors. John Joseph Sibeon died in 1948 but his grandson, Thomas Whitefoot Sibeon, who was a qualified joiner, worked in the business. Tom focussed the business solely on undertaking until his death in 1996 when it passed into the control of his son, Paul. In the early 1990, a branch was opened in Flint and a chapel of rest was built in their own grounds at Holywell.

Exchange House, 4 & 6 High Street [SJ 1853 7591]

Discoveries over the last fifty years have proved that this building played an extremely important role in market trading in Holywell dating back to medieval times. In 1702, this three-storey Queen Anne property, with a high hipped roof, was rebuilt and the date 1702 appears above the first floor centre window. Also of interest externally are the three carved figure-heads on the keystones of the first floor windows. From the latter part of the twelfth century Holywell had developed into perhaps the most prominent market town in north Wales. In the seventeenth and eighteenth centuries goods and livestock of all descriptions were brought to the town for trading and this building was probably the nerve centre for a great part of that trade — hence the name Exchange House. By the nineteenth and twentieth centuries, the premises were occupied by saddlers and, for at least fifty years, was the shop of David Roberts, grocery and provision merchants.

In March 1954, conversion work on the building revealed a Gwespyr stone pillar at the front, supporting the floor above. It had previously been boxed in by a timber covering. Although there was immediate speculation that the pillar may have come from either Basingwerk Abbey or St Winefride's Well buildings, this was discounted by an eminent archaeologist. Importantly, he did conclude that the pillar, carved with an 'egg and tongue' design cap, was several centuries old — thus proving a link with an original building from medieval times. Also found were coins from the reigns of George II and George III (1727–1820), along with

Exchange House, c1908.

tokens dating from 1788 and 1791 from the Greenfield Valley Parys Mine Copper Company. The basement revealed a fresh-water well, some fifteen-feet deep by two/three feet across.

As part of the Holywell THI scheme, these premises were the subject of a complete renovation between 2003 and 2005. Whilst the building bears a date of 1702 it is certain that it would then have been a re-build because evidence of a medieval building has been discovered in the foundations. In addition, when old plaster was removed from the top floor, oak-framed mullion windows were found, which would have originally been the external windows of 2 High Street (which would have been a wooden structure). The completed project was given a prestigious award in 2005 by the Georgian Group, a national charity dedicated to saving and protecting buildings from the Georgian period.[46]

A well-equipped restaurant, with historic artefacts was opened on he ground floor of the restored Exchange House; the two floors above accommodate four quality apartments.

The building was given a Grade II listing in 1991.[44]

Residences, Public and General Buildings
Greenfield Hall [was SJ 190 777]
After the dissolution of the monasteries in 1536, Henry VIII granted Basingwerk Abbey, its site and neighbouring lands, to Henry ap Harry of Llanasa whose daughter and heiress, Anne, married William Mostyn of Talacre. As a result, the Basingwerk assets duly passed into the hands of the Mostyns. The house was built by the Dowager Lady Mostyn, after the death of her husband in 1746. Thomas Pennant wrote that Greenfield House [Hall] was 'built by that worthy friend of mine, the late relict [widow] of Sir George Mostyn, baronet, of Talacre … It is at present in the hands of the great copper companies, being leased to them with part of the stream on which their works stand.'[22] The hall was a dower house for Lady Mostyn, and any subsequent widows of the family. The brick built hall was a fine English-looking house with an elevated position that commanded magnificent views of the River Dee, the Wirral, the Mersey and part of the Cheshire plain. However, the house was not occupied for long as the adverse effects of the local industries were soon felt by the residents. Pennant wrote that the smoke from a smelting house in Greenfield Valley 'did such injury to the fine woods belonging to Sir George Mostyn of Talacre, Bart. as to occasion law-suits between Sir George and the company.[22] We can therefore assume that, because of the ever-increasing smoke and fumes from the industrial companies located in the valley, the Mostyns decided to vacate Greenfield Hall and it was leased to managers of the companies that had caused the nuisances! Around 1784, the Mostyns leased the hall to Samuel Richardson, manager of the Parys Mine Company, and in 1818 it was sold to Dr Ralph Richardson (a descendant of Richard Richardson of Chester, died 1769) who had previously leased Kinsale Hall from the Pennants of Downing Hall and had also leased the smelting works of Pen Rho and Llanerch-y-

Môr from them.[138] By 1856, the copper manufacturers, Newton, Keates & Co., had their manager there as a tenant.[87]

Although Dr Richardson put the hall and estate up for auction on 11 August 1866, it was not until 1873 that it was all sold. Trade directories inform us that a Charles Furlonge lived there in 1874 and by 1883 the Misses Buxton were residing there.[43] The hall later became a school which prepared its pupils for admission to public schools as well as to the Royal Navy. The Ordnance Survey map of 1912 verifies the site as a school. During the Second World War, because the house had a large cellar, arrangements were made for the children from the nearby primary school to be moved there in the event of any daytime air raids.

Some parcels of land were sold off for private housing during the first half of the twentieth century and the hall was demolished shortly after the Second World War and the site, together with the remainder of the estate lands, was used for building the large School Lane housing estate.

Plas-yn-Morfa [SJ 1940 7785]
Listed by Cadw in 1991 as a Grade II building, this neo-Gothic house was constructed in the early nineteenth century just to the north of the start of Mostyn Road at Greenfield. The residence is two storeys high and originally had stables and a coach-house. It is likely that it was built by one of the Greenfield Valley industrialists but no documentation has been found to confirm this.

In 1935, J. A. Johnson, the first manager of the new Courtaulds Greenfield Works, bought it and lived there until 1984 when he sold the premises and adjoining land. The house was subsequently bought by Mrs Joan MacLean who converted it into a residential care home. She later added a new building to the complex which served as a separate nursing home.

Panton Hall [SJ 200 7545]
It has proved impossible to establish the exact date of the construction of the original Panton Hall and have to rely upon Thomas Pennant for details of its early history.

In the eighteenth century, Paul Panton (senior), an industrialist and leading figure in the civic life of Holywell, resided here. The large Riverbank Smelting Works was run by him for many years and he was also deeply involved in the lead mining industry. The energy for running the smelting works came from the then powerful stream running through it which came from the valley below the present road from Holywell to the Riverbank estate.[22] The road itself had not then been built and Panton Hall lay relatively near to the south of the works and valley. His son, Paul Panton (junior), followed in his father's footsteps and was responsible for the building of dwellings in Holywell which were named Panton Place.

Panton Hall is still in existence today as a residential establishment.

Bagillt Hall [SJ 1985 7594]
According to Thomas Pennant, Bagillt Hall was probably built around the fifteenth

century by a Henry Pennant who was the second generation in descent from Abbot Thomas Pennant.[22] Although named Bagillt Hall, it was then in the township of Holywell and not in the township of Bagillt. Upon the dissolution of Basingwerk Abbey, Henry's father, Edward, acquired the east of the Holywell township from Abbot Nicholas Pennant. Prior to 1779 the hall had been leased for a number of years to Thomas Smedley, who was also in the local lead smelting business. The history of the house is further complicated by the fact that Edward Pennant passed it, along with some of his other Holywell assets, to the writer Thomas Pennant, who had to rebuild a great part of it because of damage caused by smoke and fumes from the Riverbank Smelting Works.[22]

The hall is now divided into a number of apartments.

Glyn Abbot [SJ 1985 7598]

The name of this property is interesting — Glyn Abbot [translating as Abbot's Valley]. The land all along this area was originally part of the Basingwerk Abbey assets and, at the time of dissolution, was gifted by the last abbot to a relation, Edward Pennant.

Sited alongside the A5026 road from Holywell to Bagillt, this two-storey stone-built villa has a stucco front and a slate roof. Its construction has been dated to *c.*1830.[44] From entries in the trade directories, it would appear that Thomas Mather, the owner of the Upper Lead Smelting Works at Bagillt (but with other business interests in coal and in Liverpool) bought land from the Pennant family and then had the house built, together with two other dwellings. Those places are constructed of Gwespyr stone. The lower property was a lodge, adjoining the A5026. Adjacent to the Pen-y-Maes Road is the other property, The Mount, originally known as Top Lodge. The villa's grounds cover some six acres, located between the two roads. J. Lloyd Price, owner of St Winefred's Brewery, lived here from around 1900, having previously lived at Pendre, off Bagillt Street, and then Mertyn Hall for ten years.[134] He died in 1923. The three buildings were given Grade II listing in 1991.[44]

A Hansom cab with a coachman and horse outside Glyn Abbot in the late nineteenth century.

Perth-y-Terfyn House [SJ 1974 755]

Sited to the east of Brynford Street, this house was built about 1840 by the brothers, Henry and Charles Crockford. Perth-y-Terfyn Cottage, at the head of Brynford Street, acted as a gatehouse to the main house. During the early part of the twentieth century, it was owned and occupied by the Holywell solicitor T. C. Roberts. After he left, the premises were occupied by the Flintshire Women's Institute as their county headquarters. In 1960, the County Council purchased the house and the adjoining land and built the town's new infant school here in 1961. The house was demolished in 1971.

Plas-yn-Dre [SJ 1976 758]

This large two-storey house, with very tall gable-end chimney stacks, was built in Bagillt Street around 1700 by a branch of the Pennant family. It was sited where the present small car park is, on the left hand corner of the road to Pen-y-Maes from the Inner ring road. After the Second World War, it was the district's National Insurance Agency, before demolition in 1979.

Panton Place [SJ 196 758]

In 1816, Paul Panton (junior) of Panton Hall, High Sheriff of Flintshire, built sixteen four-roomed cottages in a 'boulevard' off High Street for occupation by professional and tradespeople as living and working quarters. The paired six-panelled doors with fan lights and vertical box sliding-sash windows (eight panes over eight on the ground floor and the first floor) gave the rows an air of elegance and reflected the fashion of the late Georgian period.[110] On the eastern corner of Panton Place, at its junction with High Street, he built Panton House for one of his agents (possibly Thomas Norbury, who wrote to Paul Panton at Plas Gwyn from Holywell to keep him regulary informed of his employer's interests here, especially the industry). That house later became Lambert's Hotel which today accommodates four separate businesses. He also built a similar dwelling on the opposite corner of Panton Place. The National Bank of England converted the premises into a bank sometime between 1839 and 1870.

The Panton Place dwellings were let out for use as business premises which included the town's first post office and the National Bank of England. The date of the construction of these dwellings, 1816, is shown in darker brickwork between two of the eastern side buildings. Between 1963 and 1968, Holywell Urban District Council demolished over 400 old dwellings in the town but, although the houses in Panton Place were in very poor internal condition, it was agreed that they were worthy of preservation. As a consequence, in 1970, a £65,000 scheme took place to convert the buildings into twenty-eight one-bedroomed flats for elderly and disabled people. The architects were Lingard & Associates of Colwyn Bay, and the contractors were Messrs Brimblecombe. The official opening ceremony was carried out on 14 October 1970. The site, being just off the High Street and the Fron Park is ideal for the residents and the project won first prize from The Times Conservation Awards

Scheme and the Royal Institute of Chartered Surveyors in 1971. All the dwellings were listed as Grade II in 1951.[44]

The Prince of Wales Cinema [SJ 1962 7592]
Built in 1921 and opened on 16 January 1922, this cinema was located on land off Station Road, just behind the Boar's Head Inn. The *County Herald* said:

> Holywell is to be congratulated upon the completion of one of the cosiest and most luxurious Cinema Theatres in North Wales, thanks to private enterprise (J. Fraser Burns and Mrs M. Clegg). The building is constructed of steel and rock-faced concrete blocks. Elaborately furnished and decorated, it has a seating capacity of over seven hundred. The pictures are projected from the rear, which is acknowledged to be the finest method of projection, obviating eyestrain.[141]

The theatre had cinematography exhibitions and variety performances, some of which attracted some of the best provincial companies. Patrons enjoyed the benefit of 'ozone ventilation' and tip-up seats. The stage was 40 ft wide x 30 ft deep and had excellent lighting facilities. During the late 1950s, although television was causing cinema audiences to fall, new management took over the cinema which they re-named the Rialto. However, just after 1980, they were forced to close, and the building was converted into a food supermarket. Unfortunately it was destroyed by fire in 1987 and the site was cleared.

The Old Drill Hall, Brynford Street [SJ 1872 7561]
In January 1860, due to concerns regarding general security in Holywell and Greenfield, the local magistrates called a meeting to consider the setting up of a local Volunteer Corps. After lengthy discussions the meeting resolved to form a Rifle Corps who were to wear grey uniforms. A red-brick drill hall was built for this unit on the west side of Brynford Street, opening on 29 June 1860. Known as the 4th Flintshire Rifle Volunteers, the corps had amongst its officers: Lord Fielding (captain); Alexander Cope (lieutenant) and Charles Crockford (ensign). By 1895 the Drill Hall was being occupied by D Company, 2nd Volunteer Battalion, Royal Welsh Fusiliers.[43] In 1907, the Territorial and Reserve Forces Act was passed whereby Militia and Volunteer units were disbanded and replaced by the Special Reserve and the Territorial Force.

After the Rifle Corps had ceased to use the Drill Hall in 1914, the premises were first used for general storage and, subsequently, a business was operated from there which sold agricultural stock for farmers, as well as potatoes and so on for the public. In 1954, a local auctioneer and estate agent, Stan H. Brown, purchased the hall for running the auction element of his business.[56] After his retirement in January 1983, sales continued to be held there by another person, before the owners of the neighbouring inn purchased the building for their own use.

The Territorial Drill Hall, Halkyn Street [SJ 1877 7571]
Of red brick and slate roof, this Queen Anne-style two-storey building, complete with caretaker's house, was built in 1914 by Sibeons of Holywell. The architect was F. A. Roberts of Mold. It replaced the former Drill Hall in Brynford Street. The front central entrance has a camber arched stone surround. Internally, there is a large hall on the ground floor. In recent years, the premises have been used by other military training units. The building was listed Grade II in 1991.[44]

The Masonic Hall, Coleshill Street [SJ 198 7574]
This brick-built, two-storey hall was erected in 1915 for the sole use of the Order of Freemasons in Holywell. Although not firmly established, it is believed that the builders were Sibeons of Holywell. The architect was F. A. Roberts, Mold. The main benefactor was Dr John Owen Jones of Bodowen Surgery and the first lodge was named Basingwerk Lodge. In later years, a second lodge was formed, with the title Beuno Lodge. The building was listed Grade II in 1991.[44]

The Tower Gardens [SJ 1866 7588]
Sited off the northern side of High Street, it would appear that, amidst the alleyways there must have been a garden area, where an observation tower was erected around O.S. grid reference SJ 1865 7588. The tower was demolished during the 1930s. The gardens became overgrown, but, when the Tower Gardens shopping precinct was built in 1955/56, the site of the original tower site became a small car park.

The Women's Royal Voluntary Service, Darby and Joan Building, Fron Park [SJ 1962 7573].
The 4 September 1963 was a prestigious day for the town's WRVS committee and members when their newly, purpose-built premises were officially opened. For some eighteen months much hard work had gone into fund raising for the project. The building cost £3,500 and a further £1,000 had to be spent on internal furnishings and fittings. The building contract had been awarded to T. H. Jones of Lloc. Mrs M. N. Maycock, district organiser, put the final touches to the foundation stone and the trowel she used, which had been donated by the contractors, was later put into a glass case within the centre.

Because the premises were no longer being used for their original purpose, they were sold in 1996 to the Fron Park Christian Fellowship.

The Greenfield Valley Heritage Park
In 1971, Holywell Urban District Council took an important and historic decision when they asked a consultancy firm to provide proposals for a seventy-acre heritage park, from the site of the former Holywell town railway station, down the Greenfield Valley to the site of Basingwerk Abbey. Included in the valley are five reservoirs. Besides being concerned about the ever-increasing dereliction of the area, it was believed that such a new and modern facility would attract visitors to the district from which Holywell could benefit. The proposals put before the council were

accepted in principle but any start on the project was delayed by the local government changes of 1974 when the district became part of the new Delyn Borough Council. A decision was eventually made to proceed with the scheme and the whole project was grant aided by various bodies. Basic land clearance was carried out under a Job Creation Programme, together with the Greenfield Valley Voluntary Action Group, starting with the area nearest the town.[100] The valley's five artificial reservoirs were dredged and the dams were rehabilitated. Archaeological investigations of industrial sites were made, resulting in the ruins of many old buildings being made sound and others being partially rebuilt. Way-marked walker's paths and routes were created, with information boards placed at strategic points. The route of the old railway down from the town station was formed into a wide walkway.[100] Prince Charles made a welcome visit to view the reclamation in the valley on 11 July 1980. He was greeted by a huge crowd in three places, followed by a celebration tea in the Assembly Hall.

Adjacent to the south of the abbey, a visitor and information centre was built on lands which had, until 1979, housed Abbey Farm. The early twentieth century outbuildings of the farm were converted to house part of a farm museum, which opened in May 1984. Its first exhibits were a variety of animals, as well as displays of old farm machinery and implements. Besides the old Abbey Farm smallholding being purchased, four other buildings used by the scheme came from sites in the old county of Flintshire. Two barns from the disused Coleshill Farm in Flint, dating from the seventeenth and eighteenth centuries, were taken down when the Kimberley Clarke paper tissue factory was built. The splendid Pentre stone farmhouse from Lixwm (parts of which dated back to the sixteenth century) was also dismantled and moved and the house was furnished with effects from that period. The fourth building to be brought down to the site was the ancient Cwm Llydan (Wide Valley) Farmhouse, which had stood on the northern slopes of Moel Fammau. A very interesting nineteenth-century cooking range, manufacured by Parry & Morris, ironfounders of Holywell (their works may possibly have been located at Bryn Celyn) has been installed in the kitchen. Where possible, all these buildings were restored stone by stone. In addition, the disused Spring Gardens Infant School, which had been built in 1877 at Well Street, Holywell, was taken down brick by brick and rebuilt close to the visitor centre. The interior of the school includes desks and furniture from the old building.

Opposite the old Abbey Farm, an Environment Centre was opened, which displays wildlife and geology and includes a viewing-point where enthusiasts can watch wildlife on the Parys Mine Pool. From within the park, a nature walk has been created up into the nearby woodland.

An interesting building by the environment centre is 'The Bakehouse' which had been used during the nineteenth century as both a store and a bakehouse.[107] It is widely believed that the building was the original gatehouse to Basingwerk Abbey, and it is built of at least three types of stone: Gwespyr stone (Moor Quarry), dark reddish stone from the Wirral and local white limestone. The walls on either side of the building are constructed from hand-made bricks of the 1780s, possibly having manufactured in the Greenfield Valley.

Part of the Lower Cotton Mill building was restored in 1993 to house an industrial heritage museum. On the lower floor is a water tank alongside a coal-fired Robey steam boiler of early twentieth century design. The steam generated by the boiler feeds up to the first floor where a 1920-design mineral water plant has been installed. This embraces bottle-cleaning machinery, a mineral water bottle-filling unit, together with a bottle-capping machine.[143 & 144]

In the early 1990s, the former Parys Mine Lodge was renovated and altered to form a lecture room and exhibition area.

The metal entrance gates to the Abbey Paper Mill, adjacent to Holywell Road, were saved and are now sited in the valley above the Flour Mill Pool.[107] There is also a viscose churn and mixer, together with driving gear, from the Courtaulds factory. Sadly, no machinery was salvaged from Holywell Textile Mill.

The valley woodlands and lakes have been developed into natural sanctuaries for flora and fauna.

The Holywell Hunt Society and Racecourse
For some years prior to 1767, gentry from Flintshire and Cheshire had been holding horse-racing meetings in the Halkyn area. On 21 November 1767, they held a special meeting in the White Horse Hotel, Holywell [now the HSBC bank building] where it was resolved to form a formal society and establish a good racecourse. The society was named the Holywell Hunt Society and the site chosen for the racecourse was alongside the Gorsedd to Babell road. Today's residences Bryn-y-Gwynt, Lower Stables Farm and Racecourse House in the parishes Whitford and Ysceifiog act as landmarks for the course, which can be traced by looking at Ornance Survey maps. The road divided the eastern and western parts of the course; the land to the east was owned by the Earl of Denbigh; that to the west by Lord Mostyn. The oval-shaped circuit covered a distance of two miles and one furlong and crossed the road in two places. The meeting also resolved that the society's headquarters would be at Calcot Hall, to the south of Brynford. Earl Grosvenor was elected as the society's first president.

Work on establishing the racecourse went ahead quickly, and in the first week of November 1768, the first races were held with a brick starting-tower having been built. It had been agreed that the meetings would be held annually for one week following 5 November, but in later years the week was brought forward to October. In 1828, a brick-built grandstand, with slated roof, was added, which had the benefit of coal-fired heating.

Ground at Ffrith-y-Garreg Wen was utilised as a training ground and a coach house with some stables at Plymouth Copse was purchased by Lord Mostyn. This was extended and used for horse stabling. Bryn-y-Gwynt, which had been a farm, was purchased and used by the society as a centre for social life; bills have been found for purchases of large quantities of alcoholic liquor. *Adams' Weekly Courier*, N[o.] 14, 1769, stated:

There was the greatest number of Noblemen and Gentlemen at the Holywell Hunt races that ever was known, who made the most brilliant appearance, and at night there was a grand ball given by the Gentlemen subscribers to the Holywell Hunt.

At first, the society strictly limited its membership to twenty-five but by 1774 this was increased to fifty. At first the horse riders were gentlemen only, but very soon professional jockeys began to appear. The popularity of the annual racing week and the growth of Chester Races attracted sportsmen and gentry from far afield. But the general public quickly acquired an interest in the meetings and many undesirable people began to attend which is said to be one of the reasons for the cessation of the race meetings. For some years, Holywell Races marked the closing of the national racing season.

The uniform for the huntsmen consisted of a red cloth coat, incorporating a plain gold embroidered vellum buttonhole, gold button, red velvet turn-down collar, white waistcoat and white cloth breeches. Royalty, in the person of Prince [later King] Leopold of Belgium (who was on a visit to Earl Grosvenor at Eaton Hall) attended in 1819.

In 1826, it was resolved to build stables more central to the course. To fund the estimated project cost of £600, members were invited to purchase £25 shares for which they would receive dividends. By 1827, the building (now part of Lower Stables Farm) was in use and included: six stables (housing fourteen horses); six boxes; a hay and corn room; a men's room; a privy; and two stove rooms. Hot air funnels ran under all the floors, the heating coming from six coal stoves. Local limestone was used for the construction of the building, which also had a slated roof.

During race weeks, bookmakers and side-shows operated alongside the course. Holywell benefitted enormously from the events as hotels and inns were packed and there would have been an obvious trade spin-off for shops and traders.

A selection of the races were: The Holywell Cup; The Gold Cup; The Champagne Stakes; The Mostyn Stakes; The Taffy Stakes; The Hawarden Castle Stakes; The Hokey Pokey Stakes. To highlight the importance of Holywell Races, a horse named the Queen of Trumps (owned by Lord Mostyn) which won the Holywell Champagne Stakes in 1834 went on to win both the St Leger and the Oaks the following year.

The last race meeting at Holywell appears to have been in 1842 after which date the National Racing Calendar makes no more references to the event. The following year, Chester Races held their first autumn race meeting and Lord Mostyn was one of the stewards.

Although the grandstand survived for another 150 years, it gradually deteriorated and had to be demolished in 1984. Part of the old racecourse is still covered by public footpaths and a bridleway and a section of one of the Whitford Community Council Millenium Walks includes an element of it.

The Holywell Hunt Club
Lord Mostyn founded the Flint and Denbigh Hunt in 1833, a separate organisation to the Race Society, although basically the same gentry were members. Being a hunt

club, they had their own hounds for the blood sport of fox hunting.

Some very interesting photographs have survived from the early years of the twentieth century which depict the scenes of the start of a hunt from the Holywell's Victoria Square.

Objects, Plaques and Items of General Interest
This section does not include any items which exist in churches and chapels.

(a) On the Pen-y-Ball Street side of the Feathers Inn, outlined in brick, is 1712, being the date of construction of the building.

(b) A wall plaque on the south wall of Halkyn Street, opposite the road entrance to the football ground and Bodowen Surgery; also a similar one nearer the junction with the main road.

(c) Decorative tiles in red Ruabon brick above numbers 75 and 77 High Street.

(d) On 22 High Street (Iceland) are decorative cartouche panels advertising the building as the former Grapes Inn. The adjoining building has decorative brick panels, with a terra cotta urn symbol as a central feature.

(e) Exchange House, 6 High Street, carries the date 1702 above the first floor centre window; also of interest are the three carved figure-heads on the keystones of the first floor windows.

(f) A stone plaque inset into the east wall of Post Office Lane bearing the name R. Sankey, the rest of the original inscription is illegible. This stone could well have been a boundary stone marking the north-eastern extremity of his land.

(g) A stone carved out of Gwespyr-type stone which was originally erected

The hunt going up Coleshill Street, c.1913.

alongside the entrance to Capel y Bryn (Bryn Seion Chapel) in 1803. The stone now stands in the grounds of Penbryn Chapel. The Welsh inscription is taken from Ecclesiastes V, verse 1.

(h) A mile stone by the post box at the entrance to Abbey Lane, opposite School Lane, Greenfield. Unfortunately, because it of Gwespyr-type stone, the inscription has been badly weathered away.

(i) A stone boundary tablet sited on the bank alongside the Holywell to Greenfield road just before its junction with the coast road. It was placed in this present postion in 1995, having been moved from its previous position when road works were being undertaken. The narration on it reads 'This stone marked 'A' was moved and resited April 18th 1903 by the Flintshire C. C. in consequence of alterations to the main road from Flint to Mostyn and is now 19 ft 3 ins northwest of the old position, being the mark as shown on the plans fixing the boundary of the Dee Conservancy Board at Greenfield.' The date of its origin has not been established.

Chapter 8

Notable Families and People

Henry Perry, Welsh scholar/grammarian
Born in Greenfield in *c*.1560, Henry Perry was a descendant of Ednowain Bendew, founder of the thirteenth of the fifteen tribes of north Wales. Ednowain's chief seat in the eleventh century was in the district of Tegeingl at Llys Coed-y-Mynydd, on the slopes of Moel-y-Parc; but he also built a motte and bailey castle at Castell Tŷ Maen, Lloc [SJ 144 769], now in the woodland named Coed Allt-y-Tywod. Perry was educated at Oxford's Balliol College from 1579. He became a Master of Arts, and a Bachelor of Divinity. After travelling abroad, he was appointed chaplain to Sir Richard Bulkeley and married the daughter of Robert Vaughan, a Beaumaris gentleman. He later served as vicar of three Anglesey parishes. He was appointed a canon of Bangor Cathedral in 1612 and died in 1617.[145]

The Panton Family
This family was very prominent in the Holywell area during the eighteenth and nineteenth centuries. Paul Panton (senior) was born at Panton Hall on 4 May 1727. His father, another Paul, who had come to the district from Bank Hall, Warrington (now Warrington Town Hall), had married Margaret, heiress to Edward Griffith of Caerwys Hall and Bagillt. She was a great grand-daughter of John Jones (1578–1658) of Gellilfdy and her ancestry can be traced back to Ednowain Bendew. Margaret Griffith died on 14 July 1728 and was buried in Holywell Parish Church where there is a memorial tablet to her. Paul Panton (senior) studied and became a barrister-at-law in 1749, becoming deeply involved in the civic and industrial life of this district with interests in the large Holway Level leadmining scheme, the Milwr leadmines, a Bagillt smeltery and the coal industry at Bagillt. On 1 March 1756, he married Jane Jones, heiress of the wealthy Plas Gwyn estate at Pentraeth in Anglesey. Paul and Jane had four children, Jane, Paul (junior), Jones and Elizabeth Maria. Paul Panton (senior) was lord of the Manor of Coleshill, High Sheriff of Flintshire in 1770 and of Anglesey in 1771. His wife died on 21 June 1764 and was buried at Pentraeth. Paul married again on 6 June 1770, to Martha Kirk, a widow, of Chester. They had a son, Thomas, in 1771 and another, Bulkeley, in 1772. Martha died in Panton Hall on 27 July 1814, aged eighty-two. Although he was deeply involved in industry, Panton was primarily noted as a literary person and antiquary. His manuscripts have proved to be an invaluable source for various aspects of the history and literature of Wales.[153] When he

died on 24 May 1797 he was buried in Holywell Parish Church where a Grecian memorial tablet was sculptured by John Flaxman (his most famous works are in Westminster Abbey and St Paul's Cathedral).[7]

Paul Panton (junior), who was born in 1758, inherited his father's estates and followed in his father's footsteps in very many ways — qualifying as a barrister-at-law in 1781 and becoming deeply involved in the local leadmining and smelting industries. He also spent a great deal of his life at Plas Gwyn and became active in the civic life of Anglesey – serving as Deputy Lieutenant and High Sheriff (1807). Panton Hall was his main residence for conducting his affairs in Flintshire and he served as High Sheriff for the county in 1815. He had Panton Place built in Holywell in 1816. He never married and he died on 24 August 1822.[77] All his possessions were left to his two sisters and his brother Jones Panton, who was the High Sheriff of Anglesey. Paul Panton's death brought to an end the family's interests in Holywell.

The Sankey Family
Richard Sankey (senior), a native of Denbigh, was the owner of Englefield Colliery and a partner in the North Wales Bank from 1790. Richard Sankey (junior) came to live at Fron Hall, from Nant Hall, Prestatyn, in about 1886 following the death of his father. He was very prominent in Holywell's civic life and gave the magnificent replacement statue of St Winefride which was placed in the niche of the original statue at the Well. He died on 22 September 1899, and was buried in the family vault at St David's Churchyard, Pantasaph.

The Crockford Family
In the mid 1840s, William Crockford and his wife, Sarah, came to Flintshire from London. They bought land adjacent to the Greenfield gasworks where they built a zinc spelter factory. Although he died in May 1844, his widow took over the business. His two brothers, Henry and Charles, built Perth-y-Terfyn House to the east of Brynford Street, Holywell. Henry had interests in both coal and lead mining, and Charles built the mineral railway between Pantasaph and Greenfield, and altered the upper part of the old Parys Mine Copper Works into a limestone crushing works, complete with lime kilns.

Emlyn Williams, international actor and playwright
George Emlyn Williams was born on 26 November 1905 at 1 Jones Cottages, Rhewl Fawr, in the parish of Llanasa. The following March, the family moved into the White Lion Inn, at nearby Glanrafon, where his father became the licensee. Emlyn's education commenced at Talacre Convent. When Picton Council School opened in June 1914, he was transferred there, only to move to Trelogan Council School because his father had given up the inn and the family moved to live in Trelogan. He passed the scholarship examination for Holywell County School and had to walk the ten miles round trip to the school daily until 1917 when the family moved to Connah's Quay where his father obtained better-paid work at Summer's steelworks. One of his

Emlyn Williams, opening the new Grove Park Little Theatre, Wrexham.
[W. Alister Williams Collection]

companions on the way to school was Whitford Roberts (later a noted Nonconformist minister). J. M. Edwards, the headmaster, and a teacher, Miss Cooke, took an exceptional interest in the potential Emlyn had and obtained for him a special concession for the train fare from Connah's Quay to Holywell to allow him to continue his education at the County School. Miss Cooke taught him French and, in time, arranged for him to go to Paris for a while for special tuition. He won an open scholarship to Oxford University where he gained an MA. His interests had by then moved him towards acting and playwriting.[16] From then on, he became a world-famous actor and gained other distinctions including a CBE; an FRSL; a LLD (Hon). On 6 November 1982, he was made a Freeman of the Borough of Delyn at the Holywell High School off Pen-y-Maes Road, the former Holywell County School. Among his most noted plays are: *The Corn is Green; Last Days of Dolwyn and Druids Rest*. In 1958 he was nominated as Best Actor for the play *A Boy growing Up.* His autobiography is entitled *George*. He died in 1987. One of the the theatres at Clwyd Theatr Cymru in Mold is named after him.

Edith Wynne, international singer
Sarah Edith Wynne was born on 11 March 1842, in Panton Place, Holywell. Her mother, who was an excellent soprano, soon realised that she had a good singing voice and, at the age of nine, she joined the Holywell Choral Society and was also a chorister at Holywell Parish Church. Her first prize for solo singing was won at the local eisteddfod the following year. She then went on a concert tour of Wales and was received with acclaim. Aged fourteen, Edith became a music student in Liverpool for some five years before going to London where she gave the first of many concerts at St James' Hall on 4 July 1862. She went to Italy for a short time where she received further training and appeared in concerts before returning to London and singing at an eisteddfod in Wales, becoming known as *Eos Cymru* (the Welsh Nightingale). At the age of thirty-three, Edith married an Armenian barrister in London and later gave birth to a girl. From then on, she devoted more time to her family and eventually retired from the professional stage in 1894. She died at the age of fifty-four and was buried in Hampstead Cemetery.[142]

Rowland Huw Pritchard, composer and publisher
Rowland H. Pritchard was born in Meirionthshire in 1811 and came to work in the Holywell Flannel Mill. Amongst his publications were the well-known *Cyfaill y Cantorion* (The Friend of Singers) and *Y Fasged Gerddorol* (The Musical Basket). Perhaps his most famous hymn tune was *Hyfrydol*, which was reputedly first sung in Pendref Chapel, Holywell. He was buried in St Peter's Cemetery in 1887.

Jonathan Pryce, international stage and screen actor
Born John Price on 1 June 1947 in a bungalow named 'Chez Nous', in Park Drive, Carmel, to parents Isaac and Maggie Price, John was the third of their three children – his sisters being Kathleen and Margaret. His parents ran Sycamore Stores, a grocer's shop, in Bryn Celyn. John Price was a pupil at Holywell Council School, from where he moved on to the Grammar School. Whilst training as a teacher at Ormskirk he chose drama as a subsidiary course which proved the start of a highly successful acting career. Turning professional, he adopted the name Jonathan Pryce.

In 1975 he won a Tony Award for his role in *The Comedians* at the Nottingham Old Vic. He later won an Olivier Award following his lead role in *Hamlet* at the Royal Court. For his outstanding performance in *Miss Saigon* he received both an Olivier and a Tony Award. He moved into the world of films, where after many performances he was given the Outer Critics Circle Award for Best Actor for his performance in *Miss Saigon* in 1991 and proclaimed Best Actor at the 1995 Cannes Film Festival in recognition of his part in *Carrington*.[146] Among his other most notable roles are in *Evita*, *Tomorrow Never Dies* and the *Pirates of the Carribean* trilogy.

Jonathan's home is in London, where he lives with actress, Kate Fahy, and their three children but he still comes back to Holywell and is proud to show his family where he grew up.

Jonathan Pryce.

Bibliography and Notes

1. *Historical Researches on the Flintshire Castles*, Edward Parry, 1830.
2. *Tour in Wales*, W. Bingley, 1798.
3. *Local Government in Britain*, Tony Byrne, 1990.
4. *The Jubilee of County Councils*, Flintshire County Council, 1938.
5. The Delyn Conservation Advisory Committee Report, August 1978.
6. *The Archaeology of Clwyd*, Clwyd County Council, 1991.
7. *Centenary Brochure, Holy Trinity Church, Greenfield, 1871–1971*, Canon David Thomas.
8. *Tours*, Daniel Defoe, 1724-1725.
9. *Black's Guide to North Wales*, 1855.
10. The Religious Census of 1852 (North Wales Volume).
11. Holywell in the Early Part of the Nineteenth Century, a lecture to the C. E. M. S., J. Lloyd Price, 1912.
12. *Spring Gardens Centenary, 1877 to 1977*, M. R. Isgar.
13. *A Topographical and Historic Description of Flintshire*, printed by Sherwood, Neely and Jones, 1810.
14. *Parochialia*, Edward Lhwyd, c.1669.
15. *Flintshire Historical Society Journal*, vol. 9, 1922.
16. *George*, Emlyn Williams, 1961.
17. *By-Gones* various issues.
18. *Flintshire*, J. M. Edwards, 1914.
19. *St Winefrides Well, a history and guide*, Rev. Christopher David.
20. Notice in St Winefrides Chapel.
21. *The Welsh Cistercians*, David H. Williams, 1969 and 2002.
22. *The History of the Parishes of Whiteford and Holywell*, Thomas Pennant, 1796.
23. *Histories of Flintshire*, J. Poole, 1831.
24. *The Beauties of England and Wales*, vol. 17, North Wales, Revd J. Evans, 1812.
25. *A History of Six Villages*, Rowland Tennant, 2003.
26. *A Diary of a Journey into North Wales in the year 1774*, Dr Samuel Johnson.
27. *A History of Wales*, Sir John Edward Lloyd, 1911.
28. *Offa's Dyke*, Sir Cyril Fox, 1925 and 1955 (note his text includes Wat's Dyke).
29. *Introduction to the Grosvenor (Halkyn) MSS Handlist*, published by Clwyd Record Office, 1988.
30. *Flintshire Place Names*, Canon Ellis Davies, 1956.
31. *The History of Flintshire*, C. R. Williams, 1961.
32. *Early Fire Service History in Clwyd Area*, D. Wheway Davies, c.1973.
33. *Royal Visits and Progresses to Wales*, Edward Parry, 1850.
34. *Anglo-Saxon England*, Sir Frank Stenton, 1947.
35. *Offa's Dyke, History and Guide*, David Hill and Margaret Worthington, 2003.
36. *Wordsworth Dictionary of British History*, 1981.
37. *The Workhouse*, Norman Longton.
38. *English Local Government: Poor Law History, part 1, The Old Poor Law*, S. & B. Webb.
39. *Before the Welfare State*, Ursula R. Q. Henriques, 1979.
40. *English Poor Law Policy*, S. & B. Webb, 1910.

41. *The County Herald*, 4 January 1895.
42. *The Buildings of Clwyd*, Edward Hubbard, 1986.
43. *North Wales Directories, 1818 to 1936*, a CD-ROM, Friends of Wrexham Museums & Clwyd Family History Society.
44. CADW Listed Buildings, list description documents.
45. An unpublished history of The Parish of Holywell, M. R. Isgar, 1993.
46. News Releases Flintshire County Council, 2003 onwards.
47. *The Wales Register and Guide*, Eyre Bros, London, 1878.
48. Flintshire County Council Annual Report Books.
49. *Report on Planning of the County of Flint*, 1935, the County Surveyor.
50. Documentation supplied Flintshire County Council Community and Housing Services Department.
51. From a lecture in Holywell on 18 April 1962, Jim H. Jones, Gas Board local manager.
52. The Parish of Holywell, historical notes, Canon David Thomas, 1964.
53. Holywell, per the internet, 2003.
54. *Chester Chronicle*, 1956.
55. *Medical Care in Holywell, 1825-1998*, Rafael Lopez, 1998.
56. *The Promoter*, a Molyneux Property Agency Guide, autumn 2003.
57. Information Boards in St Winefrides Well Exhibition Room.
58. *The Settlement of Celtic Saints in Wales*, E. G. Bowen.
59. *Flintshire Historical Society Journal*, vol. 14.
60. *Life of St Winefred*, Thomas Meyrick, 1878.
61. *St Winefride and her Well*, T. Charles-Edwards, 1962.
62. Article Derrick Pratt in *The Clwyd Historian*, October 1990.
63. *History of Shropshire* (Religious Houses chapter), A. T. Gaydon, 1973.
64. *Encyclopaedia Britannica*, 1974 edition.
65. Per documents supplied to the author by the Assistant Keeper of the Muniment Room & Library, Westminster Abbey.
66. *Holywell Urban District Town Guide*, 1910.
67. CADW Leaflet from a site visit by L. M. Bell, 21st November 1995.
68. Basingwerk Abbey, fron the publication *Citeaux*, vol 32, 1981, Rev. Dr David H. Williams.
69. *Shrewsbury Abbey, a Medieval Monastery*, Nigel Baker.
70. *The Life of St Winefride*, Thomas Swift, 1888.
71. From information given to the author by Father Mark, Pantasaph Franciscan Friary.
72. All for the Greater Glory of God, an article in the *Greenfield Valley Historical Society Chronicle*, December 1986.
73. *Chester Chronicle*, 6 February 2004.
74. *Flintshire Historical Society Journal*, vol. 18.
75. *A History of the Diocese of St Asaph*, Rev. D. R. Thomas, 1874.
76. *Medieval Stone Carving in North Wales* (section Ecclesiastical Effigies 1282–1350), Colin A. Gresham, 1968.
77. *The Dictionary of Welsh Biography*.
78. *The History of the Parish of Holywell and a Tour of the Church*, M. R. Isgar, 1992.
79. Triple Anniversary of Alpha English Congregational Church, Greenfield, 1814–1964.
80. Pendref Wesleyan Chapel, Holywell, Centenary Celebration, *County Herald*, 1 May 1908.
81. *Centenary of Moriah Chapel, Pen-y-Maes*, Noel Kerfoot Owens, 2000.
82. *The History of the Congregational Cause, now Worshiping at Tabernacle, Holywell*, Rev. C. R. Wyatt, 1970.
83. *Hanes Methodistiaeth yn Nosbarth Trefynnon*, Ll. Arthur Owen, 1910.
84. *The Welsh Baptists*, T. M. Bassett, 1977.

85. *Early Modern Wales, c.1525–1640*, J. Gwynfor Jones, 1994.
86. *Hanes Wesleyaeth Gymreig*, Parch Hugh Jones, 1913.
87. *The Greenfield Valley*, K. Davies & C. J. Williams, for Holywell Town Council, 1986.
88. *Roads and Trackways of Wales*, Richard Colyer, 1984.
89. 'The Holywell Textile Mills', Peter S. Richards in vol. 6 of *Industrial Archaeology*, 1969.
90. Britannis an illustration of the Kingdom of England & the Dominion of Wales, John Ogilby, 1675.
91. *Stage Coaches in Wales*, Herbert Williams, 1977.
92. *The British Post Office*, Howard Robinson, 1948.
93. *Flintshire Historical Journal*, vol. 21, 'Roads and Turnpike Trusts of Flintshire', R. T. Pritchard.
94. An 1812 map of the Holywell area.
95. *The Welsh Post Towns before 1840*, Michael Scott Archer, 1970.
96. *G.P.O., English Institutions*, E. T. Crutchley, 1938.
97. *The Quest for Corvo*, A. J. A. Symons, 1952.
98. *Industry in Clwyd*, C. J. Williams, 1986.
99. *A History of Wales, 1660–1815*, E. D. Evans, 1976.
100. Greenfield Heritage Park, an article Delyn Borough Council, 1982 and c1990.
101. *Clarke's Tour through Wales in 1791*.
102. Aikins England described in 1818.
103. *Clwyd Historian*, No 31, autumn 1993.
104. *The Story of the Holywell Cotton Industry, 1777–1841*, Huw Williams, 1971.
105. *Country Quest*, Huw Williams, March 1969.
106. The Holywell Textile Mills, Peter S. Richards, vol 6 of *Industrial Archaeology*, 1969.
107. *Greenfield Valley Heritage Park*, in a booklet Resources for Schools.
108. Illustrated plan of Holywell and Greenfield, *The Holywell Forum*, 1997.
109. Greenfield Valley Heritage Park Information Boards.
110. Internet web site THI, Flintshire County Council, 2006, as well as verbal detail from the THI project manager.
111. *The History of Holywell Textile Mills Ltd.*, Holywell, *c.*1971.
112. *English Local Government: English Poor Law History*, part 1.
113. *Social Administration, including the Poor Laws*, John J. Clarke, 1939.
114. 'The Holywell Hunt', A. Geoffrey Veysey, in *Clwyd Historian*, vol. 37.
115. *The River Dee*, J. S. Howson and Alfred Rimmer, 1892.
116. *Industrial Revolution in North Wales*, A. H. Dodd, 1951.
117. *A Topographical Dictionary of Wales*, Samuel lewis, 1845.
118. *Chester Chronicle*, 22 May 1965.
119. *North Wales Excursions*, Revd W. Bingley, 1814.
120. *The Copper King, Thomas Williams of Llanidan*, J. R. Harris, 2003.
121. *Greenfield Mills, Holywell Excavation*, Clwyd County Council, 1977.
122. Dissolution of the Monasteries, from an internet site, January 2006.
123. *The Mines of Flintshire and Denbighshire*, Messrs. Burt, Waite and Burnley, University of Exeter Press, 1992.
124. *Flintshire Historical Journal*, vol. 18, 1960, 'Gadlys', M. Bevan-Evans.
125. *A History of Printing and Printers in Wales*, Ifana Jones, 1925.
126. *Midland Bank, Holywell, Two Centuries of Banking, 1790–1990*, Midland Bank.
127. *Midweek Leader*, 3 August 1989.
128. *Chester Chronicle*, 10 April 1987.
129. *Chester Chronicle*, 1, 8 and 15 March 1968.
130. *The County Herald*, 15 June 1917.
131. Family history details provided Hywel and Cynthia Kerfoot Roberts, Holywell.

132. *A Short History of Modern Wales*, David Williams, 1976.
133. As per details in the rebuilt Spring Gardens School in the Greenfield Valley.
134. Philip Dykins, Butcher, Master Brewer and Gentleman, per an internet web site, March 2006.
135. *Social Administration, including the Poor Laws*, John J. Clarke, 1939.
136. *Our Children's Language, the Welsh-Medium Schools of Wales*, chapter 18, Flintshire Shows the Way, Gron Ellis.
137. *The Report on the State of Education in Wales*, 1847.
138. *Guide to the Flintshire Record Office*, M. Bevan-Evans.
139. *The Welsh Woollen Industry*, J. Geraint Jenkins, 1969.
140. *They Lived in Flintshire*, Huw Williams, 1960.
141. *The County Herald*, 13 January 1922.
142. Sarah Edith Wynne, Eirlys Wynn Tomas (the winning essay at Eisteddfod Bro Treffynnon, 1999).
143. Friends of Greenfield Valley Newsletters.
144. *The Evening Leader*, 18 February 1997.
145. A Flintshire County Council H. Q. Library information document relating to famed people from Flintshire.
146. Flintshire, a *Western Mail* Survey, 5 November 1997.
147. Greenfield Mills, Holywell, Excavation 1977, Clwyd County Council.
148. BBC web site, Early Modern Notes of Wales – St Winefrides Well, Sharon, 29/06/2004.
149. Descriptive gazetteer entries for Holywell, an Internet web site, 2006.
150. Web site advertising W. Hall & Son Ltd, 2005.
151. Caring for St Winefrides Well, St Winefride's Well Committee.
152. *Journal of a Tour through North Wales and part of Shropshire; with observations in Minerology*, London, 1797.
153. Paul Panton, literary patron and antiquary, Dylan Foster Evans, *Oxford Dictionary of National Biography*.
154. *Abbey Mills*, Grosvenor Chater Ltd, 1930.
155. *Family Business – a History of Grosvenor Chater, 1690–1977*, Michael Chater.

Flintshire Record Office Documents

R101. G/B/32/1-. Holywell Workhouse Building Accounts. R102. G/B/8g/2a. Holywell Workhouse Electric Light Comm minutes.
R103. G/B/64/3. Day of Humiliation, the Bishop of St Asaph, 10th Oct 1849.
R104. T/3/MB/4. Flints Turnpike Tolls, To be let auction 1862. R105. D/DM/223/149. Flintshire Roads Bill, session 1833.
R106. D/RD/221. Crockfords Railway

Index

References to illustrations are indicated in **bold**

Abbey Colliery: 144
Abbey Farm: 90, 128, 187
Abbey House: 126
Abbey Lane: 130, 191
Abbey Paper Mill: 119, 127, **127**, 142, 154, 188
Abbey Schoolroom: 167
Abbey Wire Mill: 130, 134
Aber: 112
Aberdo Quarry: 148
Actuary Savings Bank: 169
Addison, Richard: 113
Additional Parish Church: 90
Adeilza, wife of Hugh d'Avranches: 21
Aethelbald, King: 14, 17, 18
Afonwen Station: 115
Aiken, Arthur (mineralogist): 27, 146
Alexandra Inn: 30, 176
All Flintshire Credit Union: 173
Alma Cottage: 39
Alpha Congregational Chapel: 105–6, 126, 173
Altree, Revd Sue: 97, 102
Ambulance Service: 44
Antelope Inn: 100
ap Harri, Henri: 84
Apothocary's Hall: 57
Assembly Hall: 36–7
Ava Maria Hall: 162

Babell Road: 110
Bagillt Hall: 182
Bagillt Street: 24, 44, 49, 53, 58, 110, 116, 159, 183, 184
Bagillt-Fawr: 85
Bagillt-Fechan: 85
Bagshaw, Thomas: 159
Baker, Joe: 24, 37
Baldwin, Richard: 137
Bank Court/Place: 22, 25, 35, 114, 159, 169, 179
Barclays Bank: 50, 172
Barker, Joe: 46, **46**
Barker, John: 92
Barker, Thomas: 92
Basingwerk Abbey: 16, 17, 20, 22, 33, 51, 57, 60, 65, 69, 79, 117, 121, 124, 125, 126, 128, 135, 143, 148–9, 180–81, 183, 186–7
Basingwerk Bluff: 16, 17, 20
Basingwerk Castle; 19–20, **19**
Basingwerk Chapel: 79
Basingwerk House: 19, 126
Basingwerk Lodge (Freemasons): 186
Basingwerk School: 17, 165–6
Battery Copper & Brass Works: 128, 130, 132, 133, 138
Battery Pool: 25, **31**, **129**, 133, **133**, 138
Battery Row: 30, 133
Beauclerk, Father Charles: 75, 78, 163
Beaufort Chapel: 69
Beaufort, Lady Margaret: 65, 66, 70, 75
Bennet, John (priest): 71
Berea Baptist Chapel: 106
Berthen Gron, Y: 94
Berthen Gron Chapel, Y: 94
Bethel Baptist Chapel: 102
Beuno Lodge (Freemasons): 186
Bingley, Revd: 27
Black Book of Basingwerk: 125
Black Boy Inn: 93
Boar's Head: 185
Bodowen Surgery: 57–8, 186, 190
Boot Inn: 113
Boot Gate: 110
Brackenbury, Nevil J.: 41
Brechfa, Ieuan: 63
Bridgettine Nuns of the Most Holy Saviour of St Bridget: 163
British Gas Light Company: 49
British School: 159, **160**
Brognallt: 110, 146
Brognallt Gate: **111**
Bromley, Urias: 137
Brooks Brothers: 116
Brown, Stan H. (estate agent): 175, 185
Brown, William: 137
Bryn Celyn: 13, 22, 30, **31**, 133, 135, 140, 141, 142, 155, 157, 176, 187, 195
Bryn Celyn National School: 93, 157, 167
Bryn Celyn Post Office: 50
Bryn Celyn Stores: 30
Bryn Madyn: 92
Bryn Offa: 17
Bryn Seion Chapel: 94, 103, 191
Bryn-y-Castell: 21, 92
Bryn-y-Gaseg: 110
Bryn-y-Gwynt: 188
Brynyffynnon: 110
Brynford: 25, 34, 84, 110, 114, 116, 146–7, 179
Brynford Street: **46**, 101
Brynford Gate: 110

Brynford Hill: 113
Brynford House: 57
Brynford Road: 51, 54
Brynford Street: 51, 56, 57, 58, 94, 101, 110, 117, 158, 170, 184, 185, 193
Building Societies: 172
Burns, J. Fraser: 185
Butler, Edward: 63
Buxton, Miss: 182

Calcot: 85, 147, 179
Calcot Hall: 188
Caldy: 121
Cambrensis, Giraldus: 81
Capel Penbryn: 97, 102
Capel y Bryn: 94, 191
Capel y LLofft: 106
Caradoc, Prince: 63
Carmel: 16, 17, 108, 110, 113, 116, 124, 146, 147, 149, 195
Carnes, Edward: 176
Carnes, William: 176
Castle Hill: 34, 51, 57, 92, 93, 157, 158
Castle Hill Cottages: 93
Castle Hill School: 158
Castle Industrial Park: 48
Castle View: 21
Catherall, Jonathan: 102
Catherall, Mr: 103
Catherwood, William: 177
Catholic Convent: 30, **162**, 164
Catholic Convent School: 30, 162
Catholic Presbytery: 30
Cavanagh, James (teacher): 159, 162
Cement Works: 144
Cenwulf, King: 79
Chambers, Mrs: 125
Chapel Street: **29**, 39, 42, 105, 155, 158
Chater, A. D.: 126
Chester, Earl of: 19, 21
Chester Street: 49, 101, 110, 112
Chester–Holyhead Railway: 109, 117
Chowdhury, Dr B. D.: 58
Church House: 93
Cistercian Order: 19, 20, 22, 24, 33, 60, 62, 63, 65, 79, 80
Citizens Advice Bureau (CAB): 50
Clegg, Mrs M..: 185
Clwyd County Council: 18, 35, 36, 37
Coach & Horses: 94, 102
Coamining: 144
Cob, The: 150
Coed Ffrith: 79
Coed-y-Fron: 31, 40
Coetia-Butler Quarry: 148, 149
Coleshill: 14, 16, 19, 20, 62, 79
Coleshill Street: 24, 35, 45, 58, 89, 104, 113, 114, 169, 172, 173, 174, 180, 186, **190**
Coleshill-Fawr: 85
Coleshill-Fechan: 85
Collegiate Grammar School: 158, 159
Connah's Quay: 119, 121, 122, 166, 193, 194

Cooke, Miss (teacher): 194
Cope, Alexander: 185
Cope, H. A.: 54
Corvo, Baron: (see Frederick Rolfe)
Cottage Hospital: 54, 55, 56, 59
Cotton industry: 135
Cotton Twist Company: 125, 136
County Court: 43
Courtaulds: 39, 48, 116, 120, **121**, 149–54, **151**, 176, 182, 188
Coyney, William: 57
Crecas Quarry: (see Grange Quarry)
Crescent Mill: **31**, 118, **133**, 136, 137, 138, 141, 149
    siding: 118, 120, **120**
Crockford, Charles: 135, 148, 184–5, 193
Crockford Family: 99, 193
Crockford, Henry (Harry): 144, 184, 193
Crockford, William: 135, 148, 193
Crockford, Sarah: 135, 193
Crockford's Mineral Tramway: 39, **145**, 148
Croft, Thomas (teacher): 159
Cross Keys: 37, **38**, 73, 113, 162, 175
Cross Street: 22, 24, 32, 49, 173
Crosville: 115–7
Crown & Anchor: 50, 176
Curley, Dr: 58
Cwm Llydan: 187

d'Avranches, Hugh: 19, 21
Dafydd ap Llywelyn, Prince: 20, 62, 65, 79, 81
David, Revd Christopher: 63, 71
Davies, Revd David: 103
Davies, Edward: 159
Davies, Canon Ellis: 14
Davies, J. C.: 164
Davies, Lord of Llandinam: 139
Davies, William: 34
Deebanks: 148, 150
Defoe, Daniel: 27
Delyn Borough Council: 35, 36, 37, 41, 48, 65, 68, 154
Denbigh Asylum: 52
Dentists: 57
Deva: 16
Dewi Avenue: 31, 40
Di Pietro, Father J. B.: 65
Diana, Princess of Wales: 41
Dingle Colliery: 144
Disraeli's Inn: 175
Dock Road: 39, 47
Domesday Book: 13, 21
Donbavand, Mr: 45, 143
Douglas, John: 136, 137, 170
Douglas, Smalley & Co.: 136, 137, 169
Dr Williams School: 158
Dudek, Paul: 139
Dykins, Llewellyn: 140
Dykins, Philip Llewelyn: 40, 140, 141

Ebenezer Chapel: 106
Eden, James: 125

Edward I, King: 19, 21–2, 80
Edwards, Ann (teacher): 159
Edwards, J. M.: 194
Edwards, Thomas (of Saithaelwyd): 146
Egerton, Sir John: 22
Eldred, John: 20
Electricity Distribution of North Wales & District Ltd: 49
Elizabeth I, Queen: 71
Empire Electric Picture Palace: 37
Englefield Colliery: 125, 144, 169, 193
English Congregational Chapel: 103
English Presbyterian Church: 95
Environment Centre: 149, 187
Envangelical Church: 106
Essex, Sue (National Assembly Minister): 48
Evans, Ellen: 139
Evans, James Kerfoot: 177, 178
Evans, Peter Maelor (publisher): 177
Evans, Samuel: 54
Evans, William: 139
Evans Patent Extra & Superfine Flour: 139, **140**
Exchange House: 22, 180, **180**
Eyton, Adam: 170

Fair View House: 159
Fazackerley, Cllr Bob: 50
Feathers Inn: 98, 99, 174, 190
Fielding, Lord: 185
Ffrith-y-Garreg Wen: 188
Ffynnon Beuno: 61
Ffynnongroew: 165, 166
Fiennes, Celia: 26
Fire Brigade: 127
Fire Station: 44
Flannel Mills Band: 54
Flint and Denbigh Hunt: 189, **190**
Flint District trust: 109
Flintshire Bank: 169
Flintshire County Council: 31, 34, 36, 41, 43, 44, 45, 48, 56, 65, 90, 114, 115, 117, 123, 139, 141, 155, 159, 161, 162, 164, 165, 167, 168, 184
Flintshire Dispensary: 53, 57
Flintshire Roads Bill: 113
Flintshire Technical College: 166
Flour Mill: 139
Flour Mill Pool: 17, 25, 128, **129**, **132**, 136, 188
Foulkes, Mrs: 50
Freeman, G.: 54
Friendly Societies: 172
Fron: 40, 73
Fron Deg: 54
Fron Hall: 40, 193
Fron Park: 41, 45, 107, 184
Fron Park Christian Fellowship: 107
Fron Park Road: 30, 40, 50, 113, 114, 161
Fulbrook: 13, 16, 20, 62, 79, 81
Fulbrook Avenue: 167
Furlonge, Charles: 182

Gadlys Smeltery: 148

Gamble: Dr: 58
Garth-y-Foel: 17, 110
Gasworks: **127**
Gelli: 20, 81
Gents Boarding School: 158
Gerddi: 61
Gerddi Beuno: 40, 112, 162
Gibbons, Dr Brian (Health Minister): 56
Gloucester, HRH The Duchess of: 42
Glyn Abbot: 141, 183, **183**
Golch: 16, 108, 113
Golden Lion: 173
Golftyn: 121
Good Companions of Holywell Hospitals: 56, 59
Gorsedd: 16, 110, 112, 113, 116, 146, 147, 148
Grange, The: 135, 149
Grange Farm: 79, 148
Grange Quarry: 119, 148, 149
Grapes Inn: 190
Great Holloway/Holway Mine: 147, 149
Great Holloway/Holway Vein: 146
Great Holway Shaft: 147
Greenfield
    Business Centre: 128, 154
    County Primary School: 167, **167**
    Dock/Harbour: 16, 118, 123, 149
    Gate: 110
    Harbour: see Greenfield Dock
    No. 2 Cemetery: 45
    Railway station: 125
    Relief Fund: 134
    Valley Heritage Park: 128, 130, 149, 161, 186
    War Memorial: 39
Greenfield Copper & Brass Company: **129**, 130, 132, 133, **133**, 134
Greenfield Hall: 83, 90, 134, 181
Greenfield House: 105
Greenfield Mill: 138
Greenfield Mill Pool: 25
Greenfield Road: 49
Greenfield Spelter Works: 148
Greenfield Street: 28, 49
Greenfield Victory Club: 39
Greenhill: 140
Grenfell, Pascoe: 134
Greyhound Inn: 161
Groes Onnen Windmill: 142, 143, **143**
    Granary: 143, **143**
    Malt Kiln: 49, 143
Grosvenor, Earl: 20, 36
Grosvenor, Robert: 125
Grosvenor Chater & Co: 30, 125, 127
Grove High School: 159
Gwalia Hosiery Company: 134, 138
Gwenffrwd Avenue: 31
Gwenffrwd Road: 40
Gwenffrwd Welsh Primary School: 76
Gwenllys: 56
Gwenlo: 62
Gwynedd, Owain: 19, 20

Gyrn: 137
Gyrn Castle: 137

Hague, Miss: 92
Half-way House: 113
Halkin Cement Works: 144
Halkyn: 14, 24, 30, 117, 126, 165, 188
    Church Hill: 110
Halkyn Mountain: 14, 15, 25, 108, 109, 149
Halkyn Road: 56, 58, 106, 113, 161
Halkyn Street: 58, 113, 114, 159, 174, 179, 180, 186, 190
Halkyn Street Council School: 163
Hall's Mineral Water Works: 125
Hamer, Revd W. J.: 93
Harden, Mrs G. M.: 75
Hare & Hounds: 110
Harrison, Thomas: 157
Hawk-Forward (stagecoach): 112
Health Clinic: 44, 56
Hen Blâs: 14, 16, 19, 20, 79
Henry II, King: 19, 20
Henry VII, King: 66, 67, 69
Henry VIII, King: 21, 64, 65, 67, 70, 108, 181
Heol-y-Capel: 103, **103**, 104, 105
High Flyer (stagecoach): 112
High Street: 13, 22, **23**, 24, 25, 27, 28, 32, **34**, 37, 39, 41, 46, 49, 50, 57, 92, 110, 114, 115, **116**, 118, 158, 168, 170, 171, 176, 178, 181, 184, 186, 190
Hill, William: 125
Hillside Road: 147, 149
Hochheimer, Mr (publisher): 179
Holway (Holloway): 15, 22, 31, 45, 50, 113, 146, 147
Holway Consuls Shaft: 147
Holway District Shaft: 147
Holway East Shaft: 147
Holway Farm: 113
Holway Garage: 113, 149
Holway Grange Caverns: see Grange Quarry
Holway Level: 124, 136, 137, 147,
Holway (Holloway) Level Lead Mines: 25, 30, 137
Holway (Holloway) Road: 110, **111**, 149
Holway Post Office: 50
Holway United Shaft: 147
Holway West Peak: 147
Holy Trinity Church, Greenfield: 40, 90, **91**
Holy Well: see St Winefride's Well
Holly Hill (Bryn Celyn): 13, 30
Holywell
    Ante-natal and post-natal clinics: 56
    Board of Guardians: 34, 51–2
    Board School: 159–60
    By-pass: 113
    Circulating Library: 41
    Community Centre/Youth Club: 41
    Community Hospital: 55, 56
    Cottage Hospital: **55**, 180
    Council School: 159, 195
    County School: 119, 155, 164, 165, **165**, 179, 193, 194
    Credit Union: 173
    Dispensary: 174
    District Highway Board: 112, 114
    District Trust: 109
    Grammar School: 56, 155, 156, 157, 159, 164, 165, 166, 195
    High School: 166, 194
    (Junction) Station: 115, 117, 119, 120, **121** 149
    (Lower) High School: 164, **166**
    Library and Learners' Centre: 42, **42**
    Literary Institute and Reading Rooms: 41
    Local Board: 33, 34, 141
    Local Poor Law Board: 33
    Local School Board: 155, 161
    Public Assembly Hall: 37
    Public Cemetery: 45
    Rural District Council (RDC): 35
    Station (Greenfield): see Holywell (Junction) Station)
    Station (Town): 118, 119
    Town Council: 13, 25, 35, 36, 37, 39, 41, 54, 107, 138, 164, 173
    Town Hall: 24, **38**, **116**
    Townscape Heritage Initiative (THI): 31, 76, 77, 139, 168, 175, 181
    Urban District Council (UDC): 35, 37, 40, 41, 43, 44, 45, 47, 48, 49, 65, 98, 114, 141, 184, 186
    Union: 33, 51
    Union (Lluesty) Workhouse School: 158
    (Upper) High School: 166
Holywell Bank: 137, 169, 170, **170**
Holywell Flannel Mill: 195
Holywell Hunt Society: 173, 188
Holywell Level Company: 146, 147, 170
Holywell Level Silver & Lead Mining Company: 170
Holywell Lime Company: 90, 135, 137, 148
Holywell Limestone Company: 118
Holywell Musical Society: 70
Holywell Parish Church: see St James' Parish Church
Holywell Races: 174
Holywell Railway & Limestone Company: 118
Holywell Savings Bank: 169
Holywell Textile Mill: 39, 67, 126, 136, 138, 139, 140, 180, 188
Holywell Twist Company: 136
Holywell Vitriol Company: 143
Hope Cottage School: 158
Hope, J. A. (teacher): 157
Hotel Victoria: 94, 112, 114, 115, 174
Hughes, Elizabeth (teacher): 159
Hughes, Jane (teacher): 159
Hughes, Thomas (of Brynford Street): 170
Hyfrydle: 172

Inkerman Bridge: 39, **133**, 149
Iron Foundry: 142
Isglan Road: 22

Jacob, William: 101
James I, King: 20

James II, King: 65, 72
Jesuit College/Seminary: 50, 158
John, King: 21
Johnson, James A.: 152, 182
Johnson, Dr Samuel: 27, 124, 128
Jones, Louie Johnson (of Pistyll): 86, 89, 90
Jones, Abel: 36
Jones, Dr Arthur: 58
Jones, Charles: 142
Jones, Revd David: 103
Jones, Cllr Edgar: 114
Jones, Edward: 37, 106, 142
Jones, Edwin: 54
Jones, Dr Gruffydd O.: 58
Jones, Hugh
Jones, Revd Hugh: 89
Jones, Revd J. Jenkin: 161
Jones, John (of Holywell): 143
Jones, John (of Newtown): 137
Jones, Mrs John: 52
Jones, Dr John Owen: 57, 186
Jones, Mary (teacher): 159
Jones, Samuel: 102, 142
Jones, Samuel (of Caerwys): 94
Jones, Thomas (teacher): 169
Jones, Thomas (Glan-y-Don): 99
Jones, Thomas Lloyd (poet): 163
Jones, William: 94

Kapur, Dr: 58
Keates, William: 134
Kent, Duke of: 57
Kinder, James (teacher): 159
King's Arms: 94, 112, 113, 174
King's Ferry: 112
King's Head: 112, 113, 118, 174, **175**
Kinsale Hall: 181

Lady Mostyn (stagecoach): 112
Lambert's Hotel: 184
Leadbrook: 17
Leadmining: 146
Leisure Centre: 41
Level, The: 15, **120**, **145**, 146, 148, 149
Library: 50
Littler, William: 99
Liverpool Arms: 176
Lixwm: 94, 165
Llanasa: 24
Llanelwy: 60
Llanerch-y-Môr: 122, 144, 148, 170, 181
Lloc: 113
Lluesty (Workhouse and Hospital): 34, 44, 46, 51, 52, 53, 53, 56, 59, 78, **107**, 158
Llwyn Onn: 58
Llygan-y-Wern Gate: 110
Llys Gwenffrwd: 56, 57
Lloyd, Albert Bibby (of Flint): 55, 95
Lloyd, John: 178
Lloyd, P & O (of Bagillt): 117

Lloyd, Pryce: 117
Llwyd, Edward: 25
Llywelyn ap Iorwerth: 20, 21, 81
London & North Western Railway (LNWR): 115, **115**, **116**, 118, 135
London Lead Company: 148
Lord Mostyn (stagecoach): 112
Lower Cotton Mill: 139, 188
Lower Cotton Mill Pool: 25
Lower Mill: 136
Lower Stables Farm: 188
Loyola Cottages: 162
Lupus, Hugh: see Hugh d'Avranches
Lyon, Joseph: 134

Maes Offa: 54
Maes-y-Dre: 169, 172
Maesglas: 13
Market: 37
Market Cross: 24, **23**, **24**
Market Hall: 36, 37
Marldir: 49
Mann, Father Joseph: 73
Masonic Hall: 180, 186
Maxwell estate: 31
MacLean, Mrs Joan: 182
Mather, Thomas: 183
Meadow Cottage: 16
Meadow Mill: 16, 17, **131**, 132, 134
Meadow Mill Pool: 25, **131**
Merllyn: 113
Merseyside & North Wales Electricity Board: 49
Mertyn: 17
Mertyn Hall: 144, 183
Metcalf, Father Philip: 30
Meyrick, Thomas: 63
Mewis, Mrs Sandy (Assembly Member): 56
Mews, The: 25, 46
Middle Mill: 110
Midland Bank: 170
Milwr: 22
Moel-y-Gaer: 47
Mona Copper Mine: 128
Moor Farm: 16
Moor Lane: 92
Moor Quarry: 63, 65, 79, 148, 187
Moriah Chapel: 97–8
Morris, Dr Charles Edward: 58
Morris, Frederick Eyton: 177
Morris, Gwilym (teacher): 157
Morris, Dr Jim: 58
Mostyn: 24, 50, 144
Mostyn, Lady Anna Marie: 30
Mostyn family: 124, 125, 168, 181, 188, 189
    Mostyn, Clementina: 84
    Bishop Francis: 68, 77
    Sir George: 181
    Sir Pyers: 37, 39, 89, 105, 126, 128, 146, 148, 157
    Sir Roger: 72

Thomas: 63
Mostyn District Trust: 109
Mostyn Quay: 122
Mostyn Road: 105
Motorised bus service: 115
Mount, The: 183
Mount Glead Chapel: 30, **31**, 106
Mount Street: 159
Mount Zion: 159
Mr Cole's School: 158
Mr Phillips' Poor House: 51
Muldoone, Thomas: 159
Murphy-O'Connor, Cardinal Cormac: 68
Muspratt Brothers & Huntley: 125
Mutton, Peter: 84

National Assistance: 34
National Fire Service: 44
National Health Service: 34
National Provincial Bank of England: 170–1, **170**
National School: 30, 155, 157
Nerse Farm Smithy: 113
New Road: 21, 28, 62, 74, **74**, 94, 99, 102, 114, 159, 163
New Road Catholic School: 159, 162
Newmarket (Trelawnyd): 18, 24
Newspapers: 176
Newton, Keates & Co.: 122, 134, 182
Newton, Lyon & Co.: 134
Nichols, Ellen (teacher): 159
Nichols, H. M. (teacher): 159
North & South Wales Bank: 169
North Road: 31, 40, 42
North Wales Bank: 169, 193
North Wales Power Company: 49
Northop: 17, 24, 108, 110, 115

O'Connor, Dr: 58
Oakenholt: 17, 165
Oakley family: 169
Oare, George: 117
Offa, King: 14
Offa's Dyke: 17–18
Old Casino: 114
Old Chester Road: 110
Old Drill Hall: 185
Old Mill: 136
Old Plough Inn: 22
Old Quay: 106
Olde Boar's Head: 175
Olde Star Inn: 73
Oldfield family: 169
Ogilby, John: 109
Orme, Thomas: 157
Owain, Gutin: 80, 81, 125
Owen, John: 94
Owen Williams, Pascoe Grenfell & Partners: 134

Packet House: 176
Pant Lode: 30
Pant-y-Wacco: 146

Pantasaph: 18, 39, 74, 84, 110, 114, 116, 135, 174, 193
Pantasaph Roman Catholic Cemetery: 45
Pantasaph White Quarries: 148
Panton, Paul: 171, 182, 184, 192, 193
Panton family: 192
Panton Hall: 110, 182, 184, 192
Panton House: 171
Panton Place: 25, 39, **40**, 41, 44, 49, 50, 57, 58, 109, 113, 159, **170**, 171, 175, 184, 193, 194
Panton Place Surgery: 56, 58
Paper making: 125
Paper Mill: 128, 154
Paper Mill Pool: 25
Parish Church: see St James' Parish Church
    Churchyard: 195
Park Lane: 31, 40, 44, 56, 101
Park Works: 1278
Parkgate: 121, 122
Parry, Daniel: 52
Parry, Emma: 161
Parry, Dr Martin: 58
Parry, William: 148
Parys Copper Mine: 125, 128, 134, 135, 149, 181, 193
Parys Mine Company: 118, 130, 142, 181
Parys Mine Lodge: 188
Parys Mine Pool: 25, 149, 187
Parys Mine Works: 130
Patten, Thomas: 130
Pen Rho: 148, 181
Pen-y-Ball: 47, 146, 148
Pen-y-Ball Hill: 112, **8**
Pen-y-Ball Street: 32, 49, 98, 102, 110, 174, 190
Pen-y-Dre: 49
Pen-y-Dref: 94, 101
Pen-y-Ffordd Waen: 112
Pen-y-Gelli: 108, 146
Pen-y-Maes: 53, 97, 110, 142, 143, 158, 164, 184
Pen-y-Maes Company: 143
Pen-y-Maes Missionary School: 97
Pen-y-Maes Road: 17, 22, 54, 164, 183, 194
Pen-y-Maes Sunday School: 97
Pen-y-Pyllau: 110
Pendre: 87, 183
Pen-y-Dre House: 58
Pendre Surgery: 58
Pendref: 101, 102
Pendref Chapel: 96, 100, **100**, 195
Pendref Chapel School: 158
Peniel Chapel: 99
Pennant family of Downing
    David: 93, 95, 100, 102, 157
    Edward: 82, 130, 143, 183
    Lady Emma: 89
    Henry: 183
    John: 87
    Abbot Nicholas: 20, 65, 82, 83, 87, 142, 183
    Philip: 170
    Thomas: 16, 19, 45, 62, 65, 69, 81, 87, 88, 92, 101, 109, 112, 121, 128, 132, 136, 142, 143, 144, 146, 156, 181, 182, 183

Revd Thomas: 89
Abbot Thomas: 69, 81, 87, 183
ap Tudor, David: 81
Pennant Surgery: 58
Pentre Ffwrndan: 17
Pentre Halkyn: 30, 110, 112, 113, 114
Perth-y-Terfyn: 49, 161
Perth-y-Terfyn Cottage: 113, 152, 184
Perth-y-Terfyn House: 184, 193
Perth-y-Terfyn Infants School: 161, **161**
Perry, Henry: 192
Petre, George: 72
Petrie, John: 126
Pierce, Dan: 159
Pierce, George: 172
Phillips, Edward Henry: 116
Phillips of Holywell: 140
Pilgrims' Hospice: 77
Pin Mill: 125
Pistyll: 31, 52, 110
Plas Dewi: 28
Plas Morfa: 105, 152
Plas-yn-Dre: 184
Plas-yn-Dre Surgery: 58
Plas-yn-Morfa: 182
Plessington, Father John: 67, 72
Plessington House: 67–8
Plough Inn: 117, 176
Plymouth Copse: 188
Police Station: 43
Poole, J.: 27
Poor House: 51
Poor Law: 33–4, 51
Post Office: 30, 49, 158, 172
Post Office Lane: 41, 50, 190
Powell-Davies, Revd Huw: 97
Price, Ellice (teacher): 156
Price, Hugh: 94
Price, J. Lloyd of Glyn Abbot: 24, 67, 97, 114, 140, 141, **148**, 183
Price, James: 94
Price, John: see Jonathan Pryce
Prince of Wales Theatre/Cinema: 37, 185
Printing: 176
Pritchard, Daniel: 159
Pritchard, Rowland Huw: 195
Pryce, Jonathan (actor): 195, **195**

Quarrying: 148
Queen's Head: 176

Racecourse: 188
Racecourse House: 188
Ranulf de Gernon, Earl of Chester: 20, 63, 79, 81
Ranulf III, Earl of Chester: 20
Red Lion: 49, 113, 175
Register Office: 44
Rehoboth Chapel: 94, 95, 96, **96**, 97, 98
Rhydwen Garage: 117
Rialto: 185

Richard III, King: 63, 66, 81
Richardson, Dr Ralph: 90, 181
Richardson, Samuel: 181
Rimmer, Alfred: 24
Risley, Cllr Mrs Mair E.: 42, 57
River Dee Company: 121
Riverbank: 47, 110, 142, 182
Riverbank Refinery: 148
Riverbank Smelting Works: 182, 183
Robert of Shrewsbury: 21
Robert's Garage: 44, 53, 58, 116
Roberts, Arthur (estate agent): 173
Roberts, David (grocer): 180
Roberts, Captain Edward E.: 96
Roberts, Ellen (teacher): 159
Roberts, Hugh: 144
Roberts, Humphrey: 57
Roberts, Susanna: 159
Roberts, T. C. (solicitor): 184
Roberts, Thomas: 105
Roberts, Father Thomas: 72
Roberts, Revd Whitford: 194
Roberts, William: 58
Rock Inn: 113
Roft: 46
Roft's Tob: 15, 45,
Roleston, Miss (teacher): 159
Rolfe, Frederick (Baron Corvo): 78
Rope Works: 141
Rose Hill: 17, 94, 110
Roskell Shaft: 30
Round Building: 42
Round Memorial: **29**
Royal Geological and Natural History Society: 41
Royal Hotel (see also White Horse Hotel): **35**, 54, 173, 176
Royal Mail: 108, 109, 112
Royal Oak: 30, 133, 176

St Beuno: 15, 21–2, 60–1, 63–4, 67–8, 70
St Beuno's Stone: 64
St Beuno's Well: 61
St James' Parish Church: 20, 22, 28, 40, 51, 57, 62, **66**, 69, 84, **85**, 89, 90, 93, 99, 141, 148, 156, 158, 194
St James Place: 113
St John Ambulance: 44, 141, 161
St Kentigern: 60
St Peter's Churchyard: 45, 195
St Peter Estate: 15, 46
St Winefred's Brewery: 67, 140, 142, 183
St Winefred's Packet Company: 122
St Winefride: 13, 20, 21, 26, 60–3, 68–9, 70–1, 73, 75, 76, 81, 142, 193
St Winefride's Bell: 70
St Winefride's Catholic School: 76, 162, 163, 164
St Winefride's Chapel: 43, 65, 155, 156, **156**
St Winefride's Church: 68, 73, **74**, 179
St Winefride's Coffin: 69
St Winefride's Hall: 75–6, **120**
St Winefride's Well: **13**, 15, 20, 21–2, 25, 26, 27, 30, 34, 41,

46, 60–1, 64, **66**, 71–2, 81, 124, 136, 139, 140, 142, 148, 168, 180
St Winefride's Pilgrims Guest House: 77
St Winefride's Soap Company: 130, 142
Saha, Dr: 58
Sankey family: 142, 193
    Richard: 40, 73, 74, 143, 144, 157, 169, 190, 193
Saunders, Sister Jean: 59
Savigniac Order: 19, 79, 80
School Lane: 31, 42, 45, 49, 58, 130, 157, 167, 191
Schwarz & Sons, A.: 179
Schwarz, Antony: 179
Schwarz, David: 163
Sea View Cottages: 113
Seftons the Chemist: 57
Ship Inn (The Gletch): 176
Shotblast Engineering Ltd: 127
Sibeon, John Joseph: 179–80
Sibeon, T. W.: 74, **74**, 159, 164
Sibeon & Sons: 98, 179
Silk works: 144
Simon, James (of Abbey Farm): 99
Simon, Thomas (surgeon): 57
Siop Gôch: 148
Sisters of Charity of St Paul: 162
Smalley family: 142
    Christopher: 136–7, 157, 170
    John: 135, 169, 170
Smedley, Thomas: 183
Soap works: 142
Society of Jesus (Jesuits): 71
Spelter works: 149
Spring Gardens: 177–8
Spring Gardens Infants School: **160**, 161, 187
Spring Vale Academy: 159
Springfield: 114
Springfield Hill Gate: 110
Sproule, J.: 28
Stagg's Gate: 110
Stamford Gate: 110, 113
Star Inn: 72–3
Station Road: **35**, 37, 44, 106, 114, 118, 176, 185
Stevens, Charles: 125
Stevens, Martha A.: 159
Stillings, George: 178
Stillings, Tom: 178
Strand: 31, 54, 165
Strand House, 177
Strand Park: 46
Strand Walk: 17
Surgeons: 57
Swan & Station: 176
Swimming Pool: 41
Sycamore Stores: 30, 195

Tabernacle Chapel: 104, **104**, 173
Tai Cochion: 94
Tai Coed: 130
Talacre: 30, 37, 68, 77, 84, 87, 124, 125, 181
Talacre Mining Company: 170

Taylor, John (poet): 25
Taylor, M. V.: 16
Tegeingl: 19, 21, 63, 192
Telford, Thomas: 110
Territorial Drill Hall: 180, 186
Thomas, Revd Edward: 159
Thomas, Canon David: 13
Thomas, William: 159
Thorne, R. (Government Medical Officer): 47
Tootal, Christopher: 72
Top Lodge: 183
Tower Gardens: 37, 87, 114, 159, 186
Town Clock: 37
Travellers Inn: 110, 146
Trelawnyd (Newmarket): 18
Trelogan: 165
Tremeirchion: 24, 61
Turnpike Trusts: 109–10, **111**
Turner, Eliza (teacher): 159
Twll: 113
Tyfid: 62

Unknown Martyrs: 69
Unsworth, Richard: 125
Upper Cotton Mill (Textile Mill): 118, **133**, 136–8, 140, **145**
Upper Lead Smelting Works: 183

Vertue, Robert: 67
Vicarage, The: 92
Vickers, Joseph: 140
Vickers, William: 113
Victoria, Princess: 28, 173
Victoria Brickworks: 138
Victoria Corn Mill: 139
Victoria Cottages: 144
Victoria Square: 172, 174
Viscose Rayon Staple Fibro: 152
Vitriol Works: 143
Volunteers Arms: 57, 58
Vron, The: see The Fron

W. Hall & Son. Ltd: 22, 106, 136, 141, 176
Waen Crossroads: 113
Walden, Robert (Archbishop of Canterbury): 64
Wales Bank: 169–70, 174
Walwen: 117
Walwen Gate: 110
Walter, Archbishop Hubert: 20, 62
War Memorial Gardens: 39, **40**
War Memorial Gates: 39, **40**
Warmley & Co.: 124
Warner, Revd Richard: 27, 136, 147
Wat: 17–18
Wat's Dyke: 14, 17–18, **18**, 20
Waterhouse, Horace: 138, 139, 161
Waterhouse, Thomas H.: 104, 137, 138
Weavers Arms: 144
Wedgewood Heights: 31
Welch, John: 52

Well Chamber: 67
Well Hill: 74, 94, 99, 102, 114
Well House: 68
Well Street: 22, 24, 28, **29**, 30, 33, 34, 39, 42, 44, 62, 74, 102, 110, 112, 114, 155, 159, 161, 162, 176, 178, 180, 187
Welsh Flannel Manufacturing Co.: 100, 104, 137
Welston: 85
Westminster, Duchess of: 55
Westminster, Marchioness of: 90
Westminster Plunge Baths: 41
White Horse Hotel: 28, 54, 112, **116**, 170, 173, 188
White Quarry: 149
Whitehouse, Miss: 159
Whitford: 17, 20, 21, 33, 34, 61, 81, 83, 100, 162, 188
Whitford Dyke: 18
Whitford Street: 30, 45, 49, 76, 92, 93, 94, 95, 99, 102, 110, 112, 113, 114, 142, 159, 162, 163, 164, 174
Whitmore, George: 20
William III, King: 19
William Jones & Son: 144
William Skelton's School: 158
Williams, David (butcher): 97
Williams, Dr David: 58
Williams, (George) Emlyn (actor/playwright): 28, 119, 193–4, **194**
Williams, Gomer L.: 102

Williams, Dr James: 34
Williams, James (teacher): 159
Williams, John: 37
Williams, Owen: 134
Williams, R. Lloyd: 36
Williams, Thomas: 128, 130, 132, 133, 143
Williams, W. E.: 96, 163
Williams Brothers (of Holywell): 91
Williams, Pascoe & Co.: 134
Williamson, Major William John: 87
Williamson, Mr: 102, 103, 105
Wilson, John Marius: 27
Womens' Institute: 184
Womens' Royal Voluntary Service (WRVS): 107, 186
Wood, John (cartographer): 170, 174, 175
Woodroffe, Martyn: 41
Woollen industry: 137
Wynne, Dame Edith: 37, 194
Wynne, John Griffith: 69

Yellow Mill: 136, 137
Youth Centre: 42
Ysceifiog: 18, 21, 24, 188
Ysgol Gwenffrwd: 156, 162–4, **164**
Ysgol-y-Fron: 159
Ysgol Maes Glas: 167
Zinc Smelting Works: 135, **135**